War in the Third Dimension

ESSAYS IN CONTEMPORARY AIR POWER

Other Brassey's titles of interest

Air Power: Aircraft, Weapons Systems & Technology Series

Edited by Air Vice Marshal R. A. Mason, CBE, MA, RAF
Volume I   An Overview of Roles, Air Vice Marshal MASON
Volume II   Air to Ground Operations, Air Vice Marshal WALKER.

BARNETT *et al.*
Old Battles and New Defences: Can We Learn from Military History?

GODDEN
Harrier: Ski-jump to Victory

HARRISON
Military Helicopters

McNAUGHT
Nuclear Weapons and Their Effects

MYLES
Jump Jet, 2nd ed.

WINDASS
Avoiding Nuclear War: Common Security as a Strategy for the
Defence of the West

War
in the
Third Dimension

ESSAYS IN CONTEMPORARY AIR POWER

Edited by

Air Vice Marshal R. A. MASON, CBE, MA, RAF

BRASSEY'S DEFENCE PUBLISHERS

(a member of the Pergamon Group)

LONDON · OXFORD · WASHINGTON · NEW YORK
BEIJING · FRANKFURT · SÃO PAULO · SYDNEY · TOKYO · TORONTO

U.K. (Editorial)	Brassey's Defence Publishers, 24 Gray's Inn Road, London WC1X 8HR
(Orders)	Brassey's Defence Publishers, Headington Hill Hall, Oxford OX3 0BW, England
U.S.A. (Editorial)	Pergamon-Brassey's International Defense Publishers, 1340 Old Chain Bridge Road, McLean, Virginia 22101, U.S.A.
(Orders)	Pergamon Press, Maxwell House, Fairview Park, Elmsford, New York 10523, U.S.A.
PEOPLE'S REPUBLIC OF CHINA	Pergamon Press, Qianmen Hotel, Beijing, People's Republic of China
FEDERAL REPUBLIC OF GERMANY	Pergamon Press, Hammerweg 6, D-6242 Kronberg, Federal Republic of Germany
BRAZIL	Pergamon Editora, Rua Eça de Queiros, 346, CEP 04011, São Paulo, Brazil
AUSTRALIA	Pergamon-Brassey's Defence Publishers, P.O. Box 544, Potts Point, N.S.W. 2011, Australia
JAPAN	Pergamon Press, 8th Floor, Matsuoka Central Building, 1–7–1 Nishishinjuku, Shinjuku-ku, Tokyo 160, Japan
CANADA	Pergamon Press Canada, Suite 104, 150 Consumers Road, Willowdale, Ontario M2J 1P9, Canada

Copyright © 1986 Brassey's Defence Publishers

First edition 1986

Library of Congress Cataloging-in-Publication Data
War in the third dimension.
Bibliography: p.
Includes index.
1. Air power. 2: Aeronautics, Military.
3: Military history, Modern—20th century.
I. Mason, R.A.
UG630.W358 1986   358.4'03   86–9556

British Library Cataloguing in Publication Data
War in the third dimension: essays in contemporary air power.
1. Air warfare—History
I. Mason, R.A.
358.4'009   UG625

ISBN 0-08-031187-3 Hard cover
ISBN 0-08-031188-1 Flexicover

Cover photo of RAF Tornado F.2 reproduced courtesy of British Aerospace.

Printed in Great Britain by A. Wheaton & Co. Ltd., Exeter

Preface

Several of the articles included in this anthology have been written by senior officers still serving in either the Royal Air Force or the US Air Force. Others have been written by distinguished academics either directly or indirectly in government service. The representation of facts and the conclusions which are drawn from them are, however, the sole responsibility of the authors and they imply no endorsement from the UK Ministry of Defence, the US Department of Defense, any other agency or any other individual.

Each author has benefited not only from his own operational or academic experience, but from countless discussions with military and civilian colleagues and kindred spirits worldwide. It is impossible to acknowledge each and every one, but some have been especially helpful: in the United States, Brigadier Sam Carpenter, Colonels John Sullivan, Fred Shiner, Tim Kline, and Lieutenant Colonels Don Baucom, Craig Lamkin and Bob Erhart. In the United Kingdom the authors have received extensive research assistance from John Andrews in London and Chris Hobson at Bracknell. Several typists translated challenging manuscript into legible typing, with ineffable good humour, especially Glenna Hughes and Jean Bolton. To all of them, the authors acknowledge a considerable debt of gratitude.

Contents

List of Plates

Glossary

AAA	Anti-aircraft artillery
AAW	Anti-air weapon
AEW	Airborne early warning
AGM	Air launched guided missile
AIMVAL/ACEVAL	Air combat evaluation
ALCM	Air launched cruise missile
AMRAAM	Advanced medium range air-to-air missile
ARM	Anti-radiation missile
ASUW	Anti–submarine warfare/weapons
ASW	Anti-surface shipping warfare/weapons
ATF	Advanced tactical fighter
AVMF	Soviet naval aviation
AWACS	Airborne warning and control system
BAI	Battlefield air interdiction
BVR	Beyond visual range
C^3	Command, control and communication
C^3I	Command, control, communication and intelligence
CAP	Combat air patrol
CAS	Close air support
CBU	Cluster bomb unit
CINCPACFLT	Commander in Chief Pacific Fleet
CONAC	Continental Air Command
CTOL	Conventional take-off and landing
CVBG	Carrier battle group
EASTLANT	Eastern Atlantic
ECM	Electronic counter measures
ECCM	Electronic counter counter measures
EEZ	Economic exclusion zone
EFA	European fighter aircraft
ELINT	Electronic intelligence
ESM	Electronic support measures
EW	Early warning
FEAF	Far East Air Forces
FEBA	Forward edge of the battle area
GBU	Guided bomb unit
GCI	Ground controlled interception

HUD	Head-up display
IAF	Israeli Air Force
ICBM	Intercontinental ballistic missile
IDF	Israeli Defence Force
IFF	Identification friend or foe
IR	Infrared
KP	Russian command post
LANTIRN	Low altitude navigation and targetting infrared system for night
MAD	Magnetic anomaly detection
MATS	Military Air Transport Service
MPA	Maritime patrol aircraft
NATO	North Atlantic Treaty Organisation
OMG	Operational manoeuvre group
OTHR	Over the horizon radar
OTHT	Over the horizon targetting
PACAF	Pacific Air Forces
PGM	Precision guided munitions or missiles
PLO	Palestine Liberation Organisation
PVO	Soviet air defence forces
RAF	Royal Air Force
R&D	Research and development
R and M	Reliability and maintainability
RFC	Royal Flying Corps
ROE	Rules of engagement
RPV	Remotely piloted vehicle
SAC	Strategic Air Command
SACEUR	Supreme Allied Commander Europe
SAD	Surface-to-air defences
SAM	Surface-to-air missile
SCADS	Shipborne containerised air defence systems
SSM	Surface-to-surface missile
STOVL	Short take-off and vertical landing
TERCOM	Terrain contour matching
TVD	Theatre of military operations
UKAIR	United Kingdom air space
US	United States
USAFE	United States Air Force Europe
USCG	United States Coast Guard
VJ	Victory over Japan
VNAF	Vietnamese Air Force
VNP	Russian airborne command post
V/STOL	Vertical or short take-off and landing
VTOL	Vertical take-off and landing

1

War in the Third Dimension: Continuity, Innovation and Convergence

AIR VICE MARSHAL R. A. MASON

The twentieth century has seen the face of warfare changed by the exploitation of 'the third dimension' of the skies. It is probable that it will be changed again in the twenty-first as space itself becomes the high ground to be seized and either commanded or denied to a potential adversary. If such were to be the case, it might be salutary for those who believe that thereby warfare would be revolutionised, to reflect upon the prophecies of the early air power enthusiasts and the time which elapsed before their fulfilment. After three-quarters of a century, it can be argued that less emphasis on the 'revolutionary' aspects of air warfare and a more sturdy grafting of new ideas on to those repeatedly illustrated in the history of war on land and sea would have actually accelerated and enhanced the impact of air power. There is, however, nothing so clear as 20:20 hindsight, and it is difficult to see, under the circumstances, how the actual evolution in either East or West could have taken a different course. David MacIsaac surveys the American experience in that evolution since 1945 in a challenging style which is not only critical of many aspects of US air power application, but defines a range of problems whose resolution is unlikely to be simple. Indeed, as he amply illustrates, influences on the application of and thinking about contemporary air power have their roots deep in the traditions and habits of thought established in an earlier period.

The pioneers of military aviation were visionaries: Wells, Trenchard, Churchill, Smuts, Mitchell, Chennault, Douhet, Sikorsky, Tukhachevsky, Lapchinski. They could see beyond their military contemporaries the potential and threat offered by the skies to those who would select a military instrument to pursue a political objective. Because they were visionaries, blessed with both imagination and determination, their concepts

1

could readily transcend, but not necessarily overcome, the practical difficulties in their path. Definitions of 'air power' *per se* were seldom attempted; rather more was the specific concept of 'command of the sea' translated to 'command of the air'. The development of this and associated ideas are traced later in this volume by Air Commodore Gover and the present writer.

In all the essays, contemporary 'air power' is interpreted as the ability to project military force by or from a platform in the third dimension above the surface of the earth. The element which distinguishes air power from land and sea power is the fact that the third dimension above the earth is actually exploited to advantage by the platform or vehicle; for example, for manoeuvre, deployment, concealment or surprise rather than simply traversed as by a bullet, a shell or ballistic projectile. The grey areas—for example, a ballistic surface-to-surface missile with independently targetable warheads, and the entire field of surface-to-air weapons—do not significantly detract from the central distinction. Moreover, such a definition recognises two other qualities of air power which are sometimes overlooked. In common with sea or land power, it has a latent impact; the influence of an aircraft still on an airfield, akin to the influence of a warship over the horizon. Second, air power may apply force directly, as in bombing or air-to-air fighting, or it may distribute it, by providing air mobility or rapid resupply to surface forces, or it may amplify it by providing reconnaissance or surveillance.

The fundamental characteristic of aerial warfare was, however, first succinctly expressed not by an aviator, but by the novelist H. G. Wells, in his oft-quoted:

> In the air are no streets, no channels, no point where one can say of an antagonist. 'If he wants to reach my capital he must come by here.' In the air all directions lead everywhere.

Geographers, and sailors, had long been aware that three-quarters of the earth's surface was covered by sea; it took a little while for the realisation to sink in that all of it was covered by sky. No longer would a river, a hill, a forest, a sea or ultimately even an ocean impose an arbitrary obstacle to the conduct of warfare. In the following essays several authors refer to the use of air power in the First World War, examining different aspects of the evolution from artillery spotting through wider reconnaissance, reconnaissance denial, air combat, ground attack, deeper interdiction to the final use of 'independent' air power to carry destruction directly to an enemy's industrial heart and population. At that point a problem arose: how was the new form of warfare to be integrated with the traditional organisations designed to fight on either land or sea. It seemed, and even in the 1980s to some in the West it appears still to seem, that air power must be either independent of, or subordinate to, the traditional forms of warfare. It is the personal belief of the present writer that the West could learn more from the Soviet view that air power is in fact complementary and neither independent of nor subordinate to war at sea or on land. In 'The Russian Alternative', the evidence for that view is examined in detail.

It is, nevertheless, Western thinking about, and application of, air power which retains the greatest influence worldwide. Nor is this surprising. Freedom to develop, exchange and publish ideas internationally would alone give the West a great advantage in the spread of such influence. Added to that is the proven success in combat of Western aircraft and weapons, together with the sustained technological edge in the third industrial revolution of electronics and computer-related equipment. Inevitably, the export of ideas and equipment has been accompanied by the organisational examples which have sustained them in Britain, France and the United States. One alternative model was discarded by the world with the defeat of the Luftwaffe in 1945. Another, that of the Soviet Union, has had little to commend it to the West. The promising beginnings associated with the pre- and post-revolutionary Russian designers and strategists were lost beneath bureaucratic and ideological stultification, and subsequently concealed behind paranoic secrecy.

In retrospect, it is easy to see why there should still occasionally be diffidence among soldiers and sailors in some nations about the promises made by airmen. In the great age of doctrinal formulation between the two world wars, the three great Western 'air' powers, Britain, France and the United States, shared several relevant characteristics. In each, resources for defence were difficult to acquire, albeit for different reasons. The First World War had ended with a promise of the potential of air power, not its realisation. Armies and navies had decided the outcome, despite the flurry of panic and longer-term significance of relatively light German air raids on Britain and vice versa. If soldiers and sailors naturally saw their own dimensions to be paramount and clearly delineated, airmen, on the other hand, under-estimated difficulties of aerial navigation and target identification and over-estimated the destructive capacity of the weapon loads contemporary aircraft could carry. While France and the United States had no obvious political reason at all to pursue the development of air power, the use by Britain of aircraft for imperial policing in the residue of Empire actually retarded development. Aircraft used in the First World War, or little different from them, proved more than adequate to deal with recalcitrant tribesmen who had no air power of their own. Air supremacy in clear weather without counter air opposition offered little incentive for heavy investment in modernisation: that had to wait the threat from a resurgent Germany. It was only in the Second World War that air power began to fulfil its potential, and even then its contribution was frequently measured against its earlier promises rather than against its actual impact on warfare at sea and one land.

In the United States and Britain the need for a specialist air force was associated with an 'independent' role: primarily with strategic bombardment, operationally divorced from land and sea battles. In Britain, independence was originally stimulated and further reinforced by the need for strategic air defence also. In neither country did the higher co-ordination of defence impose a unified provision and distribution of military resources; the three major armed services competed against each other, and the closer either air force moved towards direct support of armies or navies the greater the perceived threat of assimilation by them. With the dropping of atomic weapons on Hiroshima and Nagasaki, air power reached its independent apotheosis: the age of Trenchard, Mitchell and Douhet had arrived.

Since 1945 conditions have been very different. The onset of the armed confrontation between East and West has meant that neither side has relapsed into the relative peacetime complacency which marked the post-First World War years. Both have continued to harness rapidly advancing technology to defence requirements and the result has been a qualitative enhancement of air forces well beyond the scale of the previous 40 years. The Soviet Union on the one hand, and the NATO allies on the other, have built and operated aircraft with a view to combat in a European theatre in the shadow of nuclear arsenals. Thankfully for the Europeans, they have actually seen combat in most areas of the world other than there. Slowly but surely has come the realisation that the skills demanded by military aviation do require a different kind of specialist training and a separate organisational structure to provide for direction by men who understand the complexities of aerial warfare every bit as much as their naval and army colleagues must be familiar with their own dimensions. Resource and role allocation can still prompt differences of opinion, especially in the area of maritime air operations. Group Captain Hicks's survey of the interaction of land- and sea-based maritime air power clearly identifies how and why those differences of opinion can still cause legitimate disagreement between airmen and sailors. The arguments, however, are now at the margins, not any longer over the validity or otherwise of the pervasiveness of air power in all aspects of modern warfare.

There are at least two reasons for the change in attitudes. First, the unique qualities of air power are now beyond dispute: the ability to deliver many different kinds of weapons on an unlimited variety of target arrays with a speed and destructive capacity over distances beyond the dreams of all but the most optimistic of visionaries; to extend the reach of ground forces by intercontinental airlift or by placing special forces deep behind enemy lines; to provide reconnaissance or early warning of attack many hundreds of miles behind the point of encounter on land or at sea. The fundamental significance of those attributes to the NATO alliance are examined in detail by Air Marshal Knight. Group Captain Garden narrows the focus to analyse

PLATE 1.1   F-4B Phantom aircraft from the USAF 347th Tactical Fighter Wing. It carries 2000-lb GBU-10 laser-guided bomb, a Pave Spike laser designator, six 500-lb MK-82 low-drag bombs, and two inboard AIM-9J Sidewinder missiles [USAF].

the options and complexities of air power's contribution to the air-land battle.

Second, it can be argued that airmen themselves have come to a much more mature appreciation of both the potential and limitations of air power. The unique features are rightly emphasised, but others, inherited from centuries of warfare on sea and land are given their due consideration. The defensive–offensive pendulum, epitomised by the Israeli pre-emptive strike of 1967, followed by the opening debacle of 1973 which in turn was followed by the Beka'a massacre of 1982, makes no exceptions in the third dimension. Unit costs in relation to military effectiveness are especially significant. The 'friction' in combat observed by Clausewitz is experienced by every pilot whose radio communication fails him, whose targets are not where they were supposed to be and whose 'friendly' surface-to-air defences fail to recognise his identification signals or procedures. The 'fog' of war has thickened considerably in combat enshrouded by electronic counter-measures and their counter-counter. Air power, like any other element of the military instrument, must be clearly focused on the political objective and pursue a strategy which is acceptable to the political will which ultimately commands it. Colonel Gropman's examination of the US experience in Vietnam epitomises the modern airman's view that awareness of air power's unique qualities must not obscure the military verities of the previous 2,000 years. Learning by experience may on occasion be justified; learning the same lesson twice cannot be. It is far more cost effective to learn from someone else's. This particular theme, among others, is pursued by Benjamin Lambeth in his analysis of the Israeli annihilation of the Syrian Air Force in 1982, and from it other reflections flow.

If early air power was marked by its 'independence', and if slowly but surely an awareness of its 'complementary' nature has now permeated most armed services, it is possible that 'convergence' may be a significant characteristic in the immediate future. Four aspects are already visible.

The first is the blurring of the traditional distinction between 'strategic' and 'tactical' air power as perceived in the West. The 'strategic' B-52, designed to attack an enemy heartland, participates in exercises in support of the land forces in Europe. The F-16 tactical fighter bomber, on the other hand, is used by the Israeli Air Force to strike at an Iraqi nuclear plant and at the headquarters of the PLO in Tunisia. The venerable RAF Vulcan attacks Port Stanley airfield. In-flight refuelling enables F-15 short-range 'tactical' fighter bombers to influence affairs in South-West Asia several thousand miles away from their home bases.

The second example of convergence was clearly visible in the Beka'a campaign. There, dramatically, ground forces contributed to the destruction of surface-to-air weapons, hitherto the preserve of the air forces. Such role reversal, which calls for a major change of inclination and priorities among ground force commanders, extends the logic of the land-air battle to the

PLATE 1.2   F-111 bombers of the USAF over Egypt (*USAF*).

conclusion that air defence suppression is an essential ingredient in the battle for air supremacy which in turn is of vital concern to the ground forces themselves. Taken a stage further, a large static target whose whereabouts are precisely known, such as an airfield, vehicle park or significant bridge, may well be more suited to attack by ground force surface-to-surface weapons. This theme is one of several pursued by Air Marshal Armitage in his analysis of the potential application of manned and unmanned vehicles in the third dimension. Implicit in his essay is the belief that air power is applied *by* man, not necessarily *with* man. Any air force which fails to recognise that fact is condemned to the fate of the medieval knight in armour before the longbow or the musket.

The third aspect of convergence also occurs in Air Marshal Armitage's study: the implications of transferring more of the terminal vulnerability in offensive operations from the manned platform to an increasingly 'intelligent' missile. While the need for agile fighter aircraft to contest air supremacy is unlikely to recede, in other activities there seems to be scope to develop more multi-role air frames. The Russian TU-95 Bear already flies in maritime strike/attack, reconnaissance, electronic countermeasures and cruise missile carrier roles; the Panavia Tornado, albeit with structural differences, discharges interceptor, strike, attack and reconnaissance missions. The RAF's Nimrod, developed from a transport airframe, performs maritime and early warning duties. The air superiority of the F-15 is being modified to extend its mission capabilities considerably. The inherent concept of air power's flexibility is increasingly materialising in such commonality, with ultimate economies in production, maintenance and operating costs.

Finally, and ominously for the West, there is convergence between Soviet and Western attitudes and operational procedures. From a force designed primarily to provide tactical air support after the achievement of air supremacy, hidebound by rigid procedures and preplanned missions, the Soviet High Command is now seeking to match every aspect of traditional Western air power. Offensive support is practised over rapidly increasing distances and in all weathers; maritime reconnaissance, strike and attack aircraft range over most of the world's oceans; expanding strategic and tactical airlift projects a Soviet presence to the Caribbean, the Middle East, Africa and South-East Asia as well as providing greatly increased battlefield mobility; a truly strategic bomber force now threatens the US homeland; electronic warfare constitutes an integral part of most offensive operations; and the advent of the IL-76 Candid AWACS variant may well complicate Western offensive operations and enhance co-ordination of the Soviet's own air-land battle. Fortunately, it would seem that inherent Western advantages in technology, aircrew initiative and ground crew quality will continue in the foreseeable future to offset the potential advantages of such convergence, despite strenuous Soviet efforts to reach parity in all three areas.

In the following essays, each by an author with considerable operational experience or many years' academic study of his subject, or both, all the ideas summarised above are explored in detail. None purports to be a definitive statement; indeed the discerning reader will occasionally detect varying shades of opinion. Collectively, however, it is hoped that they provide a balanced, comprehensive analysis of the impact, limitations and potential of air power on modern warfare, illustrating both the unique and traditional elements of war in the third dimension.

2

The Evolution of Air Power since 1945: The American Experience

DAVID MACISAAC

When the war of 1939-45 finally came to an end, the concept of 'air power' until then still inside quotation marks, found itself at long last advanced from dream to reality—a passage it celebrated with predictable enthusiasm and zest but little recognition of what were already emerging as determining aspects of its future. In retrospect, the suggestion that airmen did not lead the world in envisaging the technological future of warfare could be surprising. They had been doing that, with the occasional help of H. G. Wells and other outsiders, for almost half a century. They seemed by August (if not actually by April) of 1945 to have finally made their point—which had all along been, in its essence, that they saw the future of warfare better than did those tied to more traditional establishments.

When the air leaders of 1945 had been younger they had posited a third dimension to warfare—the air above the surface (whether dry or wet) from which all warfare below would be dominated. Perhaps they had not overmuch worried before 1939 with the problems that multiple, opposing air forces might generate, but the experience of the war resolved any doubts they might have held. But in the autumn of 1945, when the world finally cocked its ear in their direction, they found themselves facing a bewildering set of future imperatives involving matters as disparate as atomic weapons, the jet engine, long-range ballistic rockets, postwar economic recovery in Europe, demobilisation in the United States, the collapse of colonial empires in Africa and Asia, and the enigma of the Soviet Union. A full plate this, including much beyond the competence of airmen, and most unwelcome in a time where gains long sought and seemingly finally achieved had to be consolidated before lost to the encroachments of the more traditionally minded.

In the United States, given sole if temporary atomic dominance, the consolidation of gains became at once the first order of business. Ironically, at least from this distance in time, the marriage of two improbables of early 1941 made the case for a separate air force. The *next* Pearl Harbor, Generals Arnold, Spaatz, Eaker, Doolittle *et al.* had no difficulty convincing the Congress, would be an atomic one and could well occur in Detroit or DesMoines—let alone Boston, New York, Pittsburgh, Chicago, or Washington. The intercontinental bomber 'in the wrong hands' and loaded with an atomic weapon posed a threat unlike any the United States had faced since its infancy. The era of (relatively) free security was over; three formerly protective oceans had, at least in concept, disappeared. When one added to this gloomy equation intercontinental rockets and the impossibility of shooting them down in flight, the only option appeared to be the maintenance of a powerful (i.e. atomic armed) air force in being—fully manned, trained, and equipped to 'knock out' any enemy, preferably an unrighteous one, who might consider challenging what was then looked upon by many Americans as their 'God-given' right to supremacy in the modern world.

Much wrangling and compromising ensued, but almost exactly 2 years after VJ Day the USAF emerged as a separate service on a co-equal level with the Army and Navy. The fondest hopes of its leaders, however, proved unattainable. The pre-existing services, including the Marines, would each retain its own air arm; *the* Air Force would be one of four—a point, now more frequently acknowledged than discussed, that explains more about the subsequent history of the USAF than almost any member thereof likes to think much about. It also marks the end at the beginning, at least for the United States, of the concept of unified air power. The British, of course, had been through all this a whole war before, and the RAF became a separate service in 1918 for essentially the same reasons as the USAF in 1947: to provide a long-range retaliatory force and, when it should become possible, an air defence of the homeland.

Classical air strategy as it had evolved by 1939 met with some rude shocks in the course of the war itself. In its Douhetan formulation only two steps were required. The first was to win command of the air by destroying the enemy's air force on the ground by bombing his aircraft, bases, support facilities and factories. A second and decisive step would follow with the destruction by bombing of the enemy's industrial, governmental and population centres. The war proved more difficult. The destructive effects of bombing, both physically and psychologically, had been over-estimated; the prospects of air defence, both ground-based and airborne, proved hardier than they had appeared in a pre-radar age; and the dramatically effective employment of aircraft in support of surface forces could not be denied by the most zealous theorist of 'pure' air strategy.

Writing more than a decade after the war, the late Bernard Brodie addressed these matters.

Air power had a mighty vindication in World War II. But it was Mitchell's conception of it–'anything that flies'—rather than Douhet's that was vindicated. It was in tactical enployment that success was most spectacular and that the air forces won the unqualified respect and admiration of the older services. By contrast, the purely strategic successes, however far-reaching in particular instances, were never completely convincing to uncommitted observers. Against Germany they came too late to have a clearly decisive effect; against Japan they were imposed on an enemy already prostrated by other forms of war.[1*]

Even General Carl A. Spaatz, senior commander of the US strategic air forces during the war, was ambivalent on the question of purely strategic successes. 'Because the last war saw the weapons of all services employed in profusion,' he wrote, 'one may argue the exact degree of contribution made by strategic bombing to the final decision.' In a now forgotten article in *Life*, he went on to assert that 'the war against Germany was fundamentally an infantry war supported by air power, much as the war against Japan was fundamentally a naval war supported by air'.[2] Even the much heralded US Strategic Bombing Survey fudged the issue, declaring in its *Overall Report* (European War) that 'Allied air power was decisive in the war in western Europe'—a formulation that speaks to rather more than strategic bombing, leaves decisive undefined and geographically limits its intended scope.[3]

And yet despite such readings of the air power lessons of the war, the USAF of the late 1940s and the 1950s set its sights squarely on 'the air-atomic mission'. Several reasons obtained, over few of which the airmen had any measure of control. Demobilisation to the point of disintegration of the military services was one, presidential budget decisions another, the emerging cold war with the Soviet Union yet another. Events in Czechoslovakia, Berlin, Russia (the atomic explosion of August 1949) and soon Korea—married to disappointments at Yalta and Potsdam and mixed with liberal does of Stalinist–Leninist bombast—served to unhinge many in high places. The establishment of atomic, later nuclear, dominance over the Soviet Union was not a goal the airmen could have achieved without help from all the elements of the national government.

With severe restrictions governing the numbers of men, aircraft and weapons that would be made available, the presumably most dangerous eventuality, however unlikely, had to be prepared for first. And so, almost from its establishment in March 1946, the Strategic Air Command was given priority over the Air Defense Command and the Tactical Air Command. Several years would pass before the SAC's capabilities came to represent more than what now appears in retrospect to have been a hollow threat.[4] Once they did, however, in the years roughly between 1957 and 1962, the

* Superscript numbers refer to Notes at the end of the book.

SAC so thoroughly dominated the Air Force as a whole that other capabilities would prove difficult to revive.

The problem, to repeat, was not so much an inability to appreciate the multiple roles that air power could play as a 'co-operative permitter, expeditor, and force multiplier' across the full spectrum of warfare. Rather, it was how to mount the maximum amount of force so as to deter, and destroy if so ordered, any potential enemy bound on working its will against the United States, or so it seemed to the American air leaders of the late 1940s. A future historian might say that they succeeded beyond reason; that they became guilty of trying to make war fit a particular weapon rather than the other way round; that they were foolish to assume that a president would authorise the use of nuclear weapons in any but the most mortal of confrontations; that they had no reason to assume that future wars would be metropolitan wars between integrated societies built around vital centres; that they erred in equating deterrent capabilities with war-fighting capabilities, or at least in assuming the convertibility of the first into the second. A case can be made for all these arguments, but it is only fair to recall that the field of choice was narrower than some now assume; and that here, as in most affairs, the unforeseen and unintended consequences of decisions taken in the late 1940s were the most all-intrusive and long-lasting.[5]

1948-53: Wars Cold and Hot

The USAF was not well prepared, in the summer of 1948, when ordered to join with the RAF in an attempt to supply West Berlin from the air, in response to the Soviet decision to blockade the surface routes into Berlin from the west. Its then Chief of Staff, General Hoyt S. Vandenberg, in fact felt constrained to recommend against even the attempt, on the grounds that such long-range transports as he had available, only weeks earlier consolidated into a new Military Air Transport Service, or MATS, were already committed to support of the SAC emergency war plan. (In those days unassembled atomic bombs and assembly teams were sent in C-54 aircraft to bases overseas where the weapons were then assembled and loaded onto bomber aircraft that had deployed separately.)[6] Despite a hesitant start, the USAF and RAF, organised Second World War style as a Combined Airlift Task Force, reporting jointly to United States Air Forces in Europe (USAFE) and British air Forces of Occupation, Germany (BAFO), and eventually joined by the French, ran a successful airlift from June 1948 through the end of September 1949, airlifting more than 2,325,000 tons of food, coal and other supplies. Among the important long-range benefits derived from these operations was a new radar, the CPS-5, that quickly supplanted traditional methods of handling area traffic and this pioneered modern air traffic control procedures.[7]

The success of the Berlin airlift served to reinforce the arguments for a more balanced air force, but continuing budget cutbacks severely limited the funds made available for airlift forces and literally doomed tactical aviation to obscurity in the years before the Korean War. In fact, in December 1948 the Tactical Air Command was disestablished as a major command, its functions shifted, along with those of air defence and training of reserves, to a new Continental Air Command (CONAC). The rationale was explained by Colonel William H. Wise, a Second World War Fighter Group commander, in a 1949 article on 'The Future of the Tactical Air Force'. Colonel Wise argued that

> the tactical employment of military Air Power, being anchored to surface action, is unlikely to assume a place of importance in any major conflict of the future before the decisive action has neared completion. Since an Air Force properly organized and equipped to achieve success in the decisive phase will be capable also of performing the necessary tactical operations in the exploitation phase, the peacetime maintenance of a specialized tactical air arm at the expense of the strength and effectiveness of the decisive air echelons is unwarranted. The soundness of this concept is already widely recognized in the Air Force . . .[8]

These words are worth pondering. They reveal lines of strained logic that would affect the USAF for at least another quarter-century, most especially the idea that adequate preparation for the decisive phase of any major conflict of the future would serve by itself to satisfy the peacetime equipment needs of an air force (since, in a major conflict, the decisive phase forces would also be capable of performing tactical operations in the exploitation phase). From there it was not very far to asserting that the forces necessary for major conflict would be fully appropriate to lesser conflicts as well. Ironically enough, one year following the appearance of Colonel Wise's article, the North Koreans attacked across the 38th parallel and what began as a police action quickly became a bloody war; the Tactical Air Command was hastily reconstituted and was back in business as a major air command by 1 December 1950.

The war in Korea came as a shock to airmen as well as politicians, but perhaps even more so to the former when it quickly became evident that the latter had reservations about committing the 'decisive phase' forces. 'So far,' wired *Air Force Magazine's* Far East correspondent in July 1950,

> the Korean War is being run from the hip pocket. It isn't the slick, pushbutton affair the press had promised for the next war, with all the latest in . . . streamlined secret weapons to get it over with quickly and easily. And it isn't the kind of war where air alone can stop a

well entrenched ground army that had the time-honored military advantages of surprise, mass, movement, and offensive in its favor.[9]

The situation in the opening weeks of the campaign in Korea demanded the instant employment of all available combat aircraft in direct support of the engaged ground forces. Improvisation—airmen prefer to say flexibility—proved successful if awkward and before long HQ Far East Air Forces (FEAF) shifted its attention to classical strategic targets in North Korea, of which there proved to be few. Attention moved next to the interdiction mission where the lessons of 1944-45 in Italy had to be learned all over again: essentially, that for the aerial interdiction of the enemy's battlefield supplies to be successful, one's own surface forces had to be in control of the tactical initiative, so as to force the enemy to expend supplies in amounts and at rates he could not plan against. Without such pressure being applied to the enemy on the ground, aircraft could harass, delay, irritate—no more.

Except for some tense moments in the northern reaches of North Korea following the Chinese intervention, the attainment of air superiority proved not much of a problem—except, of course, to those who got shot at while winning it. The restrictions against attacking aircraft or bases north of the Chinese border were much decried; less remarked upon was the sanctuary status granted UN bases in South Korea. The close air support mission, as always, generated continuing and acrimonious controversy regarding its effectiveness. In the end, the low priority given to tactical aviation and doctrine between 1945 and 1950 proved costly in both lives and effectiveness. For years afterward General O. P. Weyland, Commander of FEAF, would comment ruefully to the effect that what had been remembered from the Second World War had not been written down or, if written down, had not been disseminated or, if disseminated, had not been read or understood.[10]

1954-63: Air Power During 'The Age of SAC'

In the years following Korea, the American tactical air forces went rapidly into decline once again. As early as the summer of 1951, the Joint Chiefs of Staff and civilian leaders had arrived at budget decisions that would result in the large-scale—indeed monumental—build-up of the Strategic Air Command over the coming decade. These decisions were confirmed, rather than set in motion, by the new Eisenhower administration in 1953-54 with its 'New Look' that would concentrate efforts on 'more bang for the buck over the long haul'. But more was at work here than budgetary and force structure decisions; also relevant were frustration over the limitations imposed on the air forces in Korea, a widespread feeling that the war would never have occurred in the first place had SAC been more capable and ready, a nationwide call for 'No more Koreas!', and an all but universal feeling that Korea had been an aberration—a one-time, small-scale diversion from the true path of the strategic future. (Had not the two world wars 'taught' that all future wars would be total wars—or at least capable of quickly becoming so?)

And so a host of lessons learned and warnings about the future employment of air power flooded out of the 3-year experience in Korea. Most of the admonitions passed on by the participants struck this theme: 'Don't become too wedded to the way we did things here, because we shall never see this kind of war again.'[11] In 1955 Thomas K. Finletter, who had been Secretary of the Air Force during the Korean War, wrote that the war had been 'a special case, and air power can learn little from there about its future role in United States foreign policy in the East'. The final report of the Far East Air Forces agreed, suggesting that 'any attempt to build an air force from the model of the Korean requirements could be fatal to the United States'.[12]

A few air leaders occasionally thought differently in the years between 1953 and 1957, thus far the single most tumultuous period regarding air power doctrine, running from the end in Korea through Dien Bien Phu, the first hydrogen bombs, massive retaliation (and its almost instantaneous denunciation among theorists), allegations of 'bomber gaps', the Suez fiasco, Hungary, and on to Sputnik. General Weyland, for example, stated in 1956 that he felt 'rather strongly that the most likely conflict in the immediate future will be the peripheral type. In this event it will be primarily a tactical air war.'[13] And yet, as we shall see below, he was at that very moment concentrating his efforts on creating a nuclear capability for his fighter aircraft. Similarly, when Air Marshal Sir John Slessor's *Strategy for the West* appeared in 1954, the assiduous seeker of quotations could find such thoughts as the following: 'The bomber is the primary agent of air mastery.' Or, 'Modern air power has made the battlefield irrelevant.'[14] And yet later in the same year in a widely noticed essay on 'Air Power and World Strategy', Sir John seemed to take a different tack:

> We must expect to be faced with other Koreas. . . . The idea that superior air power can in some way be a substitute for hard slogging and professional skill on the ground in this sort of war is beguiling but illusory. . . . All this is cold comfort for anyone who hopes that air power will provide some kind of short cut to victory.[15]

The mid-1950s, in short, were confusing years for those trying to think through the future of air power. If American Generals LeMay, Twining, and Power—joined by Admiral Radford—professed no doubts, O.P. Weyland and Sir John certainly did, and in good company: no one, I am convinced, experienced more severe second and third thoughts on the subject than President Eisenhower. With few exceptions, men were blinded by the nuclear spectre, growing ever larger and now almost immediately deliverable by high-speed jet aircraft and the coming missile age. In such circumstances, the last place most people looked for clues to the future was to the experiences of air forces in small, distant, no-account wars remote from industrial civilisation, involving internal rebellion, and not witness to the widespread employment of the latest in aviation technology.

The role of air power in the colonial wars following the Second World War was in no single case a determinant one. In the Philippines (1946-54), French Indochina (1946-54), Malaya (1948-60) and Algeria (1954-62) air power was effective primarily in its support modes—in reconnaissance, transport, supply dropping, liaison, and in general providing increased mobility to the side that could employ it. Each of these wars, and even Korea and later Vietnam, tended to be a one-sided affair as far as air power was concerned. The fact that its fire power role seldom proved very effective was widely taken as proof in itself that these wars were, if not atypical then certainly not appropriate for close study by the air forces of NATO and the Warsaw Pact. In the United States in particular, virtually all attention centred on preparing for large-scale war, most likely against the Soviet Union and probably beginning in Europe.

To this end, even while war raged in Korea, the USAF worked to create cross-ocean deployment capabilities and techniques for its jet fighters, along with their modification, beginning with the F-84G, to allow them to carry a nuclear weapon.[16] Some saw this as the only realistic way to compete with the SAC for the air force dollar; others worried that the Navy might impinge on (if not usurp) the overseas tactical air mission if it were to become the only service with nuclear-capable jet fighter-bombers; still others could argue that fast, forward-based jets would hopelessly confound the Soviet air defence problem—as well as help clear the way for the SAC bombers.[17] And so by the mid 1950s, USAF F-84 and soon F-100s were sitting nuclear alert at bases in Europe, primed for instant response. Most of their targets were closer than the Russian border, yet still at a range sufficient to turn any launch order into a one-way mission.

Throughout the 1950s and well into the 1960s, tactical aircraft seemed to be tolerated in the force structure only to the degree that they could contribute to strategic ambitions. Even the TAC's prized new aircraft, F-100s and later F-105s, were optimised for high-speed nuclear weapons delivery against area targets. In both Europe and the Pacific USAF tactical fighter units came to constitute a 'sort of bush league Strategic Air Command'.[18] The singular fixation on a nuclear strike role in tactical force planning was enforced in training as well, as witness the Pacific Air Forces (PACAF) F-100 training manual in 1961:

> Nuclear training will in every instance take precedence over nonnuclear familiarization and qualification. It is emphasized that conventional training will not be accomplished at the expense of the higher priority

nuclear training required by this manual. Non-MSF units will restrict conventional [weapons delivery] familiarization to the accomplishment of only one event per aircrew per year.[19]

In its concentration on the nuclear war scenario, not even the Soviet Union rivalled the United States in the postwar years. The Soviet air forces were divided up functionally from the beginning and Soviet nuclear capabilities—although it took the West rather a while to figure this out—were primarily concentrated in their rocket [missile] forces.

In Britain, the RAF's immediate postwar emphases reflected the force structure of the Battle of Britain more than the Battle of Berlin. Until 1953-54 the fighter component retained priority, at least in expenditures, over the bomber force. The decision of 1957 to create an independent British nuclear force dovetailed nicely with the new availability, beginning in 1956, of the V-bombers—Valiant, Victor and Vulcan—but the subsequent cancellation of Skybolt in favour of Polaris signalled the shift of the strategic mission to navy missiles. By 1968 Bomber and Fighter Commands would be amalgamated into Strike Command, and Transport Command would, in the wake of political decisions signalling a 'retreat from Empire', be reduced to Air Support Command.

Despite seemingly continuous budget and force reductions over a 40 year span, the RAF has retained a splendidly stiff upper lip, a capacity perhaps aided in part from their being free of the demoralising doctrinal disputes with sister services that have frequently marred the composure of their American counterparts. (The exception here, perhaps, would be the occasional exasperation of the service's politically conservative leadership with what they perceive as the ill-advised ranking of economic before military considerations in the ordering of national priorities, a situation they can no longer lay exclusively at the door of Labour governments!) In the present arrangements, with the grand record of the Falklands Campaign added to their battle streamers, the RAF retains four identifiable missions: air defence of the United Kingdom, tactical air operations in the NATO Central Region, maritime operations in 'the British Atlantic', and emergency airlift as needed. Insufficient aircraft are provided for each of these missions, but neither ally nor enemy is likely to underestimate the RAF's traditional advantages in combatant psychology.

1964-75: Wars Long and Short

When considered from the standpoint of air power theory and doctrine, the US efforts in Indochina between 1965 and 1971 must be adjudged a failure verging on a fiasco. Many reasons can be advanced to account for such a judgement, some of them welcomed by airmen, others wholly shunned.

The most welcome one, fashionable among many airmen at the time—and, regrettably, even unto today—lays the entire blame for America's failure in Indochina at the door of 'weak-kneed politicians in Washington'. These, it is implied, often in remarks addressed to a younger and more innocent generation, imposed outrageously restrictive rules of engagement (ROEs) and failed to see, in 1965, that rigorously controlled and effective pinpoint bombing of Hanoi and Haiphong (the Linebacker I and II operations of 1972 become the models in this argument) would have 'brought the enemy to their knees' 7 years earlier, thereby saving countless lives on both sides, etc.

That this variant of the stab-in-the-back theory of historical causation should be alive and well today is perhaps understandable but nonetheless regrettable in the extreme. Its promulgation blinds a rising generation of airmen to other interpretations of what went wrong and to questions regarding where it might have been that senior air leaders erred in judgement (as opposed to skill, courage, determination, and all the other heroic virtues, the presence of none of which assures the presence alongside of judgement tempered by wisdom). Surely by 1985—13 years after leaving Vietnam—it should be clear that US air power has been constrained, or limited in its application, ever since the Second World War. Among the factors that have led every administration since then to impose limits have been

  a preference for finding negotiated solutions to conflict situations;
  a prevailing concern to limit the risks of direct military involvement, let
      alone confrontation, with the Soviet Union;
  a concern to limit US military casualties so as to preserve domestic
      political support (for both the war and the continuance in office of
      the administration urging or waging it);
  a concern to limit civilian casualties whenever and wherever possible;
      and
  an attempt to accommodate the attitudes, concerns, and interests of other
      countries, especially those of actual or desired allies.

Although these limiting factors had been present during Korea as well, it would nonetheless be unfair to criticise the air leaders of the early 1960s for having failed to appreciate either their existence of significance. Korea, after all, they had been taught to look upon as an aberration; worse yet, as a mistakenly conducted war the like of which they would not see again. But surely now, 20 years after 1965, it is time to come to grips with the reality, however unwelcome or unpleasant, that warfare involving one or both superpowers in the nuclear age is to be expected to be politically restrained, surely in any conflict not directly threatening the continued existence of the nation. If this 'lesson' continues to be rejected, a future generation of air leaders promises to be as strategically unprepared for the future as the leadership generation of Vietnam was tactically unready for its own war.

The air war in South-East Asia is analysed in full later in this volume, but overall it has a tragic position in the evolution of modern airpower and especially United States air power. Its initial role in Vietnam was advisory and supporting, featuring minimally capable aircraft operating primarily in psychological warfare, transport and liaison. ('But just wait till we get a squadron or two of F-100s over here', said one visiting general. 'We'll clean this thing up in a month!') By early 1965, however, F-105s and F-4s were being launched sporadically against targets in North Vietnam. The initial goals, beyond retaliation for Viet Cong terrorist strikes against US personnel, were firstly, to pressure the government in Hanoi to withdraw support from the insurgents in the south; secondly, to interrupt the flow of supplies and men to the south; and thirdly, to strengthen the morale of pro-government forces in South Vietnam by demonstrating the US commitment to the struggle. These goals were not established by airmen, but were accepted by them despite their certain knowledge that no precedent existed suggesting air power's capacity to produce such effects when measured out in limited, sporadic doses. Even the necessary tactical decisions regarding target selection, pace, timing, routing to target, weight of attack, and the like were usually dictated by officials in Washington, not all of whom wore military uniforms. From the very beginning the rules of engagement[20] prohibited attacks against surface-to-air (SAM) sites under construction, enemy airfields, and even aircraft taking off from or landing at those fields (for fear of killing Russian and Chinese advisers at those locations, leading to possible escalation of tensions between the superpowers). If the government's concern over the possibilities for unintended escalation can be defended, the same cannot be done for its decision nonetheless to commit its airforces, including naval and marine air, to what in Washington was no more than a half-hearted effort at 'controlled, gradual escalation of limited pressure'. To repeat: no precedent existed for the transcendant efficacy of air power in the attainment of limited, essentially psychological, goal—let alone in a jungle campaign of an insurgency war directed from a head-quarters 10,000 miles away.

While most public attention centred on the air war over North Vietnam, the command and control arrangements that evolved over time, driven largely by institutional imperatives internal to the US military services, created a situation in which it appeared that five separate air wars were under way simultaneously: over the north (where the Air Force and Navy operated in separate theatres, called Route Packages), two others, mostly secret at the time, over northern Laos and over Cambodia, another in southern Laos along the Ho Chi Minh trail; and one in south Vietnam involving by far the greatest level of effort and degree of military success.

The resultant command and control arrangements made a mockery of air power doctrine. Consider, for example, the difficulties inherent in trying to sort out the question of command and control over just one of those 'separate' wars—the one over the north. Overall control was exercised by Pacific Command (PACOM), but only through a series of intervening commands: 7th and 13th Air Forces, CINCPACFLT, 7th Fleet, PACAF, Carrier Task Force (CTF) 77, etc. USAF planes based in Thailand were under the operational control of the Air commander in Saigon (Deputy COMUSMACV for Air) but under the administrative control of the Air Commander in the Philippines (13AF). Navy carrier-borne aircraft were directed from Hawaii through the Commander of 7th Fleet. The piecemeal and divided nature of the bombing campaign over the North violated virtually every tenet of air power from unity of command to concentration of force.[21]

Over South Vietnam the situation was even worse, reflecting an air war pursued simultaneously by at least six air forces (not counting the Australians), each going about its own business. At least until 1968, the 7AF Commander had charge of about 600 strike, transport, reconnaissance and liaison aircraft to support the effort on the ground. The Marines kept their 450-plus aircraft to themselves in I Corps. Army ground commanders had control of close to 4,000 aircraft (mostly helicopters). From offshore, the Navy was in charge of its 210 aircraft, some of which flew in South Vietnam. At that time the Vietnamese Air Force (VNAF) added about 400 planes to the fray. Above all these flew the B-52s, theoretically under the control of a ground officer, often a Marine, in Saigon, but under the actual control of Headquarters, SAC, in Omaha, Nebraska, through another headquarters on Guam and a liaison office (Arc Light) in Saigon. The participant air forces over Laos and along the Trail were even more numerous. Not all the blame for weakness and mismanagement can be placed on the politicians and the press.

The catalogue of conceptual bobbles that airmen must themselves answer for is not likely to be soon exhausted. Even such innovations as fixed-wing gunships and defoliation techniques revealed an underlying diffidence regarding their usefulness. The same was true of propellor-driven fighter bombers (principally the A1-E), whose usefulness could not be discounted but whose implications for the future were excessively worrisome to leaders who fretted about emerging from the war with a technologically obsolete force structure, who, in short, could not decide which war was more important, the one in progress or the one in prospect.[22] Finally, in these dreary respects came a resultant tendency to reduce strategy to targetting and, in the end, to allow the operations themselves to become the strategy. Here the airmen were willfully abetted by civilian analysts in the Office of the Secretary of Defense (OSD) with their insistent demands for a precise accounting of a demonstrably nondeterministic enterprise—namely war—

PLATE 2.1 USAF B-52 equipped with air-launched cruise missiles 'tops up' from a KC-135 tanker (*Boeing Aircraft Company*).

and their mechanistic image of war, apparently both cause and consequence of falling into the trap of equating quantitative data with significance. Here again, however, there are limits to what can be blamed on outsiders. When doctrines and beliefs, joined by hopes and dreams, come to shape rather than reflect reality, there is liable to be more than enough blame to allow all participants a share. More importantly for American airmen of today is to decide whether there is virtue in the charge that 'the bedrock error in traditional US air doctrine—the assumption that war's essential processes can be precisely and exhaustively determined—is beyond redemption'.[23]

The American airmen chafed under the restrictions applied in Indochina, but did not, with few exceptions, rebel, even in the more or less legitimate ways that 'rebellion' is allowed to occur in self-confident organisations. Resignation on principle was unheard of among senior officers; when it occurred among juniors it was usually ascribed to their having chickened out. The then Chief of Staff sought to quieten such rumblings as did arise by insisting that everything his service was about could be summed up in one sentence: 'Our mission is to fly and fight, and don't you forget it!' Other senior officers could be more wry: 'Sure it's a lousy, damn, stupid war we're in, but don't forget one thing: it's the only one we've *got*!' Most airmen kept their mouths shut and pressed stolidly on, the quiet philosophers among them only rarely sharing their thoughts. 'This, too, shall pass. And besides, if no one *else* wants to play "You bet your career", why should I? Anyway, self, no one said it was gonna be easy! Check six. Press on.'

On the other hand, when the Israeli Air Force (IAF) 'Pearl Harbored' the Egyptian, Jordanian, and Syrian Air Forces at the opening of the Six Day War in June 1967, airmen the world over saw in the Israeli example the kind of air war they understood. The Israeli government's decision for war was based on faith in the IAF's ability to achieve complete surprise in a pre-emptive strike aimed at eliminating the enemy air forces. Air superiority once attained, concentrated armour could then penetrate remaining defences and create conditions that would lead to the achievement of Israel's limited goals. Success was so swift, so complete, and so striking that most observers never noticed that the attacker's goals had been limited, never envisaging the kind of total victory that had been sought in the Second World War. Hence, one more lease on life for the proponents of *Victory through Air Power* who, in the prevailing circumstances, were not forced to notice that total victory over the Arab states—their defeat, surrender, garrisoning, and subjugation—could not be attained by air power. Instead, the lesson widely drawn was to the effect that untrammelled air power could be decisive in its own right. Another lesson, perhaps more widely noticed than openly commented upon, was that pre-emptive strike had emerged as the accepted term for what, in a more innocent age, had been called sneak attack.

Israel's success in the Six Day War of June 1967 could not be repeated in October 1973 owing both to the surprise achieved by the Egyptians and Syrians and to the quantum improvements to the attackers' ground-based air defences—principally SAM-6s and ZSU-23 tracked AA artillery—provided by the Soviets between 1970 and 1972. The Israeli loss of forty aircraft, primarily to ground fire, during the first 2 days severely shocked most observers. Film footage of jets flashing by and suddenly disintegrating in mid-air proved sobering to those watching television screens in the stag bars at Nellis, Luke, Miramar, Lakenheath and Bitburg Fighter Air Force bases.

Instant experts, mostly newsmen, forecast the end of air power in its battlefield roles. Calmer judges waited to sift the evidence more closely, but were disappointed to find it fragmentary and conflicting, a circumstance aided by conscious decisions by all participants to restrict the release of information. No one, after all, could know when the next examination would take place, nor whom the examiner might be.[24] In the end, the war's 'lessons' proved to be equivocal in all save one respect—namely, that the war of October 1973 marks the point in time beyond which the overriding concerns of air planners shifted from aircraft and engines to microprocessors, from technology as formerly understood to computerology, from air warfare as classically conceived to electronic warfare.

1975-85: Problems and Portents

In the years immediately following Vietnam, the American air forces turned their attention to increased performance in aircraft, air-to-air missiles, and to the air superiority mission in general. The F-15, F-16, F-14 and F-18 aircraft marked a quantum jump in capabilities and gave the United states an undisputed lead for at least a decade (or, roughly, from 1972 to 1982 or 1983). Recent soviet advances, in particular the SU-27 Flanker and the smaller MiG-27 Fulcrum, both looking very much like the F-15 and 'borrowing' F-14 and F-18 avionics, appear to have balanced the equation in capability and might be unbalancing it in numbers favouring the Soviet Union.[25] By 1985 the problem for the West was more and more one of spiralling costs, the Navy and Air Force tactical air and related accounts consuming close to one-half the total general purpose forces budget.[26]

But platform costs running to in excess of $40,000,000.00 a copy for F-15s were only a part of the problem. Looming on the horizon were avionics bills for the AMRAAM (advanced medium range air-to-air missile) and LANTIRN (low altitude navigation and targeting infrared system for night) that were beginning to frighten everyone except those committed to their manufacture and deployment. The prospect of LANTRIN-equipped F-15E Strike Eagle loaded with IIR-Maverick AGMs (and a couple of Amraams for good measure, an admittedly unlikely mix) conjured up among critics a vision of a $60 million package sitting at a vulnerable European airfield awaiting possible launch against a column of a half-dozen or so $10 thousand trucks. Given the Warsaw Pact plethora of ground-based air defences and the probability of pre-emptive attack options—not even to mention the existent ECM and ECCM and IFF quandaries—the much-maligned quality versus quantity issue simply refuses to die quietly.

The relevant questions, of course, are how much quality is affordable and whether quantity in itself is not a quality in so-called target-rich environments. The official American military view has been that quality, in the sense of superior combat capabilities, is required to make up for Warsaw Pact superior numbers. This in turn has led to continuing emphasis on, among other things, beyond visual range [BVR] capabilities for launch-and-leave radar-guided homing missiles; navigation and targeting avionics that will allow for low-level operations at night and in bad weather; and renewed emphasis on reliability and maintainability for aircraft systems and spare parts. All of these attributes, regrettably, are horrendously expensive and must inevitably result in fewer numbers than needed and reduced funding for ordinary peacetime training.

'How one should think about appropriate trade-offs among competing claims on limited funds' is now the most pressing problem regarding aircraft developments in both the United States and Western Europe. In the case of US fighters, Benjamin S. Lambeth has brilliantly analysed four common errors that presently stand in the way of progress. These he describes as

> confusing enemy force size with strength;
> mistaking technological sophistication for mission effectiveness;
> ignoring the importance of the human factor in warfare; and
> deriving force requirements from excessively restrictive definitions of operational need.[27]

The technical determinism that Lambeth says drives the Americans is marked by a tendency to produce statements of need based more on the outer limits of what is feasible than on what spread of performance characteristics is likely to be actually called for by most real mission demands. 'More often than not', he argues, 'the result is to overdesign against the threat by incorporating impressive capabilities of questionable practical value.'[28]

Critics less patient than Lambeth, some of them line pilots of the active air forces, also worry—perhaps too quietly—about the practical usefulness of our increasingly sophisticated systems. These are some of the comments made to the present writer:

—The world [of pilots] is divided into those who think the night can be conquered and those who don't. Same goes for low level in bad weather, where the problems amount to rather more than not being able to see.

—What I really need, like one more hole in the head, is one more element added to my HUD [heads up display]!

—It's hard to believe we're spending so much money on this BVR [beyond visual range] capability. We'll never be cleared to use it (and won't much like it if we are!).

—When the shooting starts, exceptional pilots who are also lucky become heroes, but the war is fought primarily with average pilots. Some of this gear is 'BUR' [beyond useable range] for average pilots.

—I consider the RAF to be perversely blessed with a lack of options. They have little or no ECM or all-weather avionics. They have a short list of munitions to load on a limited number of relatively old aircraft. But ironically, I believe their lack of sophistication and alternatives has focused their efforts to compensate with training that frankly would water a USAF commander's eyes.[29]

Beyond the quality/quantity/costs issue,[30] which, I repeat, will not go away, especially as the United States advanced tactical fighter (ATF) and multi-nation advanced European fighter (EFA) advance onto the drawing boards, are several others of immediate and long-range significance. Any short list of 'puzzles for air power' in 1986 would have to include all of the following:

—Is the missle vs. gun question now irretrievably decided in favour of the air-to-air missile, whether IR or radar directed? (This has happened before with a severe cost in lives.)[31]

—Above 1.2 to 1.4 Mach, is speed still to be worshipped as a god unto itself? (A fair question given new findings regarding pilot susceptibilities such as gravity-induced loss of consciousness at a time when there is talk of single-stage-to-orbit transatmospheric vehicles and Mach 20 'Aero-spaceplanes'.[32]

—Which way should we incline when faced with an actual choice between seeking to improve platform, or aircraft, effectiveness or weapons effectiveness, as with PGMs? (Even the United States might not much longer be able to pursue both technologies simultaneously.)[33]

—What can, or should, be done—if indeed anything—to create a constituency within the air forces of the West for unmanned aircraft systems, one capable of dealing with traditional institutional barriers on the level of combat effectiveness rather than bias?[34]

—For how much longer can NATO live with its airfield vulnerability problem before switching its emphasis to dirt or at least semi-prepared surfaces capable V/STOL equipment? There probably has not been a year gone by since HQ USAFE was established in 1946 that someone in the plans shop was not hard at work on the air base vulnerability problem. And yet except for some buried gasoline lines here and some revetments ('hangarettes') there, the problem has simply been defined away: there will be sufficient warning before attack. A glimmer of hope for realism in this respect surfaced in the fall of 1985 when the USAF's deputy chief of staff for logistics and engineering told a meeting of senior air national guard commanders that

> our increasingly complex weapons systems have created fragile weapons platforms that are too dependent on their support structures. These structures are tied to immobile and vulnerable basing systems that are dependent on fixed facilities, electrical power, air conditioning, spare parts stocks, sophisticated and complex support equipment, vulnerable runways, and navigation aids.[35]

How far General Marquez will get with this line of reasoning remains to be seen. But in the eyes of some he came farther in that paragraph than his service had come in 30 years.

On the American side, this list of 'puzzles' could be extended to wearying length. Unmentioned thus far is the seeming inability of the USAF to see the advantages to be gained by vastly increasing its emphasis in two areas of acknowledged strength—airlift and aerial refuelling—in both respects especially as they might reduce requirements for forward [vulnerable] basing. Also unmentioned are all the various organisational/procedural problems that have led to calls for a restructuring of the US joint chiefs of staff arrangements. Most of these are tied directly to questions regarding the control of air assets and are unlikely to be alleviated by the kinds of tinkering at the margins that the US Congress is planning to consider in 1986.[36] (To the perennial bemusement of their European allies, the Americans continue their illusory faith in the redemptive power of institutional arrangements. It is only when this touching superstition is carried over into complex, one might almost say extralegal, disquisitions regarding the 'proper' allocation and apportionment of aircraft sorties for battlefield interdiction, close air support and offensive counter air in the combat theatre, that tempers can become frayed.[37]

Finally, with regard to possible shortcomings in the American approach to war in the third dimension, is an acute unwillingness to acknowledge that US air power has been constrained or limited in its application ever since 1945 as we have seen. Current air doctrine and force structuring priorities pay this unwelcome fact little heed. Continuing emphasis on the novel aspects of emerging capabilities blind us to the elements of continuity in warfare. One of these is that in the opening stages of a conflict, military forces usually fight in a manner consistent with their prewar organisational structures, doctrinal concepts, and training patterns. And yet even a cursory analysis of current US force planning scenarios and theatre war plans suggests that our Second World War experience—major industrial nations locked in mortal combat—remains the accepted guide for projecting and assessing the role of air power in future conflicts.

Combat in and since Vietnam—in Lebanon, the Falklands, Afghanistan, Iran, Iraq, El Salvador, and even Grenada—shows us a face of war that receives scant attention in the major guidance and planning documents. These conflicts have usually been bounded by a number of political, operational, and resource constraints—even while at the same time employing techniques that range from the most rudimentary to the application of space age technologies. Many of these constraints and techniques are not taken seriously, even though it can scarcely be called unreasonable to suspect that it is in precisely these types of conflict that the United States will almost certainly become involved. The question of the relevance of air power in so-called low intensity conflicts simply has not been thought through.

For example, how does one answer the critic who says that analysis of combat in Indochina shows that air superiority was never really in doubt, but that despite this advantage the United States failed to achieve its objectives? Other cases, such as the French in Indochina and later Algeria, pose the same serious questions about the relevance of air power. The important implication is that the effectiveness of air power can vary with the pattern of conflict, available resources, and methods of employment. Today's and tomorrow's political, socio-economic, and technological environments will inevitably affect the probability of war, suggest its most likely type, and influence its outcome. Air planners of today and tomorrow must acknowledge these facts; they must place the prospect of war into context—primarily against the major threat, but also against any number of states (or other entities) in the Third World, wars that will rarely if ever be fought by the United States acting alone. The major threat justifies the department of defence budget, but the others most likely will become the tests of capability. And the fact is that in 1985 the United States was incapable of conducting special air operations in multiple remote areas simultaneously.

In conclusion, one may recall briefly the essential elements of classical air power theory as it had evolved by 1945; and then list a number of serious conceptual challenges that theory has had difficulty incorporating over the past 40 years. From these the reader can then decide for himself where help is needed.

The classical theory would hold as follows: air power can exploit range, speed, altitude, and manoeuvrability better than can land or sea forces, and therefore must be allowed to operate independently of these forces. These characteristics of air power are most effectively realised when air power is controlled centrally and executed decentrally. The principal missions of air power are strategic offence and defence, air superiority, interdiction, airlift, reconnaissance, close air support and special operations. Although priorities in their application have undergone minor shifts in special circumstances, these principles and priorities have remained basically valid in the face of profound developments in technology, strategy and international relations.

Listed below are a few tendencies and questions that airmen have had difficulty with, some of them from long before 1945 but all of them noticeable since then. No priority is meant to be inferred from their order of appearance, nor does the writer expect his readers will agree with their selection.

—A prevailing tendency to magnify expected capabilities derived from designs still on the drawing boards. This was a problem well entrenched before the Second World War, to be sure. Its more modern offshoots include a tendency to view technology and its implied performance as the lynchpin of enemy capability, while relying for one's *own* security on promissory notes of what the R&D future portends—often at the expense of needed hedges against the war that might break out tomorrow morning.[38] In some way related is the misplaced or at least questionable confidence that technical sophistication can offset numerical force deficiencies.

—A pattern of looking at the parts of the problem at the expense of the whole, a form of reductionism surely not limited to air theorists, but one evident since at least the strategic bombing campaigns of the Second World War.[39]

—A tendency to confuse destruction with control, accounting in part for a transcendant faith in the efficacy of strategic bombing and, in less brutal circumstances as over Indochina in the 1960s, the error of allowing destruction to become the end rather than one of the means to the end.

—A prevailing tendency to emphasise the fire power role of air power at the expense of its other attributes, leading to extreme difficulty in understanding that technologically advanced weaponry and vastly superior fire power will not always be sufficient to produce victory.

—Difficulty in accepting the idea that air combat engagements, no matter how successful, *can*, depending on the nature of the conflict, the goals being sought, and the means applied, prove irrelevant to broader outcomes.

—A continuing tendency to emphasise the unique aspects of war in and from the air while neglecting the elements of continuity that mark all warfare. An example that is awkward to point out to airmen is that strong wills and conflicting opinions have almost always carried more weight than theory or doctrine; although on reflection that attribute may in fact be one element of continuity in all warfare!

Finally, it could well be that airmen will be forced by circumstances to give up their long-cherished hope for the establishment of an outlook, along with an attendant vocabulary, that will allow for some measure of purity in the concept of air power or 'war in the third dimension'. Advanced technology is today giving to all kinds of weapons the ability to strike targets from great distances, thereby blurring the former distinctions between land, sea, and air power. It could even be that the old concept of air power has become an outmoded construct that has outlived its usefulness. Michael Howard (and others) have argued that the technologies of nuclear bombs, ICBMs, satellite surveillance, etc. are making air power— at least at the strategic level—irrelevant as a useful tool for strategists. The strategic questions now are what should be attacked to fulfil the purpose of the war, and from what platform—air, sea, space or land—can this be done with the greatest effectiveness, efficiency and prospects of success?

It is hoped that the foregoing reflections, admittedly idiosyncratic at times, may contribute to the definition of issues and the prompting of discussion essential to the objective assessment of the potential of modern air power.

3

The Air War in Vietnam, 1961–73

COLONEL A. L. GROPMAN

America's Vietnam War in Its Strategic Context

The Cost of Defeat in Vietnam

The Vietnam war was a humiliating, exceptionally expensive, and probably unnecessary American defeat. Between 1961 and 1973 America uselessly spilled its blood and squandered its treasure to fulfill an empty strategy. Today North Vietnam, America's adversary in that long conflict, dominates all Vietnam and Laos and is fighting a counter-insurgency in neighbouring Kampuchea.

The South Vietnamese people, those the United States tried vainly to protect, suffer greatly. Already poor, they help support the fourth largest army in the world, and political prisoners number in the tens of thousands. In the decade since the war ended, 5 per cent of the population (a million people) have fled a police state under the most hazardous conditions imaginable.[1]

The cost to the American people has also been enormous. All can count in Robert S. McNamara fashion—the dead, 58,000; the wounded, 300,000; the dollars, 150 billion[2]—but that tells little. The United States failed to gain its political objective, and it paid a high moral price—its domestic institutions were badly shaken, its youth visibly alienated;[3] its currency debased; its will and ability to use military force to protect national interests stunted for many years.

America, moreover, was a good deal less secure in 1975 when Saigon fell, than it was in 1961, when President John F. Kennedy made the first hesitant steps into South-East Asia. Between 1965 and 1973 the US defence budget nearly doubled, but the increase brought neither success in Vietnam nor added security. War-provoked inflation reduced by one-third the value of each dollar the defence budget increased. After the United States withdrew from the war, the Congress, disheartened by South-East Asia failures, appropriated less purchasing power for defence than it had done since early in the Dwight D. Eisenhower presidency.

In the meantime, America's key adversary, the Soviet Union, had now slowed its military build-up. While American defences were declining, Soviet armed forces dramatically increased their land, sea and air capabilities. The Soviet Union, moreover, appeared to have become more aggressive with its own and proxy forces in such places as Ethiopia, Angola and Afghanistan. States like Japan, Thailand, the Philippines and South Korea, furthermore, seemed to doubt the will of the United States to respond to military challenges.[4] The Vietnam war defeat contributed to reducing America's ability to protect itself and its friends.

Inadequate Strategy

But it need not have been a demoralising loss; indeed, it need not have been a defeat at all. Once they had engaged America in the war, US political leaders owed to their people and to the men they committed to battle an opportunity to achieve the country's limited objectives in Vietnam. This could have been done through the use of air power, the 'major unplayed trump card'.[5] The difficulty was not a quantitative restriction on the use of American air forces; indeed, American aircrews flew more than 1,248,000 fixed-wing and more than 37,000,000 helicopter combat sorties between 1965 and 1973.[6] The problem was not that air power was absent, but that it was squandered and misapplied. Because the political bureaucracy in the United States failed to understand the nature of the war itself and the capabilities of air power, the military strategy, especially its air component, was hopelessly flawed. And since defeats in war are, first of all, failures in strategy, a proper analysis must begin there.

The political bureaucratic decision-makers in the Defense Department and the National Security Council, beginning with the President, were ambivalent about whether they were engaged in a counter-insurgency or a sub-theatre conventional war against a foreign invasion. Throughout, they never sought even a limited victory—they tried only not to lose—and produced an objectiveless strategy that never aimed for more than a stalemate. Eventually they developed a plan to outlast North Vietnam, ignoring the fact that the North Vietnamese had a much more compelling reason to persevere than did the United States. This inadequate national strategy seriously hampered military planning, most notably the use of air power.[7]

Brevity does not permit anything like a complete analysis of the air war here. Instead we shall briefly explore the inadequacy of the air strategy and then discuss the American air campaign, with emphasis on several engagements that demonstrate air power's potency in that conflict.

Air Strategy Analysis

Confusion Over the Nature of the Vietnam War

It is difficult to simplify an essay on the air strategy of the Vietnam war. The conflict went on too long. Too many players had roles. The views of the players changed, and changed again. Some policy and strategy formulaters (mostly civilians aided initially by some military decision-makers) saw the war as a counter-insurgency and considered the defeat of the Viet Cong in South Vietnam their major objective. Others viewed the war as an effort by North Vietnam to conquer South Vietnam. As it turned out, the latter view was more accurate, as today indigenous South Vietnamese communists are nowhere near the centre of power in old Saigon (now Ho Chi Minh City).

The intent here is not to be critical of those who saw the war incorrectly, especially as we maintain that this fundamental error need not have led to defeat, because the air strategy ought to have been similar in either case. If the war was considered an insurgency, then it was necessary to shut off outside assistance to the guerrillas to achieve victory. There have been no successful counter-insurgencies without effective interdiction of outside assistance.[8] If, on the other hand, North Vietnam was considered the direct aggressor, then the war needed to be taken to Hanoi in no uncertain terms. The key in either case, therefore, was striking North Vietnam's heart and major logistic arteries and not squandering precious assets as the United States did on the capillaries in southern North Vietnam, South Vietnam, and elsewhere.

We recognise the fears decision-makers in the Johnson administration had concerning Chinese or Soviet (especially the former) involvement in the war if bombing of North Vietnam were to become intolerable to them. We recognise, but do not understand. Certainly, whatever the apprehensions Robert McNamara and his key adviser on air strategy, John McNaughton, had, those fears should have been dissolved by the lack of Chinese or Soviet overt moves during times of relatively intense bombing activity. In any case, whatever excuse Lyndon B. Johnson and his advisers had would appear not to apply to President Richard M. Nixon and his advisers, given the moves by the Chinese in 1970 to open relations with the United States and simultaneous Soviet attempts to enhance *détente*. It appears that Johnson—the president most responsible for the debacle— took advice from people who understood only the potential, abstract liabilities of air power and not its military benefits. These people took counsel of their fears and promulgated a strategy that produced disaster. They formulated an impotent air strategy that aimed only at protracting the war until Hanoi and the Viet Cong could stand it no longer. In the end, the American people's tolerance for pain without hope proved to be shorter lived than the North Vietnamese leadership's ability to tolerate destruction of superficial national assets in pursuit of their lifelong dream.

Growing Military Demand for the Unfettered Use of Air Power

The majority of the Joint Chiefs of Staff in 1964 recognised North Vietnam was the enemy and that air power was a key to success in the war.[9] The Joint Chiefs and the Pacific Command developed a strategy that aimed at sealing off North Vietnam from outside logistics support by mining harbours and attacking shipping and further hampering Communist operations in South Vietnam by severing lines of communication to the south.[10] Proponents of this strategy recognised the need to prevent Chinese and Soviet supplies from reaching guerrillas and North Vietnamese regulars in South Vietnam. But Air Force leaders also knew that attacking capillary-sized lines of communication far from Hanoi (the industrial, transportation and administrative centre of North Vietnam) would be ineffective because these were small and relatively easy to construct and, therefore, could be multiplied almost indefinitely by the enemy. Remembering Korea and the French experience with the Vietnamese, the Air Force knew that the enemy would also be able to move supplies, once they were widely distributed, at night or over well-camouflaged routes in daytime. The key was to strike ports, railroad marshalling yards and major rail and highway choke-points.[11]

Defense Secretary McNamara rejected the strategy of sealing off North Vietnam and ruled out interdicting major lines of communication close to Hanoi. He would permit striking targets in North Vietnam only near the demilitarised zone separating North from South Vietnam, but targets further north were reserved for strike only if the North Vietnamese failed to respond to US pressure.[12]

The Air Force Chief of Staff, General Curtis E. LeMay, argued forcefully for an immediate and concentrated attack against strategic targets in the Hanoi-Haiphong area. He believed interdiction elsewhere was not likely to be decisive. He was opposed by Generals Earle G. Wheeler, Army Chief of Staff, and Maxwell Taylor, Chairman of the Joint Chiefs of Staff, who preferred a more gradual increase in air pressure on North Vietnam; they believed the war had to be won in South Vietnam and that the Army should carry that burden. Wheeler also believed an air campaign should support the war in South Vietnam chiefly through close air support. The Army view in 1964 was essentially that of McNamara, who called for two main air missions (in addition to essential airlift): close air support by the Air Force of Army units and interdiction of enemy lines of communication in and near South Vietnam. The Secretary believed, without any evidence (and he persisted in this incorrect belief until he left office), that the implicit *threat* of air attacks on military industrial targets would influence the North Vietnamese to restrain their support of the Viet Cong.[13]

In mid-1964, at a meeting in Honolulu, General Taylor questioned whether the United States should attack North Vietnam at all and agreed with the Secretary of Defense that the main air effort should be designed to support the forces of South Vietnam by cutting enemy lines of communication. If an attack were to be made against North Vietnam, it should be only to *demonstrate* resolve to expand the conflict.[14] The strategy that emerged from this Honolulu conference differed in no important way from the pre-conference strategy. The Joint Chiefs of Staff, however, looking to the future, had the Defense Intelligence Agency develop a list of strategic targets in North Vietnam. Initially there were 94 key targets considered to have a direct relationship to North Vietnam's war-making capacity and the will to fight (by 1967 this list had grown to 244 targets).[15]

Gradualistic Use of Air Power

August 1964 saw the first overt American air attacks on North Vietnam. These punitive strikes, code named Pierce Arrow, were launched in response to the North Vietnamese attacks on US Navy destroyers. They struck ports, naval facilities, and North Vietnam's petroleum stocks. They marked the end of the period of strategy making that had focused on restricting American involvement in Indochina to economic aid, advice, and covert pressure against North Vietnam. Pierce Arrow was the first of a series of 'tit for tat' bombings, with targets being released for attack a few at a time, in reaction to North Vietnamese activities, rather than on the basis of a comprehensive American air strategy.

Significantly, these strikes were orientated toward achieving some particular effect upon the ground war in South Vietnam and not on destroying the will or capability of the North Vietnamese to fight. McNamara, supported by his civilian and ranking Army advisers, had argued that bombing a few targets in North Vietnam would demonstrate the potential costs to Hanoi and therefore restrain the communist government. But Ho Chi Minh's response to the Pierce Arrow attacks was not restrained. He moved thirty jet fighters from China to Hanoi's main military airfield. The air attacks did not shock Ho; they simply spurred him to start working on what was to become a superb air defence system of jet fighters, surface-to-air missiles, and anti-aircraft artillery.[16]

Further demonstrating that limited retaliatory attacks were not reducing their will to fight, the Viet Cong and North Vietnamese also stepped up attacks against American airfields. These attacks led the Joint Chiefs in November 1964 to propose a series of strikes against North Vietnam based on the Defense Intelligence Agency's list of 94 strategic targets. President Johnson rejected this proposal, but it served to put *all* of the Joint Chiefs on record in favour of more aggressive air strikes against North Vietnam. Despite the consensus among the generals and admirals, McNamara advised Johnson to continue his gradualistic approach. Johnson also retained total control of air strikes. From the first strikes in 1964 until he left office, targets were doled out 'abstentiously and with detailed personal attention in the Tuesday luncheons to which no military officer was regularly invited until late in 1967'. Johnson and McNamara 'regulated the pace of escalation personally by minimizing autonomy in the field and discouraging the development of comprehensive campaign plans'.[17]

Johnson and McNamara were stymied by their fears and their inadequate understanding of the nature of war. Johnson worried that dramatic strikes might prompt Soviet or Chinese involvement (although there had been no serious response to American attacks), that such bombing might impede chances for negotiations (when Hanoi had shown no willingness to compromise) and that bombing, in any case, was not cost effective[18] (as if defeat had no price tag).[19] The debate went on until the end of the war. It was about whether bombing was a political signal or a military means to political ends.[20]

Misapplication of Air Power: Rolling Thunder

To raise South Vietnamese morale and to increase incrementally the pressure after a series of attacks by the Viet Cong and North Vietnamese on Pleiku and Qui Nhon, a campaign called Flaming Dart was begun in February 1965. The next month it evolved into a more systematic air campaign called Rolling Thunder. The latter involved strikes on lines of communication in North Vietnam below the 19th parallel (well south of Hanoi and Haiphong) and elsewhere.

General LeMay retired in January 1965, still calling for a truly strategic air campaign; his successor, General J. C. McConnell, was no less vocal. McConnell argued that the United States needed to concentrate on destroying the centre of the North's logistics network, not its tertiary tributary aspects. Despite McConnell's view, the Secretary of Defense continued to maintain that the primary role of air power was to support ground forces in South Vietnam because McNamara was only interested in avoiding defeat.[21] But so long as the North Vietnamese paid no major price for the war and could bring all they needed to fight into the war zone and hide it beneath triple jungle canopy or in caves and tunnels, their victory remained only a matter of time.

In early 1965 the Joint Chiefs advocated a four-phase strategic attack against North Vietnam. All agreed with McNamara on the need to continue an appropriate level of close air support of the South Vietnamese and American troops in South Vietnam, but without strategic attack on North Vietnam the Chiefs knew the United States was in for a prolonged war of attrition. The Chiefs believed a strategic air attack that destroyed the ports, mined the harbours, completely interrupted the transportation net and destroyed ammunition and supply areas in the heartland of Vietnam would convince Hanoi that South Vietnam was not worth the price—destruction of their society.[22] On the other hand, civilian bureaucrats in the Defense Department argued that an all-out bombing campaign might widen the war and would 'transmit a signal of strength out of all proportion to the limited objectives of the United States in South-East Asia' and foreclose the promise of achieving American goals at a 'relatively low level of violence'.[23] But war is violence, and Hanoi had become inured to low level violence by more than 20 years of armed struggle. Only an obvious indication that the destruction of their society was imminent would dissuade them.

Hanoi's Air Defence Network

Hanoi responded to our piecemeal attacks on southern North Vietnam by building comprehensive air defences and in July 1965 shot down its first American fighter. In response to this loss, the President and McNamara authorised strikes against only those surface-to-air missile sites that were actually firing at US aircraft. Even this authority did not extend to targets above the 20th parallel.[24]

American reconnaissance, as early as April 1965, had revealed the construction of Soviet surface-to-air missile sites in North Vietnam. The military had immediately asked for permission to strike the sites before they were completed. The Department of Defense refused that permission. General Westmoreland quoted John McNaughton on Hanoi's air defence missiles: 'Putting them in is just a political ploy by the Russians to appease Hanoi.' (To McNaughton (and McNamara) it was all a matter of signals.) 'We won't bomb the sites and that will be a signal to North Vietnam not to use them.'[25] That sophistry cost the United States hundreds of lives, billions of dollars in destroyed aircraft, and the imprisonment of hundreds of American Air Force and Navy aircrew members.

The Johnson/McNamara/McNaughton Approach to Bombing

Johnson's key civilian advisers did not understand how air power had contributed to victory in the Second World War, especially in the Pacific Theatre, and how it had helped end the ugly stalemate in Korea in 1953. They also would not listen to those who did. Their complete misreading of the enemy, combined with their misunderstanding of air power, led to a series of bombing halts in the false hope that the North Vietnamese, with relief from limited pressure, would see the error of their ways and negotiate a peace or withdraw from South Vietnam. McNaughton, McNamara, and Johnson devised an air strategy of 'uncoordinated carrots and sticks' that, by smashing nothing of great value, succeeded in signalling nothing.[26] Between 1965 and 1968 Johnson halted the bombing sixteen times and publicly promulgated seventy-one peace initiatives—the last coming upon his dramatic withdrawal from the presidential campaign of 1968.[27] Hanoi was not impressed, except perhaps with their own ability to drive the American political process.

In early 1966 McNaughton wrote a memo that characterised the Defense Department view of bombing North Vietnam. Bombings, he asserted, were to interdict infiltration, bring about negotiations, provide a bargaining counter—we will stop bombing if you stop fighting—in negotiations (which he called 'minuets'), and sustain South Vietnamese and US morale. He doubted that, short of drastic action against the North Vietnamese population, an air campaign could persuade Hanoi to come to the table.

He recognised that the Air Force, using only conventional munitions, was capable of destroying industrial targets, locks and dams on the waterways, and significant portions of the population. The first he rejected because of North Vietnam's primarily rural economy; the last, because it might produce a 'counter-productive wave of revulsion abroad and at home'. Paradoxically, he thought that flooding might have some merit. But he ended up arguing against strategic bombing and supported strikes 'only as frequently as is required to keep alive Hanoi's fear of the future'.[28] McNaughton did not understand war or its principles. He looked on air power as a sophisticated 'ratchet' to tighten or loosen the pressure on Hanoi to alter the politburo's mood.[29]

McNamara argued before the Congress in 1965 that his objectives were 'limited only to destruction of the insurgencies and aggression directed by North Vietnam against the political institutions of South Vietnam'. He wanted to convince Ho Chi Minh by close air support and interdiction in southern North Vietnam, South Vietnam and elsewhere, that North Vietnam could not conquer South Vietnam.[30] Here McNamara was describing a strategy of attrition and protracted war. In such a war, there was no way that Hanoi was likely to become convinced they could not outlast the United States, a country fighting halfway around the world with its major national interests elsewhere. The Joint Chiefs, when McNamara made this comment, disagreed with his view of the conflict, saying that it was no longer an insurgency but a conventional war that demanded an air campaign not confined to South Vietnam. McNamara's view was badly flawed because, even if the war was an insurgency, no victory could be achieved so long as Hanoi could run in supplies and equipment to its forces in the South without grave risk to its own centres.[31] The task McNamara gave air power—to sever the supply system by striking only its terminal phases—was exceptionally costly and proved impossible.[32]

The Air Force wanted to concentrate bombing in North Vietnam. Having made that point clear in 1964, it never ceased calling for a strategic campaign. That service recognised the enormous tonnage being dropped on South-East Asia was largely hitting empty jungle. The Joint Chiefs argued that the only aspect of the war in which the United States could take the initiative was in the air campaign against North Vietnam's heartland and that this had to be prosecuted vigorously. McNamara repeatedly ignored this military advice.[33]

In late 1966, having rejected a strategic air campaign, McNamara counselled the President that there was no way to end the war soon and that the country needed to 'gird' itself 'openly for a longer war'. But he lost his nerve less than 2 years later and abandoned office.[34] It seemed that no civilian in the Department of Defense in 1965 and 1966, when they were counselling gradualism, recognised the frustrations building in the American population, although it had happened before within all of their memories. During the Korean war President Harry S. Truman was driven out of the presidential campaign of 1952 (as Johnson was in 1968) in large part because he could not bring that war to a rapid conclusion. McNamara counselled Johnson to take the same path as Truman—with the same result.

It should be acknowledged that the Central Intelligence Agency until 1966 advised that bombing was not cost effective. The Institute for Defense Analysis also advised McNamara in 1966 that the bombing was having 'no direct measurable effect'.[35] But the bombing they were analysing was on the fruitless targets to which McNamara had allotted to air power.

The brief analysis above shows that the strategy governing the application of air power in Vietnam was badly flawed. With this in mind, let us now review air operations between 1961 and 1972, paying particular attention to the significant air efforts in the two climactic years—1968 and 1972.

Air Power at War

The Slow Kennedy Build-up

Although American air power had assisted the French in their effort to maintain control of their South-east Asian empire, our story properly begins with the first deployments of air power to South Vietnam by the Kennedy administration. By the time Kennedy had taken office, what appeared to be insurgencies in Laos and South Vietnam were accelerating. Kennedy initially sent more military and civilian advisers to the friendly governments to stem what appeared to be an attempt by international communism to overthrow 'free' governments, continuing a programme dating back to the Eisenhower administration. In May 1961 Kennedy sent Vice President Johnson to Saigon to survey the deteriorating situation.

Subsequent to that visit, Kennedy increased US military assistance, including, in the case of the US Air Force, the dispatch of a radar mobile control and reporting post to Tan Son Nhut Air Base outside of Saigon.[36]

Later in the year the US Air Force sent a combat unit of air commandos equipped with T-28s, B-26s, and other 'vintage' aircraft. In the United States the outfit had been called Jungle Jim. When it got to South Vietnam it was called Farm Gate. Slowly, from 1961 to the end of 1964, US combat air power grew in Vietnam, but by the end of the latter year there were only 117 American aircraft in Vietnam, 50 of which were strike capable. By the end of 1965, however, there were about 500 American aircraft based in Vietnam and three US Navy aircraft carriers with more than 250 aircraft off the Vietnamese coast. Tactical air warfare in Vietnam was by then being fought on a large scale. The initial hope (but not expectation) of the Defense Department had been that the Air Force would be used only to train the South Vietnamese Air Force, but the strength of the North Vietnamese and Viet Cong compelled the United States to up the ante dramatically to prevent a South Vietnamese defeat.[37]

Hanoi's Battlefield Success Draws More Air Power

The year 1965 opened ominously. Ho Chi Minh, his defence minister, Vo Nguyen Giap, and the rest of the politburo in Hanoi saw triumph ahead. They confidently broadcast over Hanoi radio that 1965 would be 'the year of victory'. This confident judgement was based on Hanoi's assessment of South Vietnamese weakness and Washington's unwillingness to offer major assistance.[38] Apparently the American attacks made on North Vietnamese coastal torpedo bases and oil storage facilities in August 1964 and the subsequent passage of the Gulf of Tonkin resolution had not impressed Hanoi.

South Vietnam was in desperate straits in 1965, with one military coup following another and the United States anxiously trying to find ways to bolster South Vietnamese defences and morale. To improve South Vietnamese spirits, Washington openly talked about deploying additional American forces to Vietnam and the White House lifted restrictions on the use of US aircraft over South Vietnam.[39] As an exclamation point, in June 1965, B-52s dropped their first bombs on South Vietnam.[40]

During 1966 American troop strength continued to grow, reaching a total of 325,000 troops, and several American allies—Korea, Australia and New Zealand—also supplied forces. The growth of American forces apparently induced an increase in North Vietnamese forces, which in turn caused another expansion in American forces. By the beginning of 1968 there were about 500,000—approximately 10 per cent of which belonged to the US Air Force.[41]

Events in 1968, especially the Tet offensive, changed the political and social climate in the United States to the point that President Johnson dropped from the presidential campaign. It is useful here to dwell momentarily on the contributions of air power to two important military campaigns of 1968: the Tet offensive and the siege of Khe Sanh.

Air Power and the Tet Offensive: January to March 1968

During the Tet offensive, air power played a key role in keeping the enemy from accomplishing his military objectives. Beginning on 31 January, violating a holiday truce, the Viet Cong and North Vietnamese Army launched simultaneous attacks on 36 of the 44 provincial capitals, 5 of the 6 autonomous cities, 23 airfields, and numerous district capitals and hamlets. Apparently General Giap hoped the South Vietnamese army would disintegrate and the people of South Vietnam would rally to the communist cause.[42] Fortunately, because of intelligence warning, the American 7th Air Force had entered Tet on full alert[43] and was able to support South Vietnamese and American ground forces as they, although momentarily shaken, bravely fought back.

Initially the enemy seized temporary control of ten provincial capitals and succeeded in penetrating such important cities as Quang Tri, DaNang, Hue, Nha Trang, Kontum, and even Saigon, including the grounds of the American Embassy compound in the centre of the city. But except in Hue, the enemy was cleaned out after the first 2 or 3 days of the offensive. Despite the heavy simultaneous demands placed upon 7th Air Force to help defend Khe Sanh (which we will cover next), 7th Air Force, Marine, and Navy strike aviation and Air Force airlift were major factors in the enemy's wholesale military defeat.[44]

Air power did everything expected of it. Between 30 January and 25 February more than 16,000 strike sorties were flown by the Air Force, with additional thousands flown by the Marines and Navy, all in support of American and Vietnamese ground forces. And airlift—some 280 aircraft—moved troops rapidly wherever needed to thwart an enemy attack. Because of American airlift, the enemy's disruption of surface lines of communication during the Tet offensive was of little value to him. At one point more than 12,000 troops were moved in hours from the southern military regions to the most threatened area—Military Region I—to frustrate any plans General Giap might have had to separate part of that region from South Vietnam.[45]

Retaking Hue proved to be the most difficult problem. The enemy moved into the inner city and hung on. Marine, Navy, and Air Force fighters flew hundreds of sorties to support Marines and the 1st Air Cavalry Division as they battled house-to-house to drive out the enemy It took almost a month, but by the 25th of February the inner city was again in friendly hands.[46]

North Vietnamese and Viet Cong losses were exceptionally heavy. The enemy lost 5,000 troops at Hue alone. Overall enemy losses during the month-long attack were about 45,000.[47] So serious were these losses, the Viet Cong was never again a major factor in the war—the overwhelming burden of fighting now falling to regular North Vietnamese troops. Nonetheless, the Tet offensive proved to be a political disaster for the Johnson administration. Although the battle seems to have failed to have had the desired effect upon the South Vietnamese population, it caused many Americans to doubt the possibility that the United States could ever achieve its goals in Vietnam.[48]

The domestic political loss notwithstanding, American air power demonstrated to the enemy that he could not succeed in conquering South Vietnam so long as the United States retained its military forces there. American air power was flexible, and the Air Force centralised command and control apparatus functioned smoothly; rapidly moving Air Force fighters and airlifters from one end of the country to the other, shifting whenever necessary to meet the enemy. Air power denied the enemy any kind of sanctuary in South Vietnam day or night. Even bad weather provided little cover, because the enemy could be struck by radar controlled fighters and bombers. Airlift, especially the C-130s capable of working in the worst weather conditions, delivered supplies under all conditions.

Air Power and the Battle for Khe Sanh: January to April 1968

Similarly, with General Giap's siege of the Marine base at Khe Sanh, whatever his intention—and some think it was to repeat his capture of a large body of defenders as he had done in Dien Bien Phu in 1954—air power saw to it that he gained nothing while suffering enormous losses. About a week before General Giap launched the Tet offensive, he laid siege to the Khe Sanh Marine fire base located on a plateau about 30 minutes flying time west of DaNang. For $2\frac{1}{2}$ months, beginning in late January, the enemy pounded the base continually with artillery and mortars and made numerous infantry probing attacks in an attempt to overrun the 6,000 American Marines who, along with a small number of South Vietnamese Army troops, were stationed there. General Giap invested about three North Vietnamese infantry divisions in this venture.[49]

Air power's response to the communist attack involved traditional missions—interdiction, close air support, airlift—all under the command and control of 7th Air Force. Alarmed at the build-up of troops in the Khe Sanh area, General Momyer directed more than 20,000 attack sorties during December 1967 and January and February 1968 against communist lines of communication leading to the forces. More than 3,000 trucks supplying North Vietnamese forces were destroyed in this effort.[50] Interdiction was crucial because the enemy counted on his high consumption attack to soften the defences and destroy morale at Khe Sanh.[51]

Close air support was provided by fighters from the Air Force, Marines, and Navy Task Force 77 off the coast of Vietnam. Each day, 350 tactical fighters and 60 B-52s struck the enemy.[52] To effect the command and control of this many aircraft in the confines of the valley where Khe Sanh was situated was a major feat. To meet this challenge, control of all tactical air units was centralised under 7th Air Force, making General Momyer the single manager for air. During the $2\frac{1}{2}$ months of combat in that tiny area, more than 24,000 tactical and 2,700 B-52 sorties were flown, and more than 110,000 tons of bombs were dropped. Fighters were in the air day and night. During darkness, AC-47 gunships provided constant gun fire and illumination against enemy troops.[53]

The B-52s struck enemy staging, assembly, storage areas, and known gun positions. When communists were discovered digging trenches and tunnels to protect their advancing infantry, the B-52s bombed their positions, even though some were within 1,000 feet of the base perimeter.[54] The weather was an enemy ally during this campaign; more than half of the fighter strikes and all of the B-52 strikes were controlled by Air Force radar.[55]

Another major air effort at Khe Sanh was the aerial resupply of the US Marines and South Vietnamese Army troops at the camp. The runway at Khe Sanh was put out of operation by enemy artillery early in the siege. Therefore, for most of the period, the Air Force supplied Khe Sanh by airdrop and low-level cargo extraction missions. During the siege the Air Force delivered more than 12,000 tons of supplies to Khe Sanh while under constant enemy fire. Supply levels at the fire base never became dangerously low because of the air lifeline.[56]

This massive air power effort was orchestrated by the 7th Air Force at Saigon and its Direct Air Support Centre at DaNang. The actual co-ordination of air and artillery fire was directed by an Air Force Airborne Battlefield Command and Control Centre C-130 aircraft which orbited over Khe Sanh. Forward air controllers, working directly for the Airborne Command and Control Centre, directed the precise application of air power where it was most needed.[57]

General Giap's forces suffered terribly, losing probably 10,000 killed. Two of his divisions were driven out of the war for the remainder of the American involvement.[58] Activities at Khe Sanh punctuated the lesson General Giap must have learned during the Tet offensive—that he could not conquer South Vietnam so long as American ground forces supported by air power remained.

American Withdrawal and Vietnamization

Regardless of the important role air power played thwarting General Giap's plans for 1968, the political climate in the United States had become so poisoned by the length and apparent futility of the war that President Johnson withdrew from the presidential campaign of 1968. The new President, Richard M. Nixon, announced less than 6 months after taking office his plant to pull out US combat troops from Vietnam. Fighting a drawn-out, apparently pointless, war was unacceptable to the American public, and by the end of Nixon's first year in office 69,000 American troops had been removed from Vietnam—somewhat more than 10 per cent of the total.[59]

The Air Force continued to support military operations in South Vietnam and kept up its attempt to interdict enemy lines of communications. After the American ground forces dwindled and national policy dictated 'Vietnamisation' of the ground combat, air power became America's primary military arm. In the last months of Nixon's first year, B-52s struck time and time again at enemy concentrations, staging areas and fortifications to prevent the enemy from massing while American forces withdrew and South Vietnamese forces expanded. In the last 5 weeks of 1969, B-52s dropped more than 30 million pounds of bombs on enemy positions.[60]

In 1970 the first US Air Force elements began to leave South-east Asia while the South Vietnamese Air Force enlarged its force structure. By year's end the South Vietnamese had nearly 700 aircraft, including A-1s, A-37s, F-5s, AC-47s, O-1s and AC-119s.[61]

By the end of 1971 the Air Force had reduced its combat aircraft in South Vietnam to 277 (from a high in June 1968 of 737) with similar reductions of aircraft stationed in Thailand, the Philippines and Okinawa. The number of Air Force people in South Vietnam itself also declined from the peak in 1968 of 54,434 to 28,791. By the end of the year 70 per cent of all air combat operations were performed by the South Vietnamese Air Force.[62]

The next year saw some of the most dramatic uses of air power in the entire war. The US Air Force and naval air forces returned to the theatre with dramatic vengeance in the Spring of 1972 to smash the North Vietnamese attempt to conquer South Vietnam in an open invasion, complete with tanks and massed trooops.

Air Power and the Spring 1972 Invasion

The Spring 1972 invasion was in every way a more well-planned, manned, tanked, and artilleried attack than the Tet offensive. General Giap committed fourteen regular North Vietnamese divisions, virtually his entire army, in attacks across the demilitarised zone, in the central highlands, and across the Cambodian border into An Loc north of Saigon.[63]

The attack began soon after midnight on 30 March with a strike on the northernmost part of Vietnam. Here General Giap used hundreds of tanks and the largest mobile artillery pieces in his inventory to smash everything barring his way to Quang Tri City.[64] The initial attack achieved tactical surprise because the lingering north-east monsoon had lowered ceilings to the point where reconnaissance was not effective.[65]

American military manpower in Vietnam at the end of March stood at 95,000, well under 20 per cent of the peak 3 years before, with the heaviest reductions having been taken by Army and Marine combat forces. It appeared that the South Vietnamese Army and Air Force would have to shoulder the brunt of the attack, as they had, in fact, been supplying most of the combat power in South Vietnam in the previous months. However, it became obvious within hours that the South Vietnamese could not defend against General Giap's entire army, and President Nixon decided to provide massive reinforcement for the South Vietnamese in the form of American air power.[66]

On hand when the invasion began were 285 US Air Force fighters in Vietnam and Thailand, 28 gunships, 52 B-52s in Thailand, and a small number of C-130s and C-123s in Vietnam.[67] More than 100 crucial American forward air controller aircraft also remained to help conduct the operation.[68] At the time of the invasion, the Navy also had two aircraft carriers off the coast of Vietnam with a total of about 180 strike aircraft.[69]

Intelligence concerns had led the United States to build up its B-52 force—the aircraft most feared by the communists—more than a month before the invasion. Some had been sent to Thailand, but the bulk had been deployed to Guam. Twenty-nine B-52s were in place on Guam by the time Giap invaded, and twenty more were sent 4 days later. By the time the invasion was defeated, more than a hundred extra had been deployed to Guam. During the month of April B-52s flew 1,600 sorties against the communists in South Vietnam and an additional 200 against communist lines of communication elsewhere.[70]

Hanoi, according to captured documents, believed anti-war factions in the United States would preclude any strong reaction to the invasion. Rapid battlefield victories causing major losses in the remaining American Army and Air Force units would force a precipitous US withdrawal that would destroy the Vietnamisation programme and undermine Nixon's stature at home.[71]

Air Power Deployments

But, in fact, the President disregarded the anti-war movement and rapidly deployed crucial air assets to the theatre. The first Air Force and Marine fighters to arrive came from other bases in the Pacific: Korea, the Philippines and Japan. The Navy responded rapidly too, adding four

PLATE 3.1   HH-53 helicopter of 40th Aerospace Rescue and Recovery Squadron USAF over the jungles of Vietnam, October 1972 (*USAF*).

aircraft carriers to Task Force 77, the first two arriving on the 3rd and 8th of April, the third arriving on the 30th of the month, and the last arriving later because it was redeployed from the Atlantic.[72] The Air Force Tactical Air Command in the United States responded rapidly as well.

General Abrams, commander of US military forces in Vietnam, requested massive reinforcements to defeat this invasion. That request began a series of major deployments called Constant Guard—there were four in all. The first to depart, on 7th April, were F-105G Wild Weasel fighters which were designed to counter the surface-to-air missile threat. These arrived ready for combat in a week. Of course, moving a Tactical Air Command fighter unit required a massive movement of manpower and materiel to support and maintain the combat effort, and the Military Airlift Command began flying transports around the clock to sustain the build-up. The totals are dramatic. By mid-April 84 fighters and 8 EB-66 electronic warfare aircraft had arrived. In early May another 36 fighters deployed from the United States, and on 13 May an entire wing of 72 aircraft arrived from Holloman Air Force Base, New Mexico, and was ready for combat in a matter of hours. On the same day 36 C-130 aircraft arrived to augment the intra-theatre airlift structure.[73] To combat Giap's invasion, the Air Force, Navy and Marines had more than doubled their air strength in 6 weeks.

A measure of the seriousness of the North Vietnamese attack can be gained from observing the vastly expanded military capabilities that General Giap pushed into South Vietnam, including North Vietnam's heaviest and most potent anti aircraft artillery and a significant number of surface-to-air missiles.[74]

In addition to these expanded air defences were the massive armoured forces used in the North Vietnamese offensive. Both the armoured and anti-aircraft forces were without precedent in the war in South Vietnam. Although tanks and armoured vehicles were used in all phases of the invasion in the three military regions struck by Hanoi, the number involved in the attack across the demilitarised zone was especially heavy. About 400 armoured vehicles supported at least 40,000 troops in this offensive. Additionally, this invading force brought with it mobile 130-mm artillery pieces.[75]

Fortunately, the tactical air control system that had been laboriously built by the Air Force was still in place when the invasion began. The system made it possible to exploit air power's range, speed, flexibility and punch. Furthermore, many forward air controllers were still in Vietnam to direct the precise application of air power. American air power was also enhanced by the fact that many of the returning Air Force, Navy, and Marine aircrews had extensive experience in the theatre.

The first priority for the air effort was to help the South Vietnamese ground forces stabilise the ground situation. The massive force of B-52s and fighters already in the region were used to frustrate General Giap's hope for a rapid collapse of South Vietnam's government.[76]

The Attack in Military Region I

The most difficult attack to deal with was the one in the northernmost region. Here, supply of the attacking army was a simple matter for Hanoi. Certainly more tanks, surface-to-air missiles, and mobile heavy artillery were thrown into this particular effort. Perhaps General Giap hoped to sever the northern portion of South vietnam from Saigon's control if he could not conquer the entire country.

Initially the attack in the north met weak resistance; in fact, the South Vietnamese Third Division broke early in the campaign. Down through the demilitarised zone poured tanks and infantry. By 2 April all twelve South Vietnamese fire support bases between the demilitarised zone and Quang Tri City had been captured, and the communists were rapidly moving on the city itself.[77]

Dong Ha fell on 28 April, and the reinforced South Vietnamese forces fell back on their Quang Tri citadel. By the 30th the South Vietnamese were surrounded on three sides, and 4,500 rounds of enemy artillery and rocket fire pounded Quang Tri that day. The Quang Tri citadel fell to the enemy on 1 May. Because of the hasty and disorganised withdrawal of South Vietnamese forces, Hanoi captured an enormous quantity of artillery, ammunition and fuel, in addition to some tanks.[78]

But General Giap did not have it all his way. American C-130s in the theatre rapidly moved elite South Vietnamese paratroopers and marines into Military Region I to stem Giap's attack. American strike aircraft went to work early in April destroying the bridges over the My Chanh River, complicating Giap's logistic support to his forces, and many sorties were devoted to destroying the equipment abandoned by the South Vietnamese. Because Giap apparently wanted a quick victory, he moved his forces in daylight, even after the weather cleared! Long convoys of heavy tanks and artillery moved down the roads, totally exposed to air attack. American air power hit these targets, striking first the 130-mm artillery, next the tanks, followed by the smaller artillery and, last, the trucks.[79]

The high priority assigned to the 130-mm artillery was because of its high lethality. It was extremely accurate and capable of firing seven rounds per minute at a range of 17 miles. It was especially frightening to the Vietnamese foot soldiers. This weapon was towed by tracked vehicles capable of traversing the most difficult terrain.

Destroying the guns was fairly easy once they were located, but finding the guns had usually been difficult, as the North Vietnamese were masters of camouflage. Giap, moving on roads in daylight, now forfeited this advantage. Air Force fighters dropping laser-guided munitions were especially effective against these destructive enemy weapons.[80]

The North Vietnamese had seldom used tanks in the past, so their introduction at this point in the war came as a major surprise. The Air Force used laser-guided 2,000- or 3,000-lb bombs to destroy many of them, and even more were destroyed by 500-lb general purpose bombs simply because so many of these were dropped. The Vietnamese Army found that their M-48 tank was a suitable opponent to the North Vietnamese T-54 and PT-76 tank and used them in this manner. Lacking enough tanks in Military Region I, General Abrams requested the emergency airlift of six M-48s (weighing 49 tons each) from Japan to DaNang. Six giant US C-5s brought the tanks and their crews into DaNang, and the crews drove off the ramp of the C-5s directly into the war.[81]

During May and June more and more American air forces were flown in to support the South Vietnamese while air power pounded away at the communist forces and their lines of communication. Before the middle of May the South Vietnamese, supported by tactical air, naval gun fire and helicopter gunships, began to counter-attack. On the 14th of that month the South Vietnamese infantry struck south-west of Hue, with B-52s and fighters bombing the enemy ahead of the assault. By late June South Vietnamese forces had crossed the My Chanh River, and the battle to retake Quang Tri had begun.[82]

The application of air power in Military Region I had been massive. Friendly tactical fighters flew about 18,000 sorties in the 3 months beginning in April, with the US Air Force providing 45 per cent of those missions, the US Navy and Marines (combined) about 30 per cent, and the South Vietnamese the remaining 25 per cent. Additionally, Air Force B-52s flew some 2,700 sorties in that region. The Navy lost 2 aircraft; the Marines, 1; the Air Force, 20; and the South Vietnamese, 10. Air power played a key, even decisive, role in efforts to stop the communist assault. By the end of June the exhausted remnants of Giap's northern forces were pushed back into the demilitarised zone.[83]

The Battle for An Loc

Simultaneous with the attack on Military Region I, the North Vietnamese invaded South Vietnam's central highlands. Because of space limitations and the similarity of the air campaign in both Military Regions II and III, the defeat of Giap's forces in the central highlands will not be discussed so that more space can be devoted to the battle for An Loc in Military Region III where air power played a pivotal role in another major defeat for the North Vietnamese.

The communist offensive in Military Region III, that part of the country in which Saigon was located, began about 3 days after the attacks in the other two military regions, after major South Vietnamese combat units had been shifted to the northern military regions. Under excellent cover provided by the jungle, the enemy advanced on the provincial capital of An Loc using tanks to spearhead the attack. Apparently Hanoi hoped to

PLATE 3.2   AC-130 gunship over Vietnam, June 1972 [USAF].

establish a provisional government at An Loc and then to move on Saigon itself. At least three North Vietnamese and one Viet Cong division were used in this attack, aided by massed anti-aircraft artillery. The Air Force responded immediately with A-37s from Bien Hoa, some naval tactical air from the USS *Constitution*, Vietnamese F-5s and A-1s, and Air Force F-4s and AC-130s from Thailand. Around-the-clock tactical air coverage was maintained over the enemy forces from the earliest part of the attack. South Vietnamese infantry gave ground stubbornly, but the communists were able to advance.[84]

An early major objective for the enemy was the seizure of Quan Loi airfield east of An Loc, one of two airfields from which An Loc was supplied. The North Vietnamese attacked in the early evening of 7 April using, among other weapons, tear and nausea gas. The enemy succeeded in taking Quan Loi, complicating Saigon's logistic problem. The North Vietnamese then quickly moved south of the city to block Highway 13, the main road into the city.

The South Vietnamese government, using helicopters, moved a large number of elite troops—rangers, paratroopers, and President Nguyen Van Thieu's palace guard—into An Loc to hold the city. Thus, by mid April, five South Vietnamese regiments were inside the city, and the force was under attack by four enemy divisions. During the following 2 months the South Vietnamese lacked surface logistics and depended upon the air for both fire power and supplies.

The enemy attacked repeatedly with tanks and other armoured vehicles, only to be thrown back each time by ground defenders, tactical air, and US Army Cobra helicopters using anti-tank weapons. B-52s also participated in the attack whenever the enemy massed. The South Vietnamese defenders benefited from the fact that there were several nearby air bases and a Direct Air Support Centre only minutes flying time away at Bien Hoa.[85]

Another major assault against An Loc took place on 15 April, inaugurated with heavy artillery fire. At daybreak, enemy armour and infantry attacked from the north. By mid-morning, all available aircraft were in action against the attackers. At least ten of the tanks leading the assault were eliminated by tactical air and ground forces. By late in the afternoon the enemy attack had lost momentum. For 4 more days the North Vietnamese tried to overwhelm the small force inside the city. The attack failed because of the outstanding effort of air forces in support of tenacious ground defenders.[86]

An insight into the magnitude of the battle comes from realising that in the first $2\frac{1}{2}$ weeks of the attack, more than 2,500 air strikes had been flown in support of the ground forces in Military Region III. The proximity of the air bases of Bien Hoa and Tan Son Nhut and easy access to Bien Hoa as a turnaround base for fighters based in Thailand allowed the Air Force to expand rapidly its fighter sorties. Unable to take the town because of the massive air support devoted to it, the communists settled on a siege. But once the enemy fixed himself, he became even more vulnerable to repeated B-52 strikes.[87] Conditions in a siege are always ugly, and An Loc was no different; but air resupply kept the city alive.

Initially, after the closure of the airfields at An Loc and Quan Loi in early April, the Army and the Vietnamese Air Force tried to sustain the city with helicopters. This effort was given up on 12 April because enemy fire destroyed so many vulnerable helicopters. The Vietnamese Air Force tried to airdrop to the city, but the ground fire was so intense the effort was abandoned by 19 April. US Air Force C-130s were then drawn into the fracas on a full time basis. The usual drop altitude and airspeeds for supply drops, 600 feet above the ground and 130 knots airspeed, made the C-130 too vulnerable to the intense anti-aircraft artillery and ground fire in the area, and the C-130s had to employ different techniques in order to successfully sustain the city.

The drop altitude was raised progressively higher to get the C-130s out of the range of ground fire, but as the altitude went up, accuracy of drops diminished. After two losses, the C-130s switched to night drops. The major drop zone available was a soccer field only about 2,000 metres square. Trying to hit this consistently in daytime had been a challenge; at night it was impossible. The defenders recovered less than a third of the loads, and the C-130s continued to be hit (one was lost and 37 others received battle damage).

Air Force and Army troubleshooters worked feverishly at Saigon's Tan Son Nhut Air Base to improve the airdrop techniques and eventually developed a tactic of dropping the loads well above 6,000 feet and electronically delaying parachute opening until just before impact. Using this new technique, the recovery rate reached more than 90 per cent within a week. During the campaign from 9 April to 10 May, the airlift forces flew 448 missions and dropped almost 3,700 tons of supplies to the beleaguered defenders.[88] During the entire period of the siege (which ended on 18 June), C-130s dropped 7,600 tons in more than 600 sorties.[89] The C-130s allowed the defenders to hold out, preventing the enemy from establishing himself in An Loc.[90]

Realising that the air resupply could make it impossible for them to force a surrender, the enemy elected to make a mass attack beginning on 11 May. Artillery softening began on 9 May. Captured enemy soldiers had given American commanders invaluable advance information, and the air forces were fully ready for the attack when it came. B-52s arrived every 55 minutes for 30 hours. Two hundred and ninety-seven Air Force fighter-bombers were allocated to strike the enemy on 11 May, and 260 sorties were allocated for each of the next 3 days. The Marines also sent 34 fighter-bombers to Bien Hoa to join in the campaign. The B-52s struck in three-ship cells with each aircraft dropping 30 tons of bombs, covering areas that would have required sixty fighter bombers. They were especially effective.[91]

By 12 June the enemy was driven from An Loc and the surrounding area by the viciousness of constant air attacks. There is no doubt that this battle would have been lost without air support.

The spring invasion, with its 14 divisions and 600 tanks, was utterly frustrated by air power—mainly American. The Air Force, Navy, and Marines had rapidly moved potent forces into the theatre to thwart General Giap's plans. Air power interdicted enemy lines of communication, destroyed communist infantry and armour in the field, and resupplied beleaguered friendly troops. Perhaps the key to the air power success was command of the air battle by 7th Air Force. Its Tactical Air Control System flexibly and rapidly adapted to the needs of the ground battle.[92]

Strategic Bombing

The 1972 spring invasion had come in the midst of the endlessly fruitless Paris negotiations that had begun in mid 1968. Sorely antagonised by the all-out attacks, and, like Johnson, wanting to force Hanoi out of the war,[93] Nixon finally decided to strike boldly near the heart of North Vietnam with B-52s.[94] Their general misuse in the long war is reflected in the final statistics of B-52 missions. More than 124,500 B-52 sorties each dropped about 30 tons of bombs on targets in South-East Asia. But during the entire war, only 6 per cent of these bombs were on North Vietnam, and the vast majority of that 6 per cent was on targets far south of the heart of the country, Hanoi–Haiphong.[95]

Linebacker

On 8 May President Nixon announced the beginning of a comprehensive campaign against North Vietnam. The idea was to stem the flow of supplies into North Vietnam from its communist allies, to destroy existing stockpiles in North Vietnam, and to reduce markedly the flow of materials from Hanoi south. The campaign was called Operation Linebacker, and it went on simultaneously with the heavy fighting in the south. The campaign began with Operation Pocket Money, the mining of Haiphong and other major coastal points. On 10 May President Nixon approved almost all of the original 94 targets in North Vietnam for attack. Simultaneously, the President sharply contracted the no-bomb zones around Hanoi and Haiphong that had been established during the Johnson administration. With its spring offensive smashed and now faced with extensive destruction in its own homeland, Hanoi indicated that it was interested in serious peace negotiations. With that signal, President Nixon, in October, stopped the bombing in North Vietnam above the 20th parallel, fully expecting rapid progress would be made in the ongoing Paris negotiations.[96]

But once again the North Vietnamese showed their stubbornness. At home they rapidly moved supplies south; at the peace table in Paris they stalled, again testing the will of the American people. Later in the autumn Hanoi actually withdrew from the peace talks altogether. The President determined that a very strong American response was warranted. On 18 December 1972 he called for an all-out campaign against Vietnam's heartland to force a settlement that would permit America to withdraw. The interest was no longer interdiction or to demonstrate that the North Vietnamese could not win in South Vietnam, but rather to disrupt the economic, military and political life of North Vietnam so severely that the enemy would have to come to terms.

Linebacker II

For the first time since the war had begun, air power was employed strategically with the determination that had all along been advocated by US Air Force commanders. Over an 11-day period between 18 and 29 December, with a pause for Christmas Day, more than 700 B-52 sorties struck strategic targets in North Vietnam.[97] This campaign, code-named Linebacker II, motivated the North Vietnamese to conclude a settlement.[98]

It is crucial to note that the B-52s were not the only aircraft involved in the Linebacker campaign. In fact, more fighters than bombers flew against Hanoi and Haiphong. Fighter-bombers struck enemy airfields and some strategic targets, fighters flew against enemy intercepter aircraft, special fighter-bombers struck enemy radar and surface-to-air missile sites, other fighters dispensed chaff to confuse enemy radars, and other aircraft jammed enemy radars in order to protect their comrades. Additionally, more than 200 KC-135s refuelled the B-52s between Guam and their targets in North Vietnam, a distance of more than 2,600 miles. The B-52s, along with the fighters that were involved, demanded about 750 refuellings each day of the campaign.[99]

These missions required the most sophisticated orchestration. Timing had to be precise. Tanker-bomber and tanker-fighter rendezvous had to be made over the trackless ocean. To suppress the defences, specific enemy airfields and radar sites had to be attacked shortly before the bombers arrived. The success of these efforts in support of the B-52 crews is reflected in the bomber loss rate of only 2 per cent, a loss rate that was very low given the fact that no target in history was so well defended as was the Hanoi-Haiphong complex: not London, nor Ploesti, nor Berlin during the Second World War.[100]

The damage inflicted by the Guam- and Thailand-based B-52s (and by fighter bombers striking at other times of the day) was crippling. The Gia Lam railroad yard and repair facilities, the Bac Mai barracks, 80 per cent of North Vietnam's electrical power production, and 25 per cent of its petroleum stores were destroyed. More significantly, 2 days before the end of the campaign all organised air defence in North Vietnam ceased; surface-to-air missile firing became spasmodic and aimless and both the B-52s and fighter aircraft roamed over North Vietnam at will. The country had been laid open for terminal destruction, and the North Vietnamese had to do something to avoid that eventuality.

Hanoi sued for peace, and Richard Nixon and his National Security Adviser, Henry M. Kissinger, accepted. The aircrews could not understand: 'Why are we stopping now?'[101] they wondered. At least one prominent analyst has pondered the same question.

Sir Robert Thompson, probably the leading authority in the world on low intensity conflict and the key strategist in the defeat of the Malayan communist insurgency, has argued that the bombing effort should not have been stopped when the North Vietnamese sued for peace. If the goal was to drive North Vietnam completely out of the war so that the South Vietnamese could handle their insurgents and rebuild the country, the time to do that was after Hanoi's defences were depleted.[102] Douglas Pike, probably the leading authority in the West on the mind and mood of North Vietnam, believes that the North Vietnamese were truly shocked by Linebacker II and has written: 'Had a similar campaign of all-out bombing been made in early 1965' (when Generals LeMay and McConnell began calling for it), Lyndon Johnson probably could have achieved his goal of 'moving Hanoi's forces out of South Vietnam'.[103] Pike argues that although Hanoi would have maintained its objective of unifying Vietnam (just as Kim Il Sung retained his goal of 'reunifying' North and South Korea), Ho would have had to reassess the wisdom of seeking that goal through violence. The Korean paradigm is informative in other ways. Massive bombing in the spring of 1953, on a scale never before experienced by the North Koreans, forced a long truce—one that continues to this day—and has allowed the people governed from Seoul to prosper. But such was not to be the case in Vietnam.

Soon the war in South-East Asia was over for the United States, and all American forces were withdrawn. The United States had misapplied air power from one end of the war to the other. Even the 11-day campaign of December 1972—a tactical success—stopped far short of the goals it made truly achievable. Losses to the United States over the period from the early 1960s to the early 1970s were staggering: 2,561 fixed-wing aircraft and 3,587 helicopters were lost to hostile action (3,720 fixed-wing aircraft and 4,869 helicopters were lost altogether in connection with the war).[104] These losses could have been significantly reduced had President Johnson and Robert McNamara or President Nixon and Henry Kissinger used air power to its fullest potential.

Little more than 2 years after Linebacker II, Hanoi, in flagrant violation of the peace settlement that brought them relief from the strategic bombing, bounded across the demilitarised zone with tanks, penetrated deep into South Vietnam along the Laotian and Kampuchean borders, and quickly crushed the South Vietnamese. In the spring of 1975, with no American

air power to counter this naked aggression in violation of the 1973
settlement, Hanoi was finally victorious.

Bibliography

Anderson, Kurt, "Vietnam 'A Pinched and Hermetic Land." *Time*, 15 April 1985, p. 39.

Armitage, M. J., and Mason, R. A. *Air Power in the Nuclear Age*. Chicago: University of
Illinois Press, 1983.

Berger, Carl, ed. *The United States Air Force in Southeast Asia*. Washington: U.S. Government
Printing Office, 1977.

Church, George. "Viet Nam 'Lessons From a Lost War.'" *Time*, 15 April 1985, pp. 41–42.

Doglione, John A., Hogg, Donald T., Kimball, Richard D., McFadden, Julian R., Rapp,
John M., Walden, Ray Y., Wustner, Lorenz, F., Bond, Charles W., Buckner, Eugene
R., Hines, Frank T. *Airpower and the 1972 Spring Invasion*. USAF Southeast Asia
Monograph Series. Vol. II, Monograph 3. Washington: U.S. Government Printing
Office, 1976.

Fromkin, David, and Chase, James. "What *Are* the Lessons of Vietnam?" *Foreign Affairs*,
Spring 1985, p. 725.

Futrell, Robert F. *Advisory Years*. Washington: U.S. Government Printing Office, 1983.

Gelb, Leslie H., with Betts, Richard K. *The Irony of Vietnam: The System Worked*.
Washington: The Brookings Institution, 1979.

Lichtenstein, Nelson, ed. *Political Profiles: The Johnson Years*. New York: Facts on File,
Inc., n.d.

McCarthy, James R., and Allison, George B. *LINEBACKER II: A View From the Rock*.
USAF Southeast Asia Monograph Series. Vol IV, Monograph 8. Washington: U.S.
Government Printing Office, 1979.

Millet, Allan R., and Maslowski, Peter. *For the Common Defense: A Military History of the
United States of America*. London: The Free Press, 1984.

Momyer, William W. *Air Power in Three Wars*. Edited by A. J. C. Lavelle and J. C. Gaston.
Washington: U.S. Government Printing Office, 1978.

Morrow, Frank. "Viet Nam 'A Bloody Rite of Passage.'" *Time*, 15 April 1985, p. 22.

Nalty, Bernard C. *Air Power and the Fight for Khe Sanh*. Washington, Office of Air Force
History, 1973.

Office of the Assistant Secretary of Defense. Comptroller. *Southeast Asia Statistical Summary*.
Washington, 1973, Table 350A.

Peterson, A. H., et al. *Symposium on the Role of Airpower in Counterinsurgencies in
Unconventional Warfare*. Santa Monica: Rand Corporation, 1964.

Peterson, A. H., et al. *Symposium on Airpower: The Algerian War*. Santa Monica: Rand
Corporation, 1963.

Peterson, A. H., et al. *Symposium on Airpower: The Malaysian Emergency*. Santa Monica:
Rand Corporation, 1974.

Peterson, A. H., et al. *Symposium on Airpower. The Philippines Huk Campaign*. Santa Monica:
Rand Corporation, 1963.

Pike, Douglas. "The Other Side." In *Vietnam as History: Ten Years After the Paris Peace
Accords*, p. 76. Edited by Peter Braestrup. Washington: University Press of America,
1984.

Schandler, Herbert Y. *The Unmaking of a President: Lyndon Johnson and Vietnam*. Princeton:
Princeton University Press, 1977.

Summers, Harry G., Jr. *On Strategy: The Vietnam War in Context*. Carlisle Barracks,
Pennsylvania: Army War College, 1983.

Thompson, Sir Robert. "Rear Bases and Sanctuaries." In *The Lessons of Vietnam*, p. 105.
Edited by W. Scott Thompson and Donaldson D. Frizzell. New York: Crane, Russak
& Company, 1977.

U.S. Department of Defense. *United States-Vietnam Relations 1945–1967, IV, C.7.(a)*. "*The
Air War in North Vietnam*." "The Pentagon Papers." Washington: U.S. Government
Printing Office, 1971.

Wheeler, Johnson. "Coming to Grips with Vietnam." *Foreign Affairs*. Spring 1985, p. 750.

Who Was Who in America (With World Notables). Vol. IV. Chicago: A. N. Marquis Co.,
n.d.

4

Air Supremacy — The Enduring Principle

AIR COMMODORE P. D. L. GOVER

The first recorded use of an aircraft in war occurred on 23 October 1911 when an Italian pilot conducted a reconnaissance flight over the Turkish lines at Azizia in Tripoli. From the same campaign another role for an aircraft emerged with the first tentative bombing raids.

Although aircraft performance improved at an impressive pace before the outbreak of the First World War, aviation was still very much at an exploratory stage. The roles that could be performed by aircraft were therefore limited, and the perception of the day was that the primary role for aircraft was reconnaissance. Subsumed within this appreciation should have been the realisation that if it was worth mounting a reconnaissance mission, it was in the enemy's interest to prevent that mission succeeding. The springboard for air combat was therefore present at an early stage in the development of air warfare, but the First World War was some 3 weeks old before the first victory in the air was recorded. A further 6 weeks elapsed before the first air combat was fought.

On 25 August 1914 a German Taube aircraft on a reconnaissance mission of the French lines south of Mons was spotted by a flight of three Royal Flying Corps (RFC) aircraft. The British aircraft closed with and formated on the Taube. The German pilot tried to shake off the RFC aircraft, but when this proved impossible he landed the aircraft and fled the scene. The British aircraft also landed and after a fruitless search for the German set fire to the aircraft. A more significant event occurred on 5 October 1914 when a French two-seater Voisin spotted a German two-seater Aviatik reconnoitring the French lines. The French aircraft closed on the German machine and after a short battle the Aviatik was shot down. Air combat had arrived, and from this small beginning a new branch of combat entered the warfare lexicon: air supremacy.

The style and form of air combat changed little until the end of 1915. Engagements were unplanned and rather haphazard affairs of little tactical consequence except for the combatants themselves. However, two events occurred at that time that were to impact significantly on the development and future course of air warfare. The first was the perfection by the Dutch aircraft designer, Anthony Fokker, of an interrupter gear allowing a machine gun to fire through the arc of the aircraft's propeller. This development markedly improved the effectiveness of the German aircraft. But in terms of the evolution of air power, perhaps the more significant events were the changes in air combat pioneered by the German Air Force who appreciated the importance of sound tactics, the value of the cohesive formation and the need to fight for air supremacy.

With the advent of the aircraft as an essential element of a nation's military inventory, strategists and field commanders needed to understand the roles and capability of aircraft, and the employment of air power. Air supremacy is only one facet of air operations, but it is a critically important factor and an understanding, or misunderstanding, of its importance has had a significant impact on the outcome of modern warfare. While the lessons of history have increasingly highlighted the importance of air supremacy, no military strategy should be considered perpetually relevant. This essay therefore seeks to address the continued utility of air supremacy.

Air Supremacy—the Terminology

Although there is a simplicity in the expression 'air supremacy', the term is now taken in the West to apply to a specific set of circumstances, and additional terms are required to define other aspects of the prevailing air situation. The terminology in current use is as follows—

Favourable air situation. That condition in which the enemy is unable to interfere effectively with friendly land, sea or air operations,

Air superiority. That degree of dominance in the air battle of one force over another which permits the conduct of operations by the former and its related land, sea and air forces at a given time and place without prohibitive interference by the opposing force. Air superiority can therefore apply over a localised area of the battlefield for a specific period of time, or it can be associated with particular missions where highly localised air superiority forms part of the tactical situation.

Air supremacy. That degree of air superiority wherein the opposing air force is incapable of effective interference. Air supremacy refers to a wider and more extensive control of the air as in an area of operation.

Command of the air. This is taken as the absolute control of airspace in a specific theatre of operations: it subsumes the more limited concepts of air superiority and air supremacy.

The Historical Importance of Air Supremacy

Before looking at the current and future applicability of air supremacy, it is necessary to identify how important it is, how it can be achieved and what are the effects of achieving—or igorning—the concept. As the importance of air supremacy today is a function of experience, an understanding of past conflicts is therefore essential. It is accepted that the lessons of history must be treated with caution, but many aspects of warfare are pervasive: it is these enduring characteristics that need to be established. As Lord Tedder observed:

> The important thing is not to look back to the past, but to look to the future from the past.

The First World War

Fought above the mud and carnage of the trenches, the air battles of the First World War were concerned with achieving air superiority through the destruction of the enemy's air forces. Technical innovation, rapid improvements in aircraft performance and the evolution of air fighting tactics combined to produce a changing state of advantage. With the introduction of the synchronised machine gun and formation tactics, the German Air Force were the first to achieve a recognisable state of air superiority with the 'Fokker Scourge' over Verdun in the spring of 1916. The balance of advantage then moved towards the Allied Air Forces before returning to the German Air Force in 'Bloody April 1917' in which they achieved air supremacy. But with the introduction of new Allied aircraft types, an improved organisation underpinning Allied air operations and the arrival of American aircraft, Allied air power began to dominate. With the exception of their offensives in the spring of 1918, when the German Air Force achieved a degree of local success for the last time, the story of air warfare in 1918 was one of Allied domination.

Four major lessons emerged with the birth of air power from the First World War:

(i)   Air superiority had to be fought for, and a specific campaign waged to ensure its success.

(ii) Air forces could not support the land battle effectively without first achieving air superiority

(iii) The effectiveness of ground forces was markedly enhanced when supported by air power.

(iv) In a generally hostile situation, it was nevertheless possible to achieve a locally favourable air situation, and local air superiority.

The 1920s and Early 1930s

After the First World War there was an understandable slackening in the pace of technical development of military aircraft. For the first decade after the war the opportunity for testing ideas in combat was limited as the major actions that involved aircraft were the British and French colonial policing wars. Not surprisingly, thinking in European air forces tended to favour the three roles of colonial policing, air defence and anti-invasion. In the United States considerable thought and attention was given to the philosophy of strategic bombing. Furthermore, major pre-occupation of a number of air forces during this period was that they had to devote considerable energy to the consolidation of their independent, or semi-independent, status.

Despite the very clear lessons of the First World War, the 1920s and 1930s are noteworthy in that little active consideration was given to the requirements for gaining control of the air environment. However, the Spanish Civil War and the Sino-Japanese War were to introduce new parameters into considerations of air supremacy.

Sino-Japanese War

The Japanese had adopted a very cautious approach to the development of their own aircraft industry, tending to rely on imported aircraft, or aircraft built under licence. They were diligent in their analysis of aircraft design and construction techniques and by 1931 Japanese-designed and built aircraft were available for action. By the time war broke out between China and Japan in 1937, the Japanese Naval Air Force had become a highly potent weapon.

By a combination of brisk fighter battles and swift bombing attacks on airfields, the Japanese quickly overwhelmed the Chinese Air Force. Having achieved a comfortable measure of air superiority, the Japanese were then able to launch strategic attacks on most of the major Chinese targets. However, the fickle nature of air superiority was forcibly brought home to the Japanese when, on one occasion in late 1937, the Chinese Air Force caught Imperial Japanese fighter and bomber squadrons drawn up in straight lines on an airfield and succeeded in destroying some 200 aircraft. That particular lesson was frequently to be forgotten in the future by several countries, always with painful results.

Even when operating against an inferior air force, the Japanese found that if their bombers were not escorted by fighters, the attacking bombers would suffer unacceptably heavy casualties. To overcome this problem, the Japanese established forward operating bases which allowed the fighters to refuel and thereby extend their range and allow them to escort the bombers all the way to their targets. The value of the fighter escort has been relearnt many times since it was first employed by the Japanese; it remains a valid tactic 50 years later.

Spanish Civil War

In the Spanish Civil War the opportunity was taken by Germany, Italy and Soviet Russia to test their new aircraft, weapons and tactics. The Soviet support to the Republicans involved the Polikarpov I-15 biplane and I-16 monoplane fighters, and Tupolev SB-2 monoplane bombers. Italian assistance to the Nationalists consisted mainly of the Fiat CR32 biplane fighter and Savoia Marchetti SM79 and 81 monoplane fighters. Germany's early support to the Nationalists through their Condor Legion was with the Heinkel 51 biplane fighter and Junkers J2/3 transport bombers.

The early battles were inconclusive, with the Italian and Russian bombers remaining largely immune to the biplane fighters. In the air combat arena, both the Italian CR32 and the German He51 fighters were outclassed by the Soviet I-16 and the overall battle for air superiority moved in favour of the Republicans. But the arrival of modern German fighters (Messerschmidt Me-109), which were markedly superior to the Republican I-16, and bombers (Dornier 17, and Heinkel 111) quickly altered the balance of air power and allowed the Nationalist air force to gain air supremacy. In view of experiences in the early development of air combat it is surprising that initial German fighter tactics should have revolved around tight formations that proved difficult to control in the air: one of the lessons of the First World War had already been forgotten. After some early setbacks, the German fighter squadrons, under the skilful leadership of Werner Moelders, introduced the figure four formation. This loose formation was far more flexible and offered much better defensive cross-cover: it remains a basic fighter formation today.

During the latter stages of the war in Spain, the German Condor Legion was operating in conditions of air superiority bordering on air supremacy. Particular lessons that were learnt were the value of well-integrated close support and the use of bombers as long-range artillery. Indeed, so effective was the German Air Foce in supporting short-range ground operations that little consideration was given to the value of longer range penetrations and the strategic use of air power.

Battle for Poland

In 1939 the Luftwaffe's initial objective in the Polish campaign was to gain air superiority as soon as possible. In terms of aircraft strengths, the advantage was strongly on the side of the Luftwaffe, who could field some 900 bombers and fighters against the Polish Air Force's 290 aircraft. Drawing on their experiences in Spain, the Luftwaffe concentrated its activity on Polish airfields. Little opposition in the air was encountered in the early days of the conflict, as a large proportion of the Polish Air Force (PAF) had deployed tactically eastwards away from the immediate battle zone, leaving behind many of their older and less combat-effective aircraft. By the time the PAF entered the war as a fighting force on the third day of the war, the Luftwaffe had effectively won the battle for air supremacy. Of latent significance in this achievement was the fact that the result owed as much to the disruptive effect of the German bombing on Polish communications as it did to German success in destroying Polish aircraft in the air and on the ground.

Having achieved air supremacy, the next success of the Luftwaffe was in its support of the ground forces. With freedom of the skies the German Air Force provided the Army with timely and accurate reconnaissance, and used its fighter and bomber aircraft as long range artillery. The synergistic effect of this close co-operation was to add a new word to warfare: *blitzkrieg*.

Battle of Britain

Less than a year later, the Battle of Britain was the first air battle to be fought independently of a ground or sea offensive. The acknowledged German objective of the battle was quite simply air superiority over England. After the fall of France, Hitler signed the directive ordering the invasion of England, Operation Sea Lion. The responsibility for ensuring the success of the invasion rested firmly with the Luftwaffe. The Army prepared for invasion, but the German Navy could not operate effectively if subjected to attack from the air. The Luftwaffe were therefore required to gain command of the skies.

The initial German tactics were sound, in that their attacks on coastal convoys and installations forced the RAF fighters into the air to fight and hence enter a war of attrition. During August 1940 the German targeting priorities changed to concentrate on the RAF's fighter airfields, radar stations and command and control installations. Attrition on both sides was high, but the mathematical advantage was with the German Air Force. In retaliation for an attack on London on the night of 24/25 August, the RAF ordered an attack on Berlin: Hitler countered by ordering German air attacks to be switched and directed against London. The change in tactics by the Luftwaffe took the pressure off the Fighter Command airfields and control organisation and allowed the RAF to gain the initiative. The mass daylight raids on London on Sunday 15 September were effectively dispersed, and on 17 September Hitler postponed indefinitely Operation Sea Lion: the RAF had achieved a favourable air situation over southern England and by the turn of the year had gained a full measure of air superiority.

By far the most important lesson to be learnt from the Battle of Britain is that in the battle for air superiority the aim must be clearly identified and resolutely maintained. In all of its previous conflicts the German Air Force had acted in concert with ground forces. In these joint operations, planning had been detailed and thorough, but when fighting a pure air battle their aims were much less clear. In changing targeting priorities the Luftwaffe lost sight of the primacy of the air battle and accordingly lost the Battle of Britain. There was, however, a further significant element: in retrospect, it is clear that German Intelligence reports were frequently inaccurate. Such a weakness was, and remains, as critical a factor in war in the third dimension as in the other traditional environments on land and sea.

El Alamein

Remembered in history as primarily a crucial land battle, El Alamein is also important from the perspective of the development of air power thinking. In the desert campaign a wide-ranging battle for air superiority had been fought, including the use of aircraft to interdict the supply and fuel lines supporting Field Marshal Rommel's forces. At El Alamein, General Montgomery and the Army recognised that their best protection from the Luftwaffe lay in offensive sweeps and attacks on the enemy airfields, since this would—and did—achieve air superiority. Testimony to the effectiveness of the air effort is expressed in the view of Field Marshal Rommel who stated that:

> British air superiority threw to the winds all our operational and tactical rules.

Experience gained in the desert campaign in achieving air superiority, and in the use of air power when in a position of air superiority, proved so valuable that the Desert Air Force formed the model for all future tactical air forces. Specifically, acceptance and belief in the importance of air superiority over the active and support areas of the battle zone was to underpin military planning for the rest of the war.

Overlord

In the context of air supremacy, the Overlord operation, and the Allied campaign following the landings on 6 June 1944, is significant for two reasons. First, it demonstrated unequivocally that an inferior ground force operating under conditions of air supremacy could triumph. Such was the magnitude of Allied air supremacy that over 10,000 sorties were flown on 6 June without a single loss due to Luftwaffe action.

Second, Allied air supremacy denied any aerial reconnaissance to the German High Command and without accurate intelligence on the invasion's landing Rommel's strategy was driven to a concept of mobile defence. This strategy has parallels with the problems facing NATO in the Central Region, where the movement of large forces and reinforcements will be vulnerable to air power. During the Normandy campaign Allied Command of the air severely restricted the movement of German ground forces, and 6 days after the invasion Rommel commented:

> Our own operations are rendered extraordinarily difficult and in part impossible to carry out due to the exceptionally strong and in some respects overwhelming superiority of the enemy air force.

Air Supremacy—an Official Statement

By the beginning of 1943 the principles for the employment of air power had been firmly established, and the importance of air superiority fully appreciated. On 21 July 1943 the US War Department published the Field Service Regulations governing the Command and Employment of Air Power, FM 100-20. The doctrine stated:

> The gaining of air superiority is the first major requirement for the success of any major land operation ... Air Forces must be employed primarily against the enemy's air forces until air superiority is obtained ... Counter air force operations in the theatre must be carried on continuously and intensively to gain and maintain air supremacy ... .

Maritime Lessons

Meanwhile, as in the land environment, the advent of the aircraft was having profound effect on naval warfare. Indeed, the effects of air power at sea were in many respects more dramatic and pointed. No longer could warships and merchant navies operate with only the surface and sub-surface threats to consider; when within range of aircraft the air threat assumed paramount importance.

All the major sea battles involving air power in the Second World War had a common theme. From the efficacy of the Swordfish attacks at Taranto against the Italian Navy; the Japanese strike at Pearl Harbour, the sinking of the *Prince of Wales* and *Repulse* by Japanese land-based aircraft, to the effectiveness of the Luftwaffe attack on the Arctic convoys, the pervasive lesson was that sea power could be rendered inconsequential by air power.

The major influence of the aircraft at sea was to require that the air threat needed to be contained before naval power could be usefully employed. The great battles in the Pacific at Coral Sea, Midway, Guad-alcanal and Leyte Gulf between the Japanese and American carrier groups were primarily battles for air supremacy. Some surface and submarine action was also involved, but the primary strike weapon was the aircraft. In winning control of the skies the US Navy prepared the way for victory at sea.

The maritime environment also provides a graphic illustration of how a position of local air superiority can be established and utilised. When the German battle cruisers *Scharnhorst* and *Gneisenau* decided to run the gauntlet sailing through the English Channel in February 1942 the RAF had clear air superiority in the area. But with careful planning in providing the ships with an impressive fighter escort, with more than a little luck from the weather and with the assistance of poorly coordinated Allied aerial reconnaissance the German fighters were able to protect the ships without a single hit being scored.

The Jet Era

Although the jet fighter was developed and tested in the air combat arena during the latter stages of the Second World War, it was not until the Korean War that jet aircraft were used in any significant numbers. In many respects the employment of jet combat aircraft differed little from their propeller predecessors. While operating heights, speeds, range, turning performance and weapon release parameters were different, the underlying principles for the use of air power did not change with the introduction of the jet engine. Using the experience gained during the Second World War, the transition to the jet era should have been uneventful. But as in the aftermath of the First World War, many lessons were forgotten, and the ever-broadening aspects of air power itself were to introduce new factors into the air power equation. Subsequently, the lessons were modified in the wars in Korea, Vietnam, the Middle East and the Falkland Islands.

Korea

In Korea from the outset the UN air forces gained air superiority over the battle area, and at no time during the conflict was there a serious threat to the ground forces from North Korean or Chinese aircraft. While some impressive air battles were fought along the Yalu river between MiGs and Sabres, the battles were more symbolic than consequential. The UN (largely American) air forces were limited in the areas they could conduct bombing and offensive operations, and fought 'face-saving' operations to maintain air superiority south of the Yalu. Nevertheless, a measure of the

magnitude of Allied air superiority can be seen from the ratio of kills
between the MiGs and the Sabres of some 12:1 in favour of the Sabre.

The effect of having air supremacy over the ground battle zone was that
the Army never had to operate in a situation where it had to consider the
possible effects of enemy air action. Considerations surrounding air
superiority therefore fell from the thinking and activities of the Army and
close air support became the main concern and primary consideration.

Without having to wage a dedicated campaign to first gain air superiority,
the US forces did not have the spur to ensure that all their air effort was
co-ordinated to the best possible degree. As a result, the largely independent
air effort of the US Air Force, Navy and Marines was not as effective as
it should have been. The principles of centralisation of air power had been
forgotten or overlooked through inter-service rivalries.

A further lesson to come from the Korean War was that air supremacy
will not by itself guarantee the success of an air interdiction campaign.
Against an enemy that is not highly mechanised, who does not rely on an
infrastructure network for mobility and who can retain sufficient initiative
on the ground to match his efforts to his rate of supply, an interdiction
programme can absorb a great deal of air effort for little apparent result.
If, however, the enemy loses the initiative and becomes more sensitive
to his supply position, a skilful interdiction programme can have a decisive
effect. At that point the relationship between air supremacy and interdiction
is re-established.

Vietnam

The US air war with Vietnam had a number of similarities with the
war in Korea. Interdiction campaigns, as typified by the Linebacker I
operations, against largely unmechanised guerrilla-style forces, again
involved considerable air effort for marginal results. Political constraints
on the application of air power allowed an enemy sanctuaries from which
to husband and marshal forces, and hence significantly to dilute the
effectiveness of the air effort. But when the political restraints were
removed and air power was allowed to focus its fire power, the results
were impressive. The haste with which the North Vietnamese opted for a
cease-fire after some 11 days of the Linebacker II campaign was testimony
to the efficacy of concentrated air effort.

The fact that the United States could wage such an intensive air
campaign was due to the fact that in the classic air-combat sense the
United States had air superiority. At no time did the North Vietnamese
MiGs present a serious threat to the attack aircraft, and fighter engagements
were not on the same scale as in the Korean War. But the possibility, and
sometimes the reality, of an engagement with enemy fighters required a
return to the fighter escort tactic that had been developed over the skies

of Europe in 1944.

Despite their superiority in the air, the US forces could not operate within the strict definition of the term 'air superiority'. The new factor to enter the air equation was the Surface-to-Air Missile (SAM). Although SAMs had been in the military inventory for some time, and plans to operate within a SAM environment had been worked through, their large-scale use in Vietnam was nevertheless to have a marked effect on air tactics.

Countering the SAM threat involved both a change in operating concept and the development of scientific means of countering the missiles. The passive detection of a missile threat and the techniques of actively countering such a threat is rather outside the scope of this chapter. Nevertheless, the effect was to require that consideration—both in terms of aircraft configuration and force composition—had to be given to this aspect of air warfare. The US experience in Vietnam was that in a heavy missile threat environment the support force to attack force ratio could be in the order of 4:1. Consideration also had to be given to the need to suppress the enemy's Early Warning (EW) systems and inhibit his SAM sites. In short, maintaining air superiority was a complex task involving aggressive attacks against SAM and EW systems as well as evolving tactics for the employment of large support forces and the use of passive and active counter-measures. Hitherto, the contribution of air-to-ground defence to the achievement of air supremacy had been marginal, even with radar laid guns. Now, however, the struggle to acquire it was clearly no longer the prerogative of the fighter pilot.

The Middle East Wars

Israeli planning for the 1967 war was founded on the Israeli Defence Forces' belief that the first priority of the battle was the attainment of air superiority. The totality of their success is now part of the history of air warfare. In the space of some 4 hours almost three-quarters of the Egyptian combat aircraft had been destroyed, most of them on the ground. Air supremacy over the whole of the intended battle area had been ensured: air power had made its most dramatic contribution to the outcome of a war since Hiroshima and Nagasaki.

So obvious were the errors of the Egyptian Air Force in contributing to the success of the Israeli Air Force (IAF) that the circumstances surrounding the Israeli victory were probably unique and unlikely to be repeated in any future conflict. But historically the effectiveness of an unexpected air strike had already been clearly demonstrated by the Chinese Air Force's attack against the Japanese in 1937, and the Japanese attack at Pearl Harbour in 1940. Admittedly, after the 1967 war all the major air forces of the world took action to reduce the vulnerability of aircraft on the ground, so the ease of the Israeli Air Force's success is unlikely to be repeated. But the efficacy of the pre-emptive air strike—which was the cornerstone of the Israeli strategy—will undoubtedly remain a valid tactic for many years to come. Moreover, as explained elsewhere, a similar concept remains an essential ingredient of Soviet strategy. Subsequently, the Egyptian Air Force had the wisdom to learn from its mistakes. Above all it learnt the importance of air power in any future Middle Eastern conflict. Accordingly, Egyptian rearmament plans centred around the containment of Israeli air activity over the ground forces by the close integration of SAM, AAA and fighter aircraft. A much lower priority was given to the acquisition of a capability to offensively engage the IAF. The effectiveness of the strategy was put to the test in October 1973.

Three lessons can be drawn about air supremacy in the Yom Kippur War: two from Israeli action on the southern front against the Egyptians, and one from the intense activity on the Golan Heights against the Syrians.

Although the Israeli Air Force had experience of the earlier generation of Soviet supplied SAM-2 and SAM-3 systems, and had evolved measures to reduce the weapons' effectiveness, the performance of the SAM-6 and ZSU23-4 came as an operational surprise. The initial effectiveness of the Egyptian Air Defence umbrella severely inhibited the operations of the IAF, with the result that the Egyptian ground forces established well-defended bridgeheads and territory across the Suez Canal. However, with both technical and tactical improvisation, the IAF found that the new threats could be endured, and a defence suppression and counter-air programme was therefore conducted. As the Egyptian Air Defence system degraded, so Israeli Air Force air superiority improved. Of the combined Arab losses of some 450 aircraft, over half were accredited to the IAF. The second lesson to emerge from this campaign is the importance of air space management. The Egyptian and Syrian forces both operated comprehensive ground-based air defence systems. It has been estimated that 15–20 per cent of Arab aircraft losses were due to their own air defence forces. With losses of this magnitude, the need to identify friend from foe becomes vitally important.

In the north, the speed of the Syrian advance in the Golan Heights was such that the Israeli Air Force did not have the opportunity to wage a counter-air programme. The available IAF air effort was devoted to close support of their ground forces and as such was instrumental in checking the Syrian advance. The significant point about this action is that the Syrian Air Force did not engage in a counter-air campaign against the IAF to reduce the effort being applied at the front: had they done so, the result could have been significantly different.

Falklands Conflict

The Falklands conflict was characterised by two differing approaches to the role of air power. From the outset the UK Task Force was particularly aware of the air dimension and of the requirement to mount an aggressive campaign to engage the air threat. Contrastingly, the Argentinian Air Force did not appear to have an air strategy: it certainly did not display an understanding of the need to press at the earliest stage for a degree of air superiority.

At the start of the conflict the Argentinian forces had in excess of 110 Air Force and Navy aircraft in the medium-range fighter-bomber and bomber categories. To counter this potential threat the Task Force Commander had an initial deployment of some 22 Sea Harriers. A variety of ships' missile and gun systems were also available for defence of the Task Force.

After the early air combat encounters on 1 May 1982 in which Mirage/Dagger pilots fired air-to-air missiles with rather more bravado and hope than skill at Sea Harrier patrols, the Argentinian Air Force did not seek to engage the Sea Harriers in any form of contest for control of the air. Even more fortuitous for the Task Force was the fact that the Argentinians did not engage in a concerted counter-air programme. Instead of fighting a campaign in which the numerical advantage of attrition was in their favour, the Argentinians opted to use their air effort to disrupt the Task Force landings in, for them, an ever-worsening air defence situation. Whether they lacked the endurance to engage in air-to-air combat or whether their failure to do so was because of a strategic miscalculation remains uncertain, but whatever the cause, it rendered nugatory the considerable individual skill and bravery shown by the Argentinian pilots

Air Supremacy—The Current Position

This brief survey of the evolution of the concept of air supremacy illustrates that today its attainment is no longer a simple function of air combat between aircraft. It is a complex operation involving a wide spectrum of air and surface forces in a variety of roles, demanding attention to both offensive action and defensive measures. Weakness in the former will make it difficult to achieve air supremacy in the forward battle zone, while neglect of the latter will make it easier for the enemy to gain advange. Some of the more important considerations can be readily identified.

Offensive Action

As the Israeli Air Force showed so convincingly in 1967, the pre-emptive air strike can be devastatingly effective. The focal point of all aircraft operations remains the airbase complex. Within this generic term is included the aircraft carrier and the dispersed sites which characterise field operations for aircraft such as the Harrier. As an aircraft that is confined to its airbase does not pose a threat, the counter-air mission is the most

PLATE 4.1 Air superiority *par excellence*: McDonnell Douglas F-15 Eagle with Sparrow and Sidewinder missiles (*McDonnell Douglas Corporation*).

potentially effective action that can be employed in mounting a campaign to achieve air supremacy. But after the lessons of the 1967 war success will not be easy, as in likely conflict zones aircraft are now operated from hardened shelters. Also, much of the operational support structure including fuel, spares, weapons and control centres are hardened, and many airfields are equipped with rapid runway repair facilities. In short, even with the introduction of airfield denial weapons such as the JP233, the closure of an airbase is not assured and is, at best, likely to be temporary.

An important point to be appreciated in waging a counter-air programme is that initially the results are likely to be unspectacular. The Luftwaffe made the mistake in 1940 of stopping their counter-air offensive at the point when Fighter Command was at breaking point. If air resources are such that only a single campaign can be mounted at any one time, then priority should usually be given to the counter-air mission. However, there may be occasions, as on the Golan Heights for the Israeli forces, when the urgency of the tactical situation may be such as to require exceptional concentration of close support effort.

But in the terms of strategic priorities the counter-air battle has a fundamental primacy over all other missions against an enemy who himself possesses a formidable air arm.

Defence Suppression

Complementary to the counter-air mission is the need for defence suppression, since in a dense air defence environment it is essential to reduce the effectiveness of the defences and so enhance the success of the counter-air mission. In broad terms, there are three separate elements involved in successful defence suppression: threat identification, defensive counter-measures and threat engagement.

Threat identification and defensive counter-measures are technologically driven aspects of modern warfare. Both are subjects that merit—and receive—specific discussion, but in the air supremacy context it is their contribution to the overall counter-air mission that requires recording. Sensitivity and responsiveness in the electronic environment is a necessary and key aid to survival.

The active engagement of enemy air defence systems is not a new aspect of air warfare. In the First World War aircraft on both sides attacked anti-aircraft gun emplacements. At the tactical level little changed until the advent of the surface-to-air missile. During the Vietnam War the US Forces found that specific and detailed attention had to be devoted to countering the SAM threat. The identification of a new and specific threat led in turn to the development of specialised defence suppression weapons. The US experiences in Vietnam, and the Israeli actions against Egyptian and Syrian SAM systems, point to the requirement for careful integration into the overall counter-air mission of the defence suppression task. A further consideration is whether a counter-air attack force should of itself be fully self-contained with aircraft within the formation carrying countermeasures equipment together with defence suppression and primary attack weapons. Clearly, judgement decisions need to be taken in the light of the prevailing threat, but past experience suggests that the defence suppression mission is a specialisation in its own right. The USAF has acknowledged the special nature of the defence suppression task with the establishment of its F-4G Wild Weasel Squadrons. The European nations, who are now becoming more aware of the importance of the defence suppression mission, are currently deciding on their tactical approach to the task: the indications are that some form of dedicated mission may be necessary.

Fighter Escort

As an integral part of the counter-air mission, consideration must also be given to the requirement for fighter escort. Ideally, the attack force should be able to operate without an escort, and in many instances a correctly configured and tactically deployed attack mission should, in theory, be able to operate unescorted. But the practicalities of life are such that to the aircrew of the attacking force the fighter represents a highly unwelcome and persistent threat. Static defence systems can be mentally and tactically prepared for, and they do not induce an urge to jettison weapons to counter the threat. Engagement by enemy fighters is most unsettling to attack crews—particularly the less-well-trained and disciplined crews—and hence the presence of a fighter threat can frequently produce results quite disproportionate to the actual threat imposed. Experience from the First World War, the Spanish Civil War, the Battle of Britain, the Strategic Bombing offensive against Germany, the Sino-Japanese War, the Vietnam conflict and the Middle East Wars all suggest that the attack mission is greatly enhanced when supported by escort fighters. It is therefore surprising that in most of today's modern air forces the tactics of fighter escort are seldom practiced; there is evidence to suggest that the Soviet Air Force may be an exception.

Defensive Measures

The obverse to the foregoing is the requirement for an air defence system over one's own air space. In a stable peacetime environment the establishment of such a system commands no mystique. The requirement is for a comprehensive detection and early warning system, a Command and Control network, an integrated defensive system including fighters, SAMs and AAAs, and a high degree of survivability of the enemy's primary counter-air targets. Pervasive to the entire system is the need for a reliable identification system. Finally, the fundamentals of the system

PLATE 4.2   American F-16 fighters over Egypt (*USAF*).

can be markedly enhanced through the incorporation of Airborne Early Warning and tanker aircraft.

The bill for attempting to provide a comprehensive air defence system is enormous and readily prompts the question is it worth it? In the past air power has frequently been over-sold. In the 1930s the great weight of American thinking on air power was given towards the importance of the strategic bomber. While the very capable B-17 Flying Fortress was the direct progeny of this thought process, neither the great effort that went into the Allied strategic bombing of Germany in 1943–45, nor the US bombing of Japan, or Vietnam, had the effect that the strategic planners had anticipated. With the exception of nuclear weapons, air power could not by itself win a war. But as the Battle of Britain illustrated, a capable air defence could prevent defeat.

Developments since that period have been such that air power is now a more formidable and genuinely strategic instrument of war. The precision with which weapons can currently be delivered in all weathers ensures that air power has the capability of inflicting devastatingly accurate punishment. The need to protect against such attacks is essential and underscores why, for example, the United Kingdom identifies as one of its four national priorities the defence of the United Kingdom—and why so much effort is being taken in modernising the ground radar network; improving and expanding the fighter defences, enhancing its air-to-air refuelling forces and introducing Airborne Early Warning aircraft.

Air Superiority at Sea

Since the First World War major battles at sea have involved aircraft, and it has largely been the battle for air superiority at sea that has eventually decided the outcome of a particular conflict.

Most warships have a self-defence or full air defence capability. In theory, this allows a protective bubble to be established around a surface action group. But such a system is inevitably reactive to the enemy's initiative, and the shorter range and more reactive the system, the more likely it is to be penetrated. The aircraft carrier and carrier attack group concept allows the protective zone to be expanded to the radius of action of its fighter aircraft. With large US carriers embarking over 100 combat aircraft, of which typically half could be air defence aircraft, the carrier group has the air power to operate under a formidable air defence umbrella. However, as airfields are vulnerable to attack, so too are the carriers—but they are intrinsically more susceptible to incapacitating damage. The battle for air superiority at sea will therefore be critical, with victory likely to go to the side which gains ascendancy in the air.

Is Air Supremacy Achievable Today?

The simple answer to the foregoing question is a categoric 'Yes', as the Israeli example illustrates. However, the question is very scenario dependent. In broad terms air supremacy can evolve from three separate situations: by default, through indifference and through offensive and defensive action.

An extant example of air supremacy by default is that of Afghanistan, where the Afghan rebels have no air assets of their own, and only limited quantities of very basic anti-aircraft weapons. As a result, the Soviet Air Force has complete command of the air. What successes the Soviet forces have achieved in Afghanistan have stemmed largely from the use of their air power to strike at rebel positions, or for mobility of their ground forces. The benign air environment has also allowed the Soviet Air Force to mirror the Condor Legion's experiences in the Spanish Civil War in the testing of aircraft, weapons and tactics. Another example of air supremacy by default can be drawn from the Falklands War. As the Argentinian Air Force did not seek to engage the Task Force's aircraft, or to mount an effective counter-air programme, they accorded the Sea Harriers *de facto* superiority in the air.

Air superiority through indifference is a term appropriate to those conflicts where both sides have attack and fighter forces, but neither side appears willing to engage the other to formally contest air superiority. Such a situation exists in the Iran–Iraq War where air strikes are used largely for political propaganda purposes. The unwillingness of both countries to engage in an air supremacy conflict suggests that the air weapon is mutually regarded as the national strategic weapon: its loss could herald defeat. In some respects, this philosophy represents an advanced appreciation of the importance of air power. It could also indicate that the aim of the conflict is not immediately associated with military victory.

The achievement of air supremacy through offensive and defensive action is the essence of the application of air power. It can be attained, as the Israeli Air Force demonstrated in 1967, 1973 and more recently in 1982, when some 80 Syrian aircraft were destroyed for the loss of a single Israeli fighter. With the speed, range and striking power of modern aircraft a pre-emptive strike can administer a devastating blow. While airbase and aircraft survivability measures can do much to lessen the damage inflicted, the initiative in the application of air power is perhaps the most powerful force multiplier in the military inventory.

Air Supremacy—The Future

While some speculation is inevitably involved in forecasting the future, there are, nevertheless, two aspects of aviation about which there can be some degree of certainty. The first is the increasing use of the air as a war-fighting medium.

During the first 60 or so years of aviation the vast majority of military aircraft were directly associated with the combat mission. Civil aviation, while growing in numbers and overall capability, was nevertheless limited in the tasks it could perform. With the dawn of the jet airliner, but particularly the wide bodied jet transport, the ability of civil transport aircraft to perform a worthwhile strategic function increased dramatically. Equally important, the general public have become much more 'air conscious'. The military consequences of this spectacular growth in capability have led to US reinforcement forces for Europe now relying on the Atlantic air bridge, the Soviet troop rotations to East Germany being conducted by air and the Soviet invasion of Afghanistan being largely an airborne operation. The strategic mobility of personnel and material by air is now a fundamental part of war planning.

The ready availability of large aircraft has also assisted the development of air-to-air refuelling and Airborne Early Warning aircraft. Both of these aircraft are considered to be 'force multipliers', and are now important elements in the strategic military inventory.

The acceptability and utility of the helicopter has followed a similar growth pattern. Most modern defence forces rely heavily on helicopters for battlefield mobility, intelligence and short-range attack capability. In times of tension, the considerable civilian helicopter assets can also provide a useful boost to a nation's lift capability and mobility.

The foregoing trends are certain to continue into the foreseeable future. But pervasive to the use of these forces is that to operate at full effectiveness they require a benign air environment. If reliance is placed on the use of these forces, then it is axiomatic that a degree of air superiority is required in one's own air space.

The second fundamental change is that aircraft and weapons have become much more capable. The ability of aircraft to engage targets with pinpoint accuracy in all weathers throughout the day and night is an aspect of air power that will undoubtedly increase. Allied to the vastly enhanced capability of the aircraft itself, is improved weapon performance and the ability to better match weapon to target. The net result of these changes is a quantum increase in the effectiveness of air power, and comparatively modest air assets can command a strategic significance. The trend for the future is therefore for the need for a greater awareness of the importance of air supremacy.

A further advantage of the new technology is that aircraft can be made easier to fly and operate. As a result, much of the skill requirement for competent operation and weapon aiming can be eliminated. The acquisition of modern aircraft can therefore give an otherwise minor or unsophisticated air force the ability to command considerable fire power. Not only could such an acquisition significantly alter the power structure with a region, it could also influence the superpowers' view of a local military balance should they wish to intervene.

Future Fighter

Air supremacy started with the fighter: it will continue with the fighter as a key element until well into the next millennium. The United States is well into a re-equipment programme with its 'Teen' series of fighters, as well as actively considering the next generation of fighter; the Soviet Union is in the early stage of introducing its third generation jet fighters, Fulcrum and Flanker; and the European nations are introducing new fighter aircraft as well as looking ahead to a consortium European fighter.

The great changes between the second and third generation fighters stem from improvements in aircraft manoeuvreability and power, cockpit visibility, aircraft handling and target engagement capability. Such is the difference in capability between the two generations that exchange ratios of better than 10.1 are obtained in mock combat. In the European context the benchmark aircraft is the F-16: other aircraft fight to survive; the F-16 fights to win. It invariably succeeds.

The trends set by modern aircraft for manoeuvreability and ease of operation will be continued for the next generation of fighters. In a tight air environment the great advantage of manoeuvreability is that it gives the fighter the initiative to engage—or disengage—from the fight, it provides more target engagement opportunities and it makes the enemy's task much more difficult. Although Beyond Visual Range (BVR) weapons have their place in the fighter's armoury, in a dense electronic environment they are difficult weapons to use—particularly in the presence of an imperfect identification system. Where some form of visual identification is necessary, air combat takes place in a more compact area, thereby placing a premium on manoeuvreability.

Since current aircraft performance already borders on the limits of human physiological tolerance, future developments are likely to seek to expand the tolerance envelope rather than raise the structural limits. Ultimate top speed is therefore less likely to command a high priority, as it is considerably easier to impart the necessary speed to an air-to-air missile. But perhaps the most important area of improvement in the future will be associated with target detection, identification and engagement, where speed of response with minimum workload will be important if the pilot is to retain full awareness of the air situation.

Space

Although the absolute extension of the third dimension is into the infinity of space, the qualifying refix of 'air' to supremacy should theoretically limit discussion to activities in the atmosphere. However, recent developments in the space environment have produced echoes of the early days of aviation which merit comment.

The first of the parallels is unexceptional, in that much of the activity in the early years of both aviation and space was associated with developing knowledge of the new environment. The second parallel, however, is more intriguing: the use of the new medium for the reconnaissance task and the broad gathering of intelligence. To date, space and satellite systems have been invulnerable to enemy counter-action. But in line with the maxim that 'if a reconnaissance mission is worth mounting, it is in the enemy's interest to prevent that mission succeeding', it is not surprising that development is currently taking place into anti-satellite weapons systems. Current technology limits consideration to target systems in low earth orbits or trajectories, but is unlikely to remain so.

On the aviation scale of evolution, the foregoing parallels would place the use of space around the late 1915 period. The recent change that has upset the space equation has been the US Strategic Defence Initiative proposing the development of space weapons capable of engaging ballistic weapons in space. With such a system the United States would be in a position to conduct a campaign for supremacy in space: the comparison with aviation would then be around the early 1916 period and the introduction of the synchronised machine gun.

So very similar has been the development of aviation and space that it is difficult to see at what point they will diverge. Despite the pace of modern technology, the time scale for space development will nevertheless be considerably longer. But without legislation to prohibit—and be enforced—the use of space for offensive military action, it seems highly likely that space will continue to mirror the development of the 'air' environment. Space supremacy is likely to be as important, if not more important, than air supremacy: the principle will endure, albeit in an even greater enivronment.

5

Air Power in the NATO Alliance

AIR MARSHAL SIR MICHAEL KNIGHT

For over 40 years now there has been comparative peace in Western Europe, and for all but the first four of those years that peace has been guaranteed by the North Atlantic Alliance—now composed of sixteen sovereign nations, differing widely in historical, social and cultural perspective, but united in defence of their national freedoms by supranational means. Air power, for its part, had undoubtedly come of age in warfighting terms during the Second World War, and the air forces of a number of the Western nations had emerged from that conflict with a new-found sense of confidence in their ability to contribute flexibly, effectively and often decisively to the waging and winning of any future war. Ironically, but happily, since 1945 air power has played a different role in that cockpit of conflict which is Western Europe. There it has been a vital component of the West's deterrent strategy—and was indeed, for many years, its only credible component. Even today, certainly at the sub-strategic level, NATO's air forces confer on the Alliance its only guaranteed immediate reaction capability and its whole deterrent strategy is underpinned by the capacity of air power to be directed with minimum notice, whenever and wherever a threat may emerge. If deterrence were ever to fail and Europe to be flung into the cataclysm of all-out nuclear war, the air would also have its grim part to play alongside the other (primarily naval) components of strategic deterrence. But in the belief that this ultimate folly will never come to pass, these thoughts are directed to the part played by air power in the prevention, and, if that were to fail, in the containment of a European war at the lower levels of escalation.

The Ingredients of Alliance Strategy

Deterrence is, at once, a philosophy and a number of strictly practical measures which together form and strengthen it. These range from capable and well-equipped fighting forces, trained and practised to maintain the highest levels of readiness, through in-place supporting forces, again

81

highly trained and ready to receive and absorb very large numbers
of reinforcements from out of theatre, to continuous and increasingly
sophisticated means of reconnaissance and surveillance providing timely
indication and warning of any developing threat and the adequate protection
of civilian populations against that threat. Above all, in an alliance of
democratic nations credible deterrence relies on the maintenance of the
political will to act in resolute and timely manner for and in the best
interests of that alliance, and on the continued understanding and support
of the majority among the peoples of its member nations. None of these
elements can be neglected in the face of a threat which has grown stronger
and itself more credible year on year. Whether or not the Soviets and their
Warsaw Pact allies intend to launch an offensive on the Western Alliance
or on any of its constituent parts, it is a fact that they have continued to
build up the capability so to do. Were, in the event, one or more elements
of NATO's overall defensive strategy to be so weakened in Soviet eyes as
to justify the very grave risks of attack, a former Deputy SACEUR[1] has
identified the critical requirements for the successful defence of Western
Europe as being:

> early decisions to bring in-place forces up to wartime strength;
> the rapid introduction of reinforcements into all three regions of
> Allied Command Europe;
> the attrition of Warsaw Pact air forces through offensive and defensive
> counter-air;
> successful defence of the Atlantic and Mediterranean lines of com-
> munication and of the European ports and the UK base through
> which reinforcements will pass; and
> the delay, disruption and destruction of Soviet follow-on forces
> before they can be introduced into the battle.

The Nature of the Threat

Of course, these requirements have to be set against the threat, and
although other studies have covered that aspect of the subject in detail,
some broad generalisations are useful here as a means of putting the
problems of NATO's air forces into some sort of perspective. It has
become something of a truism—but, for all that, a sobering fact—that the
forces available to the USSR and her Warsaw Pact allies are immensely
strong 'across the board', with modern, technologically advanced equipment, and with personnel well-trained for all conditions of modern war,
now more flexibly controlled and generally well motivated to 'the cause'.
They would make formidable opponents were they to be led into an attack
on the West. And they would have some very real advantages were they to

PLATE 5.1 Airborne early warning for NATO: five E-3A AWACS early warning aircraft parked at the NATO airbase at Geilenkirchen, West Germany. With its long-range airborne radar, the AWACS performs special surveillance, primarily searching for threats that could go undetected by conventional ground radar. Multinational crews transmit the data to NADGE (NATO Air Defence Ground Environment) ground stations equipped with AEGIS advanced data processing equipment and special communications equipment. At these sites, commanders direct their own nation's fighter interceptors and surface-to-air missiles to protect their national borders from low-level threats

(Huges Aircraft Company).

do so with little warning—advantages which would include numbers, battle-preparedness, reserve strength, a measure of standardisation which NATO might envy, a degree of centralised direction which it would not (but which would, nevertheless, be very useful in bringing the Pact to war) and comparatively more easily manageable problems of re-supply.

In air force terms, not only have the Soviets maintained—even increased—their quantitative superiority as the years have gone by, they have, more recently, greatly enhanced the flexibility of their forces by a now well-publicised reorganisation of their frontal aviation. And long gone are the days when the West could gain comfort from a knowledge either of the Soviets' technical inferiority or inadequate training standards. Even were that not to be so, there are practical (if unquantifiable) limits to the degree by which advanced technology can counter-balance sheer weight of numbers. In an essay[2] put together by two American students of air warfare, that latter fact was adduced as being one of the main lessons re-learnt from the very comprehensive series of AIMVAL/ACEVAL tests carried out by the United States in the late 1970s, and the authors went on to suggest that, by as objective a measurement as could be applied in this case, the qualitative gap behind NATO's combat aircrews and those of the Warsaw Pact had, anyway, steadily narrowed to the point at which the Western Alliance could no longer confidently claim the edge. There is no denying the argument that people still count, but when generally higher standards and, specifically, regular and realistic advanced combat training have become increasingly the order of the day in the air forces of the Pact, then that is an important development which NATO's commanders cannot ignore. Indeed, they may even learn (as some member nations of the Alliance have already learnt) that the Soviets' tendency to specialise early in role and to remain long in a given specialisation have much to commend them in terms of the maintenance of operational standards.

Of course, the Soviets have some obvious advantages in all of this which stem from aspects of their situation which the West would not wish to copy. The exercise of personal initiative has never ranked high among the qualities expected of the Eastern bloc's combat aircrew, and whilst this is scarcely consonant with the most flexible application of air power, it must do something to overcome such modern 'Western air force' problems as the wish of aircrew to influence their own career patterns or to opt in favour of altogether different careers. There are not too many indications that the Soviets and their allies are losing to civil aviation the increasing numbers of combat-trained aircrew now leaving NATO's air forces. Indeed, it is unlikely that such a situation would be tolerated by the air commanders of the Warsaw Pact. In the West the process is part and parcel of personal freedom, and as such is willingly accepted. However, there is a consequent weakening of combat capability, whether that be in the loss of trained personnel *per se* or in the deflection of too many experienced front-line aircrew—and, every bit as important, ground personnel—to the continuing task of training new people. The situation shows every sign of worsening in the years immediately ahead, and it must be matched by positive measures to improve retention by enhancing the quality of life for serving personnel and perhaps by some innovative thinking about 'composite careers' which allow a freer passage both ways between the military and civil sectors. The problems may seem very great, but the cost of not solving them is likely to be even greater.

The Functions of Air Power for NATO

All that said, there is much that is right about the air forces of NATO, and, indeed, a refreshing will to tackle the difficulties. Airmen, as a breed, tend towards optimism, and the 'can do' spirit is still very much alive. What, then, are we asking our people to do? What, in short, are the functions of air power for NATO which must be practised in peace if they are to work in war?

Broadly speaking—and in a reasonably coherent chronological order—they include:

air reconnaissance in all its forms. Monitoring activity in every element from space to sub-surface would play a vital part in helping to gain the maximum warning of attack. Of course it would continue to be of importance throughout the course of any subsequent hostilities but it is perhaps in the early-warning phase that its contribution would be of greatest value—if only because a swift and firm response to an emerging threat may give the enemy both cause and opportunity to withdraw. If that were not to happen, then

combat air reinforcements would have to be very rapidly moved forward from their home bases to the theatre of operations, supported by

the carriage in transport aircraft, both military and civil, of essential personnel and ready-use supplies, well in advance of the passage by sea of the balance of material not already pre-stocked in theatre.

As the threat developed, so would the need for the defence (including, of course, air defence) of vital installations, and this would almost certainly include, at an early stage of any conflict,

offensive counter-air activity designed to limit the effectiveness of the enemy's primary means of attack.

PLATE 5.2   USAF Lockheed C-5B long-range strategic transport (*Lockheed Aircraft Company*).

With the advance of his land forces would come the need for air interdiction, both behind the immediate battle areas and deep into those of his rearward support.

Depending on the perceived requirements of army commanders and the degree of priority which could be accorded to each, the close support of Alliance ground forces, both in the application of airborne firepower and in the provision of tactical airlift are well-practised and well-understood roles for air power in war, whilst

at sea, operations against submarines, surface shipping and the enemy's long-range aircraft (including stand-off missile-carriers) would represent a continuing priority call on NATO's air forces.

To equip, train and prepare for this great variety of tasks is not only a daunting but a very expensive proposition. However, it is not one that has to be taken either in isolation or from a 'standing start'. Give or take a few patchy areas, perhaps too thin a cover here and there and some evidence of less than robust logistic support—NATO's air forces do, between them, still contain some of the world's best equipment and some of its best trained personnel. Faced with a steadily increasing threat, no prudent military man would rest content with what he has, and the demands will properly be for more capable equipments and for the people to use them effectively. But NATO's commanders also recognise that there are many conflicting calls on the wealth available to their respective nations, and that no effort can be spared in the search for the every greater cost-effectiveness of military man and machine. In that context, air forces have never been slow to meet the pace of technological change and a willingness to exploit the inherent benefits of increased standardisation across the whole gamut of activity, from weapons procurement to training, must continue to work to the advantage of the Alliance.

Current Capabilities

To examine in a little more detail the base-line from which NATO's air forces can develop and improve in the years ahead: reinforcement is certainly one of the biggest practical problems that would face the Alliance were it ever required to move speedily from a purely defensive posture to a war-fighting capability. In the transition from their peacetime locations to their in-theatre operational bases, there can be no doubting the ability of air forces to move very rapidly indeed. Not only are extremely detailed plans already drawn up and constantly up-dated, the necessary real estate, works services and, in many cases, logistics support packages are now in place, the concept of collocated operating bases is well developed, and squadrons and units regularly practise their reinforcement roles—whether that be across the Atlantic or in the movement from one to another region of Allied Command Europe. Significant numbers of supporting personnel, troops and quantities of priority freight can also be moved by air, and, here again, peacetime planning and exercise activity have confirmed the practicality of enhancing a purely military airlift capability by the resources available in the nations' civil aviation fleets.

Of course, the greater problem of reinforcement is not that of establishing a timely presence and a basic war-fighting capability whenever it may be needed. Rather is the practical difficulty that of transporting, often over long distances, the enormous tonnages of heavy equipment and war consumables which would be needed to give large-scale army reinforcement a capability for sustained operations. It is a problem which, for obvious reasons of capacity and cost, can be solved neither by the air nor by the permanent basing of still larger regular forces and their equipments on the continent of Europe. That said, air power can help in other less direct ways. On the one hand, early and effective air operations can blunt the edge of enemy attack and, hence, buy a little of that always precious commodity—time. This would be achieved, not least, by limiting the capacity of enemy offensive air for decisive action in the early stages of the land battle and by early attempts to prevent the necessary flow of his reinforcements to the front. NATO's air forces would also undoubtedly play a major role in the maritime battle, where a primary aim would be the protection of very large numbers of surface ships carrying reinforcements and supplies across the Atlantic and North Sea. Perhaps of particular significance would be the role played by maritime air in anti-submarine warfare—that most difficult of war-fighting arts, but one in which NATO's air forces are well practised and on which technology may have begun to swing the delicate balance of advantage slightly the way of the hunter in recent years.

Whilst that crucial battle was being fought over, on and below the seas, it would certainly be the case that the in-place and immediate reinforcement forces in Europe itself would be under increasing pressure from the numerically superior forces which faced them. Soviet doctrine has consistently maintained that a prime and early objective in war is the destruction of the West's ability to escalate, and that presupposes determined efforts to take out NATO's nuclear assets, its early-warning capability, its communications, its command structure and its war reserves—probably in that order. In that they pose a clear threat to the success of any offensive, the West's air bases must also be considered prime targets for Soviet/Warsaw Pact attack in the early stages of any war in Europe—whether that be in the Central Region or on the flanks. Perhaps slightly less pressing in timescale, but of growing importance were the fighting to continue, NATO's reinforcement ports, airfields and lines

PLATE 5.3 An RAF Tornado strike/attack aircraft dropping airfield denial and destruction munitions during trials (*Hunter Engineering Ltd.*).

of communication would also come under attack.

The tasks for NATO's air forces within Europe are, therefore, broadly two-fold, and they encompass the classic roles of defence and offence. Of course, the two are now so inextricably interwoven that each works in the direct interest of the other. For example, the lack of an effective air defence would positively invite attack which, in that particular scenario, could only be countered by offensive action against the enemy's air assets on the ground. On the other hand, the strongest possible air defence cannot wrest the initiative from an attacking enemy, it can only blunt the edge of his attack and, at best, force him to reconsider his tactical objectives.

All that said, it is a *sine qua non* of deterrence—particularly within a strategy of flexible response and against a wish consistently to raise the nuclear threshold—that as high a priority as possible be given to air defence. Effective and balanced air defence will be at a premium in periods of tension, transition to war and the early stages of war itself. Early-warning and control facilities, which have been given a step increment in recent years by the deployment of a NATO Airborne Early Warning (AEW) force, must continue to receive priority for the funding of state-of-the-art improvements—whether they be in detection capability, performance in a degraded electronic warfare environment or physical protection against enemy attack. If NATO could rely on the continued effective functioning of its AEW and air defence ground environment facilities, if it could continue to develop a mix of active and passive measures, including dispersal and repair of damaged airfield pavement, if it could up-grade its surface-to-air forces and equip its fighters with advanced air-to-air missiles which, *inter alia,* had genuine capability beyond visual range, above all, if it could break the log-jam which has for so long blocked progress towards a thoroughly effective and foolproof system of identification to assist the resolution of today's problems of airspace control—then it might count itself in a strong position either to sow enough seeds of doubt in the minds of the opposition as to stay the attacking hand or, were that not to happen, then to inflict an unsustainable loss-rate on his offensive aircraft.

The other side of the coin is, of course, the enemy's defensive threat to the Alliance's offensive air power. The need for that offensive air to be directed against counter-air targets—including runways, hardened aircraft shelters, dispersed aircraft, fuel and weapons stocks and command, control and communication (C^3) facilities—becomes imperative if the enemy has not been deflected by the effects of the Alliance's air defences. In this article, and in the contributions of others, it has been stressed that it is offensive not defensive action that wins wars; but even before the war-winning stage, only offensive air operations offer any real prospect of destroying the enemy's air assets before he can use them to force his own victory. Without straying too far into the detail of the land/air battle (which is the province of others in this compilation of essays), it is probably true to say that, for some time to come, disruption of the enemy's offensive air bases will continue to provide the most immediate relief against attack on our own vital installations. There is much debate as to whether the most lucrative targets in the complex that makes up a modern air base are runways, command centres, stocks, aircraft or personnel. However, it is unlikely that an attack on the West would have been launched by the Soviets without adequate reserves of aircraft, air and ground personnel, spares and munitions—which would tend to place their destruction in the second order as a quick-acting relief for NATO.

On the other hand, runways and airfield pavement can be repaired, and Soviet combat aircraft, though increasingly sophisticated in performance, are probably still rather more ruggedly constructed than many of Western manufacture—and thereby capable of operation from partially degraded surfaces. The most that can be said is that offensive air bases must be high-priority targets in any European conflict, and that any attack on them would almost inevitably have to be repeated every 36 to 48 hours for its effect to be marked. When that consideration is set against the great number of offensive airfields and emergency operating strips available to the Warsaw Pact, the conduct of the counter-air campaign can be seen for what it is—not only the most important, but by a large margin the most demanding facing NATO's air forces.

Another possibility—that of attempting to take the battle to the enemy in the air over his own territory—would seem to have even less to commend it to NATO's planners. A third option within the broad objective of negating the enemy's offensive air threat might be in the disruption of his command and control of that threat. However, this is probably best considered as an adjunct of other options rather than as an aim in itself. The total disruption of the Warsaw Pact's C^3 and intelligence ($C^3$1) networks is now (and will probably long remain) an immensely complex operation, which could not be guaranteed to succeed and which could, anyway, increasingly be countered by resort to more autonomous operations.

Of other possible applications of offensive air power by NATO, interdiction (including battlefield air interdiction) and close air support are dealt with in some detail elsewhere. Suffice it here to comment merely that deeper interdiction has recently acquired high visibility with the development of the doctrine of 'follow-on forces attack'. SACEUR[3] has himself drawn attention to the 'serious repercussions on Pact mobilisation and deployment flow' which would result from the interdiction of the Soviets' vital (and comparatively vulnerable) reinforcement patterns. However, he has recognised (and NATO Ministers have accepted) the need for some fairly substantial improvements by the Alliance if it is to become capable of achieving this highly desirable aim—improvements which include better real-time surveillance, target acquisition and intelligence means, a more survivable and responsive C^3I system and conventional weapons systems which can accurately and effectively engage targets well to the rear of the forward edge of the battle area (FEBA).

Aspects of Deep Interdiction

In an interesting and detailed study[4] of the role of conventional air power in NATO Europe, interdiction is assessed as being probably the most effective against an enemy on the offensive and relying on rapid movement and massive fire power—which certainly typify what we know of Soviet military thinking. Many commentators have drawn attention to the practical difficulties which the Soviets would face in maintaining the momentum of advance. However, for the West, the overriding problem lies in its ability to withstand the massive force which the Soviets could undoubtedly bring to bear before the effects of interdiction began to bite. By most calculations, Europe would be in for another very 'near-run thing'.

It is, nevertheless, both relevant and instructive to examine the possible effects of deep interdiction, particularly in the context of likely developments in technology which could, given time, make it a more viable option for the conventional phase of war in Europe—rather than, as now, most probably one for the employment of tactical nuclear weapons. There is no doubting that targets would be there to be hit; indeed, they would be both numerous and potentially lucrative in terms of slowing down the momentum of the enemy's attack. They would include critical bridges and similar choke-points; railway marshalling yards—particularly where delays were incurred by the need for guage-change; troop and vehicle assembly areas; support airfields; and rear command posts. Time bought by conventional attacks on such targets would be trebly valuable for NATO in lengthening the period during which in-place forces could withstand the first weight of attack, allowing the Alliance's own reinforcement plans to be brought into effect and giving the politicians of both sides the chance to negotiate—with the continuing pressure of military activity to remind them of the awful consequences of their failure.

Of course, almost by definition, all of this would be taking place at a time when the Alliance's available combat strength was still some way short of its potential; and, in consequence, the proper allocation of priorities as between scarce offensive resources would be a particularly difficult problem. There could, for example, be no question of any exclusive concentration on deep interdiction whilst the Alliance's ground forces were being sorely pressed by the power and weight of a Warsaw pact onslaught. Patently, that would not serve the purpose of 'buying time'; and SACEUR[5] himself presents the attack of follow-on forces as a 'complementary and mutually reinforcing' operation to that of defence at the General Defensive Position. Again, the aim of raising the nuclear threshold may not be met by the dedication of all dual-capable resources to deep interdiction at the conventional level. Even were attrition losses to be kept within reasonable limits, such tactics might persuade Soviet commanders of the need to mount pre-emptive attacks deep into NATO territory, which would effectively precipitate the Alliance into early escalation. It is also a fact that, certainly in the foreseeable future, there would be major cost implications for NATO in acquiring a guaranteed capability for the effective conventional attack of sufficient 'follow-on force' targets to stop a major Warsaw Pact offensive in its tracks. Indeed, technology may not yet be capable of overcoming all the very real practical problems which currently beset this most complex requirement.

All that said, there are very many theoretical advantages to be gained from the concept; and it is certain that a great deal of development work will continue—as it must if major advances are to be made across a whole range of highly complex technologies covering, *inter alia*:

> the protection of delivery vehicles in an increasingly hostile defensive environment;
>
> the development of improved target-acquisition sensors capable, in all weathers, of effective discrimination against very advanced decoys and other deceptive counter-measures and capable, also, against targets moving less than predictably;
>
> real-time intelligence-gathering, collation, analysis and dissemination—ideally to delivery vehicles or crews already airborne;
>
> flexible target allocation and weapon/target matching—again in flight; and
>
> a range of precision-guided and target-optimised munitions, including airburst, impact, armour-piercing, anti-personnel and delay.

Truly, there will be no shortage of problems to attract the attentions of tomorrow's hi-tech wizards, or, indeed, those of the day after and not the least of those problems will be the development of technologically feasible systems at a cost which can be borne by defence budgets which are, at best, severely constrained and which may, in real terms, even reduce in the years ahead.

Beyond the Central Region

Of course, the battle may not be one exclusively fought in the Central Region of Europe; whilst much of the foregoing comment is generalised, it does have perhaps a readier application to Central Europe than to the Alliance's other European regions. However, an exclusively Central Region battle is not the only conceivable scenario. Even if that were to be the Soviets' primary objective, it seems inconceivable that simultaneous attacks—if only to confuse, distract and disrupt NATO—would not be mounted in the North or South, and probably both. Nor does it in any way minimise the crucial importance of a Central Region battle (should that come to pass) to suggest the possibility of fighting in, for example, the Northern Region/EASTLANT/UKAIR areas of interest with the major combattants in the Centre continuing to face each other, fully armed and 'ready to go'—but not actually fighting. If (purely as one possible option) the Soviets had determined that, at a given time, a combination of NATO's current force dispositions, some evidence of a lack of political cohesion and perhaps the temporary diversion of attention to another of the world's trouble-spots, favourable weather and the movement forward of Warsaw Pact forces for 'exercise' purposes in the North and Centre— all combined to make a swift attack on Northern Norway a viable option, with the risks acceptable in the light of the possible gains, then the Alliance could be faced with almost a *fait accompli* in the North while the Centre was being held in a form of stalemate—the Soviets not intending and the West not prepared to move forward across borders. And, of course, exactly the same scenario might be drawn for the Southern Region of Allied Command Europe.

The Advance of Technology

All of which serves to underscore the need for NATO's military planners, and especially the air planners, to be not only aware but adaptable, and prepared to view the Alliance's relatively limited available war-fighting assets in the most flexible manner. Here it seems likely that emerging technology will provide a useful bonus, though not perhaps quite the panacea that some would have it—and certainly not available 'on the cheap'. At the lower end of the technological spectrum, advances in computer-aided design and manufacture, in the computer-controlled testing of components and in the development of new fatigue-resistant materials should all help reduce the frightening costs of inadequate reliability and difficult maintainability in defence equipments. As an aside, it is now more than ever necessary that those who specify the operational requirements for all new equipments should place reliability and main-tainability (R&M) alongside performance, cost and timescale and not allow the two first objectives always to be sacrificed to the demands of the other three. In the long (and, in some cases not all that long) run, inadequate attention to and insistence on improved R&M will lead directly to lower front-line numbers by reason of escalating procurement and through-life costs. The generally sound policy of adjusting the balance of aircraft platforms versus weapons more in favour of the latter could be wholly distorted were the platforms to become too costly either to acquire or own.

On a more positive note, a whole range of developments is now either in hand or under serious study in the battle to improve system R&M. They range from the injection of 'front-end' money to meet tighter R&M goals set at the early project stage, to the incorporation of built-in test into sub-systems—a technologically complex and costly (but potentially both time-saving and rewarding) exercise; from the provision of ever greater redundancy in aircraft controls and systems to still largely undeveloped computer-based techniques of 'self-cure' by use of multi-function control surfaces; and, as an adjunct of all this, very worthwhile developments in the techniques of battle-damage repair.

As to weapon development itself, it seems likely that the principle of making the weapon do more of the work will become increasingly attractive—again with reference to the balance between investment in platforms and in weapons. Whilst exciting developments continue to take place in airframe and engine technology and design, there is relatively even more potential for improvement in weapons technology. Among the many important projects currently affecting weapons manufacture and delivery are improvements in navigation and guidance systems; satellite and other communications; electro-optical, infrared and radar sensors, reconnaissance and surveillance systems; warhead technology; the development of remotely-piloted vehicles (for a whole variety of roles); and immensely accurate cruise missiles, especially when enhanced by the flexibility afforded by air-launch. There is now not only the incentive but the means to extend the flexibility and adaptability of air power by harnessing missiles and their associated technology to improve both effectiveness and cost-effectiveness.

That flexibility and adaptability will continue to call for the manned aircraft in most situations of war or near war—if only because, as Scott Crossfield long ago reminded us, 'man is the most efficient and flexible control device you can install in an aircraft'. However, the manned aircraft may increasingly become the carrier, positioner and final releaser of weapons of ever greater stand-off capability, and extreme agility may be built into the weapon rather more easily than into the aircraft. The inherent advantages of air power (speed of reaction, flexibility in application and concentration on target)—these advantages will be enhanced rather than replaced by the right combination of man and missile. And it must surely make every sense to seek to allocate the most difficult, dangerous, expensive, but vital part of any given war mission to what is potentially the least expensive component of the overall weapons system—the weapon itself.

Towards the Next Century

So what of the future, beyond the next span of years, and on into the twenty-first century? It would, of course, be brave if not fooolhardy to speculate within too clearly defined a NATO scenario.

There are few signs of any slowing down of the pace of change—indeed, rather the reverse. But, given that the world is spared its own destruction, one or two pervasive factors will undoubtedly be in evidence as far into the future as anyone may wish to look. Despite the best efforts of the peacemakers, man will continue to fear, envy, to seek power over and, from time to time, to fight man. Technology will continue to force the pace of development and potential achievement, and air forces will continue to be among its early beneficiaries—necessarily so, as we move ever more deeply into the jungle of electronic warfare. Europe may well remain the arena in which East and West will confront each other with the world's most sophisticated aircraft and weapons.

Whatever the ways in which future technology may assist the attacker, it seems likely that the increasing depth, variety and capability of enemy defences around such large and important fixed targets as airfields will continue to make the task of conventional counter-air both hazardous and complex. Success could well be bought at high cost and, at worst, it might still not be guaranteed.

The solution to this dilemma must be sought in the development of successive new generations of increasingly accurate and lethal stand-off weapons optimised for the comprehensive cratering of airfield surfaces, the disruption of repair and recovery and, as accuracy and lethality increase, the destruction of hardened aircraft shelters themselves. Such weapons are still at a comparatively early stage of development, and it has yet to be shown that they can be made cost-effective for the key role of neutralising enemy airfields by conventional means. Assuming that they will, eventually, be so developed, future weapons such as these would be carried towards their targets by manned attack aircraft, so that every early advantage could be taken of surprise, evasive routeing, tactical timing, force concentration and the option of alternative targetting en route. But the 'first wave' attacks would be the province of the stand-off weapon, if necessary followed by defence suppression and re-attack by the launchers of those first weapons.

The same tactics could, of course, be used against enemy shipping and such other high-value, highly defended targets as headquarters, vital communication centres, second-echelon logistic areas, transportation complexes and choke-points, which take us well into the business of interdiction. The point is that to the flexibility of the future manned offensive aircraft must increasingly be added the sophistication which technology can bring to the range of weapons carried by it, as, of course, to its identification, deception and penetration equipment. The argument is not whether the missile can replace the manned aircraft: a mix of the two must offer the most cost-effective option against a range of future targets, and, indeed, offensive roles.

Nearer the battlefield, the situation is rather different, though in its own way no less complex. Developments in aircraft capable of short take-off and vertical landing have more immediate application to close air support and battlefield air interdiction, though the concept itself becomes increasingly attractive for other combat aircraft, as a means of reducing dependence on runways and their associated fixed installations. In the immediate support of land forces, the problems of the future are likely to be different only in degree from those already all too well known. To the difficulties of identification (both of target and attacker) are added the proliferation of the enemy's mobile defensive systems, the confusion inevitable in any fast-moving conflict and the need for accurate and timely intelligence as a prerequisite of priority tasking. All of this postulates the development by land and air components of ever more closely co-ordinated activities. Ground forces must be prepared to take out the enemy's surface-to-air defences just as air-delivered weapons are expected to be used against tanks; suitably armed helicopters must work in close concert with artillery and then 'double' as high-speed armoured personnel carriers; fixed-wing aircraft equipped with new-generation synthetic aperture sensors and 'launch-and-leave' weapons could, certainly in the early stages of the battle, operate effectively against enemy concentrations from relative safety behind the FEBA; and developments in perhaps the most fruitful area of new technology—the acquisition, processing and dissemination of information—will ensure the required degree of co-ordination between air and ground forces.

Among the earliest and still most crucial of roles for air power are those of reconnaissance and surveillance. As has already been suggested, they are important during peace, vital in any period of transition to war and, certainly if the most cost-effective use is to be made of offensive and defensive systems, crucial in war itself. Timely and accurate intelligence of the enemy's preparations, movements, force concentrations and deployments will continue to be necessary for the successful conduct of air operations over land or sea, and post-attack analysis will have an equally important role to play in helping to ensure that later missions are impaired as little as possible by 'the fog of war'. In the fields of reconnaissance and surveillance, there have long been the most optimistic hopes for the use of unmanned systems, but in looking towards the turn of the century and beyond, it would seem likely that these hopes will be fully realised. In the first place, satellite surveillance has already been developed to a fine art and its product is of high quality. It can obtain intelligence through a wide variety of sensors—visual, electro-optical and radar among them—and that intelligence can be relayed, analysed and disseminated in a relatively quick time. It seems certain that this timeframe will be further reduced as advanced technology continues to work over the problem, and that developments in microwave transmission and data-processing will make high-definition, real-time intelligence a fact of life. Indeed, the greatest problem will then be not in acquisition, but in analysis and dissemination to front-line units and their controlling headquarters. Current-generation satellites have certain limitations—specifically in all-weather operation, cost and vulnerability. However, not only are their operating limitations already subject to a great deal of research, with every prospect of their being overcome in the relatively short term; but, even in an age of so-called 'Star Wars', their vulnerability is likely to be less than that of the existing alternative—manned aircraft systems—and the cost of not having satellite-acquired intelligence could well become many times greater than that of providing it.

There would still be a need for surveillance systems to operate in the tactical sense—both over land and at sea. Here again technology is already able to offer much—and will, in the near future, give more. It is no longer a pipe-dream to believe that vulnerable, manned, tactical reconnaissance aircraft will give way to light-weight sensors carried aboard unmanned drones—themselves the beneficiaries of exciting advances in airframe materials and construction, low noise/low heat propulsion systems and the micro-miniaturisation of electronics.

One aspect of airborne surveillance is already well developed and shows every sign of continuing that process. The monitoring of enemy air activity and the control of forces to counter it are functions now safely lodged in large airborne systems, and with development concentrated on reducing their vulnerability, such systems will well serve both commanders and combatants in the years ahead. They may be used to detect and plot surface shipping and, as necessary, to direct attacks on it. And, within the constraints of their primary roles, such tasks may also be carried out by aircraft formally concerned with the detection, tracking and eventual destruction of enemy sub-surface vessels. As in all the other activities which in combination spell air power, anti-submarine warfare continues to reap the benefits of advancing technology.

Equally important is the maintenance of a viable force for the air transportation of men, material, war-fighting equipment and supplies. Here, as much as anywhere, it will be necessary to keep open the options by investing in versatility. Excluding support helicopters (which already have a range of specific roles, mainly in the direct support of ground forces), NATO's future airlift capability must be built around genuine multi-role support aircraft. In addition to the traditional tasks of air transport, these will necessarily be capable of the vital air-to-air refuelling (and, in the future perhaps, even air-to-air rearming) of both defensive and offensive aircraft. They would also be fitted with extensive suites of electronic counter- and counter-countermeasures, batteries of self-defence systems, including weapons, and, as an extension of the latter, almost certainly the capacity to launch anti-radar and other stand-off attack missiles.

Conclusion

Technology has been the repeated refrain of these collective thoughts. But there is nothing suprising in this for technology has, from the earliest years of air power, worked closely with and for it—the one acting as catalyst to the development of the other. The founder of the Royal Air Force, Lord Trenchard, once commented that economy lay in expanding the power of material and personnel without increasing either. It is this sort of economy which is even more important today—and, in the final analysis, it is technological advance that can most surely bring it to pass.

This has been something of a 'wide-angle' view of air power in the NATO context, which must necessarily be read beside the more detailed contributions of others. No attempt has been made to identify the problems of individual regions—let alone of individual air forces of the Alliance, but rather has the aim been to examine the current state of NATO's air arm and its potential in the years ahead. The picture is, of course, not a consistent one throughout the Alliance's area of interest, but these thoughts may act as a back-cloth against which to view specific aspects of NATO's constituent parts.

6

The Soviet Alternative: Air Supremacy, Aerial Preparation and Air Accompaniment

AIR VICE MARSHAL R. A. MASON

In four decades of uneasy peace between East and West, military strength has been a constant factor in the equation of power. Conventional forces on land, sea and in the air, plus nuclear weaponry in all three dimensions, have been monitored as the balance of advantage has been perceived to tip from side to side. The evolution of Soviet air power in that balance has been well documented, from its early postwar concentration on air defence of the motherland and provision of tactical air support to the land forces, to its emergence in the second half of the 1980s as a balanced force equipped not just for the two earlier roles but able to threaten NATO territories and sea routes, to provide long-range support for client states far beyond Soviet boundaries and to maintain a presence in Africa, the Middle East and South-East Asia. In 1985 the US Department of Defense summarised the Soviet combat order of battle as 900 bombers, 7,300 fighters and 1,600 aircraft in *Soviet Naval Aviation*.[1] Moreover, there was no doubt that the technological advantages held by the West for so long in most aspects of airframe, engine and weapon design were being whittled away. And yet, despite similarities in equipment, roles and doctrine, it might well be the differences between Soviet and Western air power which would have the greater influence in any confrontation.

Occasionally the novelty of warfare in the third dimension has tended to obscure the fact that it is also heir to the traditional elements of war at sea and on the land. The armed forces of any state are a product of many influences and air forces are no exception. In fact, all remain imperceptibly interrelated although it is a matter for the historian, the economist, the political scientist or the sociologist to determine the relative weight of each. They include the nature of the parent society from which the servicemen are drawn. The armed services may not always be a mirror of that society. Indeed, in some cases the military may come to dominate the civilian, but there seems to be general agreement that in most respects the Russian air forces fall into the former category, as do those of the West.

A second influence is the geopolitical circumstances of the state. No more than a glance at an atlas followed by a reflection on comparative size, nature of frontiers, type of terrain, climate and proximity or otherwise of perceived threat or objectives points the different influences at work, for example, on the Soviet Union and the United States.

Falling out of the geopolitical factors may be overriding strategic principles: in the Soviet case, the well-documented emphasis on surprise, concentration of force and sustained momentum. Again, that may be compared with the essentially defensive posture of the Western democracies. Strategic principles should, in Clausewitzian terms, be in harmony with political objectives. Commentators in East and West would no doubt disagree in this aspect of the analysis, but the view from the West is one of Soviet expansion of power and influence:

> The Soviet Union inherited the product of many centuries of Russian expansion; it is a country obsessed with its own security but insensitive to the security concerns of others. These traditions, and the great importance given to military power which goes with them, have been combined with an ideology dedicated to the ultimate victory of communism. The evidence suggests that these ideological goals will be pursued with caution and discretion, but that opportunities will be grasped if the price limited and acceptable.[2]

Even clearly defined strategic principles and political objectives, however, may not be sustained unless sufficient resources are made available to the armed forces. Despite a slowing-down in growth in the late 1970s, the scale of Soviet investment in defence continued to grow in real terms during the next decade.

In 1980 it was estimated that 40 per cent of the Soviet defence budget was allocated to items associated with air power. Exact figures remain difficult to obtain because the government of the Soviet Union has no public pressure upon it to publish detailed Western style defence budgets. Nor is there any public debate about the priority to be afforded the defence industry in the Soviet economy as a whole. The implications of that priority for the Soviet armed forces are far-reaching. The Soviet officer enjoys a comparative status and prestige not always enjoyed by his contemporaries in the West. His aircraft and associated equipment will be the best that the Soviet industrial base can produce, but they will also be subject to the limitations of that base and the quality and quantity of the engineers required to maintain it.

Finally, the Sovier Air Forces will, like any other well-established force, be strongly influenced by their own traditions: the habits of thought and action which have evolved over 70 years. Indeed, the Soviet Air Forces, like the Navy and land forces, pay considerable attention to their past for a source of operational and doctrinal wisdom as well as for the more universal purpose of fostering a sense of corporate tradition and esprit in a new arrival to the regiment.

In sum, most of the traditional influences at work in the Soviet Air Forces—societal, geopolitical, strategic, national priorities and objectives, technological and traditional—differ considerably from the same generic factors at work in the West. If their implications are included in a net assessment of contemporary Soviet air power, a more comprehensive analysis of the East–West air power balance can emerge than one which either relies on a purely quantitative and qualitative hardware comparison or one whose conclusions are tarnished by 'mirror imaging'. The latter is the product of interpreting Soviet Air Force activities, doctrine and organisation as if their formative influences were the same as those in the West; they manifestly are not.

Air Supremacy: The Significance of Initiative

Elsewhere in this volume the evolution of the Western concept of 'Command of the Air' is traced, emphasising an awareness that all operations on land or at sea are at risk unless protection is given against disruption and destruction from the air. The Soviet view is similar, but is marked by important differences of emphasis and means of achievement. As early as 1932 'command of the air' was expressed as 'absolute air supremacy' and was believed to be generally 'unattainable'. 'Temporary, local superiority', on the other hand, 'is possible'.[3] That theme has been consistently sustained for over 50 years. In 1970 'Foremost in the independent air operations (in the Great Patriotic War) was the achievement of air superiority ... the destruction of enemy air power along a particular strategic axis or in the entire theatre of operations ... .'[4] Ten years later, in a definitive article on 'Air Supremacy', Air Force General P. Bazanov emphasised the need to neutralise enemy aviation to make it possible for land, naval and home front forces 'to cope with their missions without enemy hindrance ... air supremacy is indispensible for success both in each military operation and in a war as a whole'.[5]

The distinction between those sentiments and those of Fullerton, Trenchard and Douhet in the West is not semantic. In Russian eyes, air supremacy is not an abstract concept to be fought for in general terms, but inextricable from combat in the other two dimensions. It is an integral element in combined arms operations and, unlike views sometimes held in the West, it has never been regarded as the sole responsibility of the fighter pilot. In 1932 '... it would be prejudice to think that air supremacy is achieved through the efforts of aviation alone. Both air and land forces participate in achieving (i). ....'[6] It is therefore misleading simply to examine the numerical strength of Western and Soviet fighter-interceptors to arrive at a neat assessment of potential combat impact—quite apart from other qualitative analysis—because of their different roles. To achieve air supremacy over a 'strategic axis' or 'theatre of operations', when the land forces are configured to mount and sustain large-scale, highly mobile operations, presupposes offensive sweeps, not simply the protection of national air space for which Western fighters are largely procured.

Moreover, in 1980 interceptor units of the ten Air Defence Districts of the independent Soviet air defence force, *PVO Strany*, were reallocated on a geographical basis so that the military district commanders on the periphery of the Soviet Union assumed responsibility for all air defence. Thereafter, should his forces be required to move forward into other theatres of operation to support an offensive, mounted for example by the armies of the Group of Soviet Forces in Germany, the ground force commander would move in theory at least with fighter regiments which had trained alongside the ground forces and ground attack aircraft which they would be expected to protect. The remainder of the *PVO Strany* units were retained in five Air Defence Districts to cover strategically important regions in the Russian heartland.

It is a truism in military history that it is the loser who takes most to heart the lessons which are available to him. It may be that the Soviet Union has remembered more about the ingredients and importance of air supremacy. On 5 October 1941 an official Soviet statement acknowledged the loss of 5,316 aircraft, tacitly conceding the probability of earlier German claims to have destroyed 1,811 Soviet aircraft in the first 24 hours of Barbarossa in June. For several months Soviet fighters fought desperately over the Ukraine, Moscow and Leningrad to reduce the impact of the Luftwaffe on the ravaged Russian ground forces. The lesson is recalled regularly in Soviet military publications. In the West, on the other hand, the Allied armies moved back into Europe under massive air cover, facing a Luftwaffe debilitated by 3 years of incessant combat not just in the East but against the combined British and American bomber offensives. Western air superiority in 1944–45 was held by the fighters of the tactical air forces, but their victory had been largely prepared by the attrition inflicted by the bomber crews. In any foreseeable conflict between NATO and the Warsaw Pact the contest for air supremacy would not be preceded by 3 years of attrition; it would be decided by the forces in the theatre at the time. Those forces, moreover, would not all be in the skies.

From the days of the 1917 revolution, anti-aircraft batteries on the ground have enjoyed greater prominence in the Soviet Union than in the West. The second battery of the first anti-aircraft battalion in Petrograd, for example, formed in October 1917, is now known as 'The Order of Lenin Guards Putilov-Kirov Air Defence Missile Regiment' and participates regularly in military reviews in Red Square in Moscow. Indeed, for most of its history since 1917 the Soviet air defence system, including the interceptors, was commanded by a soldier, usually an artilleryman. It was, however, not until 1960 that the contribution of surface-to-air defences (SAD) made a dramatic impact on activities in the third dimension which was to prove from the outset very ambivalent, for aircrew in general but especially for Soviet fighter pilots.

The shooting down of Gary Powers en route from Peshawar in Pakistan to Bodo in Norway was received with acclaim in Moscow and foreboding in the West. The demise of the manned aircraft was confidently forecast by Western cognoscenti as indeed it has been forecast on several subsequent occasions. Until Penkovsky's later revelations, however, it was not known that fourteen SA–2 missiles were launched at Powers: and despite their careful siting below his expected track, twelve missed and another destroyed a MIG-19 which was trying to intercept him. The accuracy of SAD in both East and West has improved considerably since 1960, but the problem epitomised by the fate of the MiG remains. Since 1960 the umbrella of SAD, ranging from the ZSU 23-4 radar laid guns and short-range optical, infrared and radar-guided missiles to the long-range high-altitude SA-5s, has been spread over the Warsaw Pact forces back across the frontiers of the Soviet Union to cover large tracts of the heartland itself. In a theatre of operations the SAD are in theory complementary and overlapping, and the overall organisation is expected to be sufficiently mobile to accompany an armoured offensive. Ideally, their operations should be 'precisely co-ordinated with those of fighter aviation, with the air defence resources of the senior chief, and with the operations of adjacent units and sub-units receiving cover. Co-ordination must be continuous.' All this in a fast-moving environment which demand manoeuvre, rapid response and the achievement of surprise against a low-flying enemy by 'roaming air defence units'.[7]

The contribution of SAD to air supremacy is ambivalent, because while clearly their presence inhibits hostile offensive air operations, they do not do a great deal for the peace of mind of friendly fighter pilots either. They have, in short, enormously complicated problems of aerospace management and could well aggravate one traditional problem peculiar to Soviet aircrew: an apparent reluctance to develop individual initiative. The problems can be readily envisaged. Friendly Soviet aircraft can be expected to be departing for or returning from deeper offensive sorties; they would be providing close air support or complementing the SAD over ground forces committed to a mobile offensive. The SAD, however, are expected to be deployed wherever possible in ambush positions, as well as along the ground forces' line of march; they are to manoeuvre and change position frequently. They are aware of their vulnerability to jamming, spoofing and anti-radiation missiles; they are acutely conscious of the need to get in the first shot, and they are largely manned by conscript troops. In such an environment, traditional methods of aerospace management by safety heights, speeds, lanes, times or electronic identification all become very speculative. It is not surprising that Soviet pilots become accustomed to close control, when in the combat zone, under such conditions, individual initiative could carry a high penalty.

There is no doubt that the Soviet fighter pilot is marked by a lack of initiative when compared with his Western counterparts; there is too much criticism of the shortcoming in Soviet military journals for it simply to be a product of Western wishful thinking. Soviet writers frequently explain it by reference to operational or technical circumstances pertaining at some particular time and proceed to argue that the circumstances of the 1980s demand a very different attitude. Yet neither the weakness, if such it be, nor the recommended improvements are new to the 1980s, as even the most cursory survey illustrates. The presence of SAD may inhibit Soviet aircrew initiative, but they are only the most recent inhibiting factor.

In the Great Patriotic War the disasters of 1941 had a traumatic impact. Inferior aircraft, a leadership decimated by purges, death in combat and by firing squad for failure, inexperience and lack of cohesive organisation, all combined to produce combat pilots whose characteristic features in the eyes of their German opponents were 'a tendency towards caution and reluctance instead of toughness and stamina, brute strength instead of genuine combat efficiency . . .'.[8] When fighter pilots neglected their escorting duties and scattered at the first sight of the opposition, the solution was to be the rigorous enforcement of flight and formation discipline based on rigid training and detailed, comprehensive pre-flight briefings which sought as far as possible to anticipate and plan for the circumstances likely to be faced by the tyro pilot. As the Soviet forces moved on to the offensive in the later years of the war, the desire to concentrate ground attack aircraft against a target array at a particular time and place led to a further reason for adhering to a plan and the discouragement of independence, although, as will be noted later, there was one operational exception to provide a precedent of a different kind.

Overall, therefore, the Soviet Air Forces emerged from the Second World War convinced of the need for air supremacy, but not prepared to rely on aircrew initiative to contribute a great deal towards it. Since then several other operational factors have conspired to inhibit its acquisition. In the air defence of the Soviet heartland, for example, interceptor pilots were, and in 1985 still were, heavily dependent upon ground radars and fighter controllers to place them at the correct position in azimuth, height, speed and heading from which to make their interception. Thereafter the air-launched missile would in theory do the rest. As airborne intercept radars improved, the autonomous combat radius of the interceptor increased, but never to the extent of completely autonomous operations. When Foxhound, Fulcrum and Flanker are operating with 'look down shoot down' radars, acquiring low-level targets beyond the scan of the ground controller, their crews will be called upon to act much more upon their own initiative. With the operational entry of Candid-AWACS, however, even that modicum of independent action will presumably be curtailed as the interceptor pilots respond to the longer range, more comprehensive defensive survey of the airborne radar controllers.

In sum, it is possible to explain a comparative lack of initiative, by Western standards, in terms of traditional training patterns and operational circumstances. If that were the whole story, however, the situation would be acceptable to Soviet air commanders, and it manifestly is not. Not only have several articles in the early 1980s dealt with specific tactical circumstances where more fighter pilot initiative was required, but several very senior commanders have expressed concern about stereotyped training and attitudes.

Independence of tactical thought and action has been encouraged by relatively junior officers in articles which have been given wide publicity, not just in the specialist journals such as *Aviation and Cosmonautics*, but in the national armed forces daily, *Red Star*, for example in October 1984:

> Stereotyped habits shackle an airman's initiative and noticeably reduce the effectiveness of assigned missions accomplishment.
>
> After another instructive air battle, we specifically and thoroughly discussed the need to more boldly take intelligent risks in combat and make more active use of aircraft equipment capabilities and new air combat tactics. It is no secret that some pilots prefer not to go beyond the bounds of tried and true air combat methods, referring to the fact that everything is spelled out by appropriate documents, and the pilot's task allegedly remains simply to follow them to the letter.[9]

In the widely recognised conventions used by Soviet military writers, for 'some pilots' read 'a disturbingly large number of pilots', and for 'appropriate documents' read 'going slavishly by the book'. But not all middle rank officers thought like that author. Earlier in 1984 the Commander in Chief of Air Defence Forces Aviation (APVO) used his own 'in house' journal, *Air Defence Herald*, to launch a blistering attack on the training methods and all-round effectiveness of many of his interceptor regimental commanders. On many occasions they had failed to get to grips with the challenges presented by new aircraft, new weapons, new avionics, new command and control systems and especially with the threat posed by a low-flying enemy adept in electronic warfare. One individual was named, but the account of his misdemeanours must have prompted at least a twitch on several other air bases across the Soviet Union:

. . . we still find commanders who continue to work in the old fashioned way when working out complex forms of tactical employment; they lack creative initiative and wait, as the saying goes, for prompting 'from higher up', and, in the event of failure, are prone to complain about so-called objective difficulties.

Specifically, this kind of approach was characteristic of the supervisory staff in the fighter air regiment in which Lieutenant Colonel V Nikonov served as deputy commander.

For example, at one time the diversification of the different forms of weapons employment here proceeded at a snail's pace. This, in turn, led to simplifications in working out problems for destroying small, low-flying targets and gave rise to a series of other problems, as well as neglect. This, it goes without saying, would not have happened if the regimental supervisory staff had displayed a greater sense of responsibility in working out the assigned tasks, including complex forms of tactical employment, and had shown greater imagination and initiative in the use of existing resources.

Successful development of flying personnel's practical skills in complex forms of tactical employment of modern aviation systems is possible only through a radical overhaul of the work methods used by air unit commanders in organizing flight training. It is essential to use a new approach in using trainers, one involving the simulation of air and jamming situations as applied to the problems being solved.[10]

This lengthy extract clearly illustrates one of the contradictions in Soviet fighter organisation. The overall system may be well co-ordinated, but regimental training and operational conversion are the responsibilities of individual commanders and staffs. Initiative and creativity are all very well when they are successful, but it is much safer in a high visibility exercise to discharge only the demands of the book with maximum effectiveness and publicity. That way probably lies promotion; not every C-in-C may think like General Moskvitelev, the author of that critique.

And yet there may be signs that an increasing number of senior air force officers are trying to change traditional habits. In August 1984 the Commander of the Pacific Fleet Air Forces reflected on the shortcomings of Forger pilots and their training. Interestingly, after reflections on anti-shipping operations, including those of the Skyhawks in the Falklands, he also referred to the use of the Royal Navy's Sea Harriers in air defence. The day may not be far distant when Forger will begin to land off the parent carrier and be armed with air-to-air weapons. If so, the need to improve training will become even more important:

Unfortunately, however, not every tactical air exercise and sortie is used in the best possible way to develop creativity and initiative in crew commanders and group leaders. What exactly is wrong? Primarily, in our view, the reasons are stereotyped procedures and lack of discipline....[11]

The time-honoured preparation for a flight by seeking to examine all eventualities may reduce the incidence of the unexpected, but it carries a penalty:

Conventionalities planned beforehand dampen the enthusiasm of crews, give rise to a highly overconfident attitude, and do not further improve skills. Therefore, an individual officer's skill level grows more slowly. They lose previously acquired skills and routinely act in a stereotyped manner.[12]

The remedy proposed by the general is intriguing, to say the least, in a Soviet environment. He quotes Academician P. Kapitsa: 'the nurturing of man's creative abilities is based on the development of independent thinking', and doubts the efficacy of sending down orders from Command headquarters for pilots to produce research papers. Instead, the squadron commander should write them, nurturing innovative tactics, checking them 'hundreds of times' and kindling 'a fire in his subordinates so that they will think and suggest more, and become innovators in developing tactics'. 'Original decisions are born only in a creative atmosphere.'[13] Sadly for the peace of mind of the squadron commanders, the General does not end on that note. Instead, he explains the success of the 'outstanding' squadron led by Pilot First Class Guards Major Tomilov, 'who year in and year out' complete all missions and lead the socialist competition. Their recipe for success, however, is not rooted in an atmosphere of creative thought, but in 'a natural union of training and education', valuable assistance from 'the deputy commander for political matters', and 'party and Young Communist league activists', in 'socialist competition' and in basing their theoretical knowledge, flying and tactical skills on 'unswerving fulfilment of the training manual provisions' which 'generates the high, stable results achieved both in the course of every day flights and in tactical air exercises'.[14]

In sum, the Commander of Naval Aviation in the Far East is no nearer resolving the dilemma of how to inculcate creative thinking within the straitjacket of Marxist bureaucracy and dogma than any of his predecessors. It would, however, be foolhardy for potential opponents to draw too much comfort from it. There is no argument in the Soviet Union about the need for air superiority, and no discussion about how many resources to allocate to its achievement. The new generation of fighter/

interceptors, Foxhound, Fulcrum and Flanker, are likely to participate in combat in such numbers and under such ground and airborne control as to make the possession or otherwise of individual pilot initiative of far less consequence that it would be in the West. Of much greater significance, as noted by both PVO and SNAF generals, is the ability of Soviet pilots to keep their tactical thinking ahead, or at least abreast of, technical innovation and Western operating procedures. In that area there are probably grounds for much greater Western optimism, and until the Soviet political system changes its own habits of thought and rewards for conformity the problem in the military is likely to remain endemic.

It is against that background that all assessments of the Soviet search for air supremacy should be viewed. But there were reports in 1981 that an air firing and tactical training regiment had been established at the Yeisk Higher School for Pilots, near Volgograd, at which presumably tactical doctrine could be consolidated and developed. Such an institute could in the longer term induce more widely applied tactical innovation. Encouragement of initiative by senior commanders might erode the constraining influence of the regimental political deputy. The prestige and perquisites extended by the Soviet Union to the fighter pilot would continue to ensure that the air force could choose the most talented of many thousands of volunteers each year. It was probable that the technological gap between MiG-29 Fulcrum and F-16 was closer than that between MiG-21 and F-4, and that between SU-27 Flanker and F-15 even closer. The West had advantages in tactical innovation—provided that lessons of earlier wars were not shrouded in complacency—and still in technological edge, although by 1985 it was narrowing. But perhaps above all, Western advantage lay in technological depth: the ability of well equipped, well-motivated ground crew backed by comprehensive engineering and logistic support to sustain operations flown by strongly motivated aircrew in high-performance aircraft. Similar factors were present in the balance of advantage in offensive air operations.

Offensive Operations

Since the Royal Flying Corps was commanded in France by Major General Hugh Trenchard in the First World War, the spirit of the offensive has permeated the British Royal Air Force. The leading pioneer of US military aviation, Mitchell, was strongly influenced by a 2-day meeting with Trenchard in France in 1918. The ability of air power to reach out 'independently' beyond the front lines, to strike not only at the enemy's reinforcements and reserves but at his industrial heart and civilian morale was a concept shared by both with Douhet and which proved to be a major factor in the emergence of a third service, independent of Army or Navy, in both Britain and the United States. In Russia, long-range offensive

PLATE 6.1   MIG-23C operational trainer of the Polish Air Force.

aviation has until the mid-1980s invariably been associated with combat on land or at sea. It may not be a coincidence that both the United States and the United Kingdom were fighting far from their own frontiers, although the United Kingdom felt at first hand in both wars the impact of strategic bombing. The Soviet Union, on the other hand, faced enemies either across or within her frontiers. Her armies were her sword and shield, and for the greater part of her history her offensive air power has been a complement, if not always subordinate, to her forces on land. Frequently, when the likely contribution of Soviet offensive air power to any future conflict has been assessed in the West, that fact has not received the attention it deserved.

Soviet hagiography would have us believe that Soviet heavy bombers played a major role in the Second World War.[15] In fact, despite a promising inheritance in the First World War with the Sikorsky Il'ya Murometz four-engined bomber, and an effective Tupolev heavy bomber development in the 1930s, the great majority of Soviet offensive investment in the air has gone into tactical support. Until 1981 most light, medium and fighter bombers were controlled by Frontal Aviation, an approximation to Tactical Air Command of the USAF. The heavier, longer-range regiments were usually the cinderella of Soviet military aviation.

Aerial Preparation

Tactical offensive operations, defined as activities in direct or indirect support of the ground forces, have been the second major preoccupation of the Soviet Air Forces, after the achievement of air supremacy, since 1942 when the control of the Eastern European skies was slowly wrested from the Luftwaffe and up to 6,000 ground attack aircraft could be committed to a theatre of operations at any one time. Since then a coherent body of offensive doctrine has been written, and a recognisably constant pattern of operations exercised. Perhaps, surprisingly, there is a good measure of agreement between East and West on how offensive operations would be mounted by the Warsaw Pact in a conflict in Europe. In July 1984, for example, Western analysis at a seminar in Bonn suggested that:

> A Warsaw Pact air operation would take place on three separate fronts in Western Europe with Pact forces attempting to clear two or three separate air corridors per front. Each corridor is intended to be an area 25-30 miles wide and 100-150 miles deep. The plans call for rendering NATO air defense missiles and aircraft virtually ineffective in each corridor, allowing nearly free movement by Warsaw Pact aircraft. Presence of the corridor would allow Pact aircraft to slip through NATO air defence belts, then spread out and attack relatively unprotected rear areas. ...Radar and com-

munications systems would be attacked by a combination of electronic counter-measures, chaff and physical attack ... by a combination of standard ordnance and the Soviets' increasing inventory of AS-12 anti-radiation missiles.[16]

In the *Soviet Military Encyclopedia* just such an operation is defined, in abstract, as 'aerial preparation'. It is not an 'independent' operation in the Western sense, but clearly linked to an imminent ground force offensive:

> Aerial preparation involves making simultaneous or consecutive strikes by frontal (tactical) aviation units and formations against objectives located at tactical and close operational depth. Such objectives can include those which cannot be destroyed by missiles and artillery, those capable of changing location just before strikes are made against them, and those requiring powerful aviation ammunition for their destruction.
>
> Long-range (strategic) aviation can also take part in aerial preparation. Nuclear strike resources, aircraft at the nearest airfields, control posts, tanks and artillery in areas of concentration and in fire positions, strong-points, centers of resistance, and water crossings are destroyed primarily by aviation during aerial preparation.[17]

The specific target arrays associated with NATO air and nuclear resources were spelled out by a Polish writer in December 1981.

> NATO war plans [the author observes] envisage the deployment of powerful groupings of armed forces in the European theatre of military operations. These groupings include a considerable amount of aviation of various types as well as missiles and nuclear weapons, which even in peace time are constantly maintained at a high level of combat readiness. . . .
>
> The experience of the most recent wars has shown that the air forces have always substantially affected the course of the combat action of their own troops. Consequently the problems of combatting air forces have been given much attention, and deserve still more, because a breaking up or serious weakening of the enemy's air force and nuclear missile groupings leads to a fast decline of his capabilities. By ensuring supremacy in the air, it creates favourable conditions for the action of troops taking part in the operations in the TVD. . . .

To secure this

The aim of an air operation intended to rout (weaken) air force and nuclear missile groupings can be attained through:

—the destruction of aircraft and aircrew on airfields;
— the destruction of enemy aircraft and aircrew in aerial battles;
— the destruction of aircraft carriers at sea and in port;
— the destruction of operational-tactical missiles;
— the disruption of the command and control system and enemy aircraft guidance systems;
— the destruction of nuclear warheads, storage sites, fuel dumps, conventional weapons and material and technical supplies;
— the destruction, blocking and mining of airfields. . . .

The operation will be conducted under one single overall command and in accordance with a single concept of plan, so as to achieve a speedy routing of air force groupings and missile resources as well as to reduce the enemy's nuclear potential. It follows from this that an air operation has a combined arms character. . . .

Enemy air force and missile groupings should first be routed in those areas where the principal tasks of the war are being implemented, i.e. in the main TVDs where the strongest groupings of ground forces and air forces are deployed. The West European TVD is one of them. Therefore it can be stated that in no other theatre will the course of the operation depend so much on the situation in the air, on the skilful use of own air force, and on the breakup of enemy air forces. This is so because he who seizes initiative in the air will dictate his conditions.[18]

Air Accompaniment

Once the grand offensive has begun, another concept derived from the Second World War, 'Air Accompaniment' will probably be implemented.

> 'Air accompaniment' began to be employed during the Great Patriotic War as the final phase of air support when troops advanced deep within enemy defenses. It usually took the form of sorties by frontal aviation subunits, chiefly ground-attack aircraft, either scheduled or called in from the command post. In crucial periods of battle, (when troops are overcoming defensive lines at operational depth, warding off enemy counter-attacks, overcoming water obstacles from the march, etc), successively alternating ground-attack aircraft sub-units were employed continuously over the battlefield for a prescribed time (1-2 hours or more).[19]

In the context of that conceptual framework, several developments in Soviet air power in the 1970s and 1980s assume considerable significance. The first was the advent of 'third generation' offensive aircraft such as the later marks of MiG-21 and SU-17, the MiG-23/27 family and SU-24

PLATE 6.2   MIG-21PFMA fighter of the Polish Air Force.

whose greater range, heavier fire power, greater accuracy and increasing night/bad weather capabilities greatly enhanced the offensive threat of both the aerial preparation and the air accompaniment. Second was the entry of the attack and assault helicopter forces: the Mi-8 Hip and the Mi-24 Hind. The third was the reorganisation in 1981 of all Soviet overland offensive aircraft, coinciding with the assertion by Marshal Ogarkov that the basic operational area in a future war would not be the traditional 'front' but a 'theatre of military operations' or TVD. Such theatres appeared to comprise North-Western, Central and South-Western Europe, Southern and Far Eastern. Five bomber air armies were deployed, comprising one with all the very long-range Bears and Bisons controlled from Moscow, one with medium-range Badgers, Bisons and Backfires which could be deployed towards any TVD, two light and medium bomber armies assigned to the central and south-western areas and a fifth, composite, army in the east with medium and light bombers. The fixed wing fighter bombers were assigned to the commanders of military districts and the helicopter regiments were placed under direct Army command. Thereby all offensive air assets were under command commensurate with their combat radius. By the mid-1980s Soviet offensive air power had the aircraft, the weapons and the organisation to discharge its doctrinal responsibilities. Pursuit of a doctrine of combined arms warfare was sustained by a military organisation constructed and controlled in such a way as to minimise corrosive inter-Service wrangling over roles and role driven budgets. There was, therefore, no need in the Soviet Union for a massive doctrinal and operational revision such as that in the West which produced the counter-offensive thinking of the early 1980s. There was indeed a blurring of roles which in the West had tended to be neatly compartmented as 'tactical' and 'strategic'.

Or at least so it seemed until 1985, when an interesting convergence between East and West became recognisable. A new variant of the TU-95, Bear H entered service, more or less at the same time as B-52s began to exercise in support of NATO ground forces in Europe. Bear H was a cruise missile carrier, and regularly flew to positions in the Northern hemisphere from which it could simulate the launch of nuclear-tipped missiles against the United States. Nothing there relating to aerial preparation: just good old fashioned 'strategic' operations instantly recognisable to Douhet, Mitchell and Trenchard had they lived to see them.

After three decades of dependence for strategic bombardment on ICBMs from land and sea, the introduction of Bear H gave the Soviet Union for the first time a realistic manned bomber threat to the United States. Much had been made earlier of the 'potential' of Backfire, Bison and earlier marks of TU95, but such assessments in the United States had sometimes been viewed with scepticism in European aviation circles. Not any more. Bear H was upstaged in the international press by the B1 lookalike

'Blackjack', but while the latter was still stuttering through its development stages Bear H was entering regimental service with its war load. It was an odd coincidence that as the Soviet Air Force introduced her first really 'strategic' bomber, the US Air Force intercontinental B-52 was deployed forward to bases in the United Kingdom and flew tactical missions in support of NATO ground forces in exercises in Western Europe.

It is, however, one thing to have coherent doctrine, appropriate aircraft and weapons and a logical command chain, but quite another to get sufficient aircraft to the point of operational significance in the right numbers at the right time. Just as creativity and responsiveness might be the Achilles heel of the Soviet reach for air supremacy, so other, peculiarly Soviet, weaknesses might inhibit the timely concentration of force necessary for both successful aerial preparation and sustained air accompaniment.

The effort required by the Soviet Air Forces and their Warsaw Pact allies to provide aerial preparation would be formidable, even if target arrays were initially restricted to those associated with NATO air power. Permutations of scenarios are endless, but it is likely that blinding of early warning and paralysis of command and control would be early objectives. In which case anti-radiation missiles (ARM) launched against ground and airborne early warning radars from across the inner German border could present complications to rules of engagement for NATO interceptors or SAD. Assuming a conventional phase to the conflict, which by the mid-1980s the Soviet Union was clearly doing, the main attack following immediately behind the ARM launch would require close co-ordination to ensure concentration of force over targets, accurate timing in sequence and in concert with other attacks, accurate navigation and target acquisition and comprehensive post-attack reconnaissance provision to seek to avoid both overkill and omission or evasion.

Some of the ingredients for this complex recipe were available in 1985, but by no means all. Stand-off ARMs could be carried by a variety of Soviet aircraft operating regularly in peacetime from bases in Eastern Europe: SU-24 Fencer, for example. Blinding of NATO air defences by ECM could be attempted either by specialist aircraft such as converted AN-12 Cubs, specific marks of Badger or Bear or by on-board jamming equipment carried by many medium and heavy bombers. Shorter-range NATO defences could receive additional electronic interference from specialist ECM Hips. Soviet attacking aircraft could probably begin to rely on airborne control and guidance from their own AWACS aircraft, IL-76 Mainstay, which was beginning to deploy in Eastern Europe and could stand off behind the offensive, looking in. In theory, the numbers of aircraft necessary for saturation raids were available; about 65 per cent of Soviet offensive aircraft were concentrated near the western and southern TVDs, comprising some 600 bombers and 3,750 fighter bombers, reconnaissance and ECM aircraft. Associated offensive training had begun to change slightly, but perceptibly: larger formations of aircraft were used in exercises, with escorting fighters, over longer distances. This tendency was particularly noticeable in Soviet naval air force exercises when combinations of Bear, Badger and occasionally Flogger were launched against simulated NATO carrier task forces. The Soviet Union seems to recognise very fully the considerable conventional and nuclear strike power of the US Navy carrier groups and would presumably include those in European waters in the target arrays in the aerial preparation phase. Indeed, in such exercises the further value of central direction from Moscow can occasionally be seen when aircraft from both SNAF and the Air Armies participate in the same simulated attacks.

Unopposed exercises are one thing, however; achieving aerial preparation without alerting NATO peacetime reconnaissance and early warning agencies and subsequently in the face of even degraded NATO defences, and then sustaining the required efforts in the face of traditional combat friction: that would not be quite so easy. Isolated ARM attacks could probably be mounted without giving too much away to routine NATO electronic and other forms of reconnaissance. Preparation and mounting of a large-scale offensive would be much more difficult to conceal. The days are long gone when a massive bomber formation could assemble undetected over England, rumble across the North Sea and suddenly breach radar defences near an enemy frontier. Satellite and other early warning systems would probably detect not only the signals traffic preceding aerial preparation, but the bomber and escorting formations themselves while still hundreds of miles away from missile launch. In passing, then vulnerability or otherwise of reconnaissance satellites clearly is of paramount importance to Western air defences in such scenarios.

However, if the offensive did avoid detection, the Soviet regiments would need to raise their flying effort considerably above normal peacetime levels. Bomber crews seem to complete only a very small number of sorties each month. Moreover, almost all bombers and fighter bomber regiments absorb new aircrew direct from flying training units. Larger numbers of aircraft per squadron than in the West, and, probably, a higher crew-to-aircraft ratio, conceals the amount of operational training which must be carried out on the squadron rather than on a conversion unit as in the United Kingdom. On the other hand, aircrew turbulence seems to be less in the Soviet Air Force than in the West; it is not uncommon for pilots and navigators to spend many years on one type of aircraft if not on the same squadron, moving on primarily for promotion or, occasionally, on to new aircraft types which are not yet re-equipping their own squadron. But as in the fighter squadrons, training standards are uneven, reflecting the quality and effectiveness of the squadron or regimental commander. Reports on medium or heavy bomber activities are not as common in the Soviet military press as those relating to the more glamorous and perhaps more debatable tactical operations. Occasional glimpses, however, confirm the constant exhortations to follow the paragon of the month. For example, Lieutenant Colonel Anatoliy Maksimovich Kuribets, commander of an unspecified but possibly Backfire or Badger squadron:

> There is also much concern for the dissemination of advanced experience. Let's say that new tactics are used in firing a missile. The squadron commander, together with the political worker and party bureau secretary, immediately arrange for a demonstration, analysis, and exchange of experience with other crews. And this is beneficial. Officer I Pelipenko's aircrew, for example, delivered a precise missile strike against an 'enemy' target during the next tactical flight exercise by employing experience gained by his comrades in arms.
>
> The work experience of this vanguard squadron commander has been synthesized and adopted in other units. Anatoliy Maksimovich has spoken on numerous occasions at party committee meetings, party meetings, and job-related conferences, and has shared his ideas on improving the training methods of crew and detachment commanders. His suggestions in essence consist of making the monitoring of aviator training continuous, effective, and extremely demanding.
>
> Other communist leaders can learn much from this commander whose squadron has earned excellent ratings.[20]

This extract suggests the lack of any organisation such as the RAF's Central Tactics and Trials Unit or many similar units in Western air forces whose task is to identify and disseminate tactical guidance on new weapons and equipment. It may well be that faced with a constant, widespread reluctance of aircrew to innovate, the Soviet Air Force will concentrate what little creativity exists in a central unit for tactical evaluation and innovation. It is difficult to see how existing training facilities can avoid impairing operational effectiveness, and the advent of even more complex aircraft in the last decade is unlikely to have softened the 1976 senior officer perception of squadron training standards:

> A large role in further developing and improving the training facility belongs to innovators in the units. Thus, in the military collective headed by officer B. Kononenko, via the efforts of efficiency experts, classrooms are equipped with working test benches and models which provide visual aid in studying the special features of a working principle and the principles of operation of the more complicated units and systems on the aircraft. They make it possible for flying personnel to develop skills in the use of armament, equipment, and

radar navigational devices, and for technical personnel to master the sequence for carrying out operations during an efficiency check of the units and systems. One should note that such a training facility as was created in this collective can confidently be called exemplary. . . .

At the same time isolated military collectives still exist where the necessary attention is not accorded to the development of a training facility. Sometimes in technical classrooms one can see test benches, charts, and posters which do not contribute to a thorough understanding of the physical processes taking place in one or another assembly or sub-assembly or to a clarification of the interdependence of their physical properties and quantitative parameters, showing operating time in various modes. At times visual training aids do not reflect changes made or modifications, and as a result, the special features of equipment use. Methods for instrument monitoring of the status of components and sub-assemblies are poorly described. There are no posters devoted to the characteristic equipment malfunctions occurring as a result of misuse or to methods of detecting and eliminating these discrepancies. There are not enough visual aids to instruct checking and adjustment, tuning, and dismantling and assembly operations. Although rarely, all the same it happens that essentially good classrooms which have been equipped with enthusiasm, simulators, ranges, and other elements of the training facility are used episodically and not effectively enough.

The task of commanders, political workers, technical personnel, and party organizations consists in making the training facility in all units a model in content that is universally and completely used to further improve the technical and practical skills of the personnel.[21]

The usual code is employed: 'isolated exceptions', 'sometimes . . .', 'although rarely . . .', but the weaknesses which are pinpointed crop up again and again in military journals. Moreover, as the then Chief of the Soviet Air Forces observed in 1955, when it was politic to prefer missiles to manned bombers, 'long range bombers are expensive to build, man and maintain . . . they tie up large numbers of maintenance personnel . . . (and) need a complicated supply and servicing organisation'.[22]

The Soviet Union can give great industrial and economic priority to the production of advanced military aircraft. By acquiring Western technology, by observing Western aeronautical developments, by listening to Western aeronautical debates, they can often reduce the time taken in the West for comparable aircraft production; indeed, Soviet expertise in several areas can compete strongly on even terms. But even with the considerable expansion in the technological literacy of the Soviet people, the comparative quality of Soviet ground crew remains lamentably low. Offensive operations depend upon career aircrew and largely conscript ground crew. An attempt to encourage retention among enlisted men by the creation of warrant officer rank has only succeeded in producing warrant officers who discharge duties performed in the West by junior enlisted men. As is often the case, it is the senior Soviet military commanders who are the sternest critics of their men's shortcomings. 'We must decisively eliminate the present shortcomings of technical personnel', observed the Commander of the Air Force Aviation Engineering Service in 1978. Since then his conscript ground crews have had to cope with later marks of Backfire, Bear H, Fencer C, D, Fulcrum, Frogfoot and subsequently Blackjack and Flanker. And the degree of difficulty?

> For example, in checking the panel of one of the radars, the operator must perform more than one set of ten switchings in a strict sequence. This is why it is now so important for specialists to have high qualifications, to be exceptionally industrious, and to take a creative approach to maintaining aviation equipment and monitoring gear.[23]

High qualifications? Specialists? For a switching sequence? It is easy to read too much into one example, however typical. It is equally easy, however, to imagine the response of the average RAF junior technician if he were to be exhorted to take a creative approach to instrument checks of that simplicity.

One must therefore question the impact of uneven training and limitations in maintenance on the ability of the Soviet bomber regiments to mount and sustain a large-scale aerial preparation operation equal to the theoretical sum of the potentially operational numerical parts. This, however, is little consolation to NATO planners, because, as is explained elsewhere, the Alliance relies very heavily on its air power to redress the imbalance of conventional forces in position on the ground. Even a partially successful aerial preparation by the Soviet Air Force would create serious defensive problems for NATO and make the second offensive phase, air accompaniment, that much easier for the Soviet Air Force to carry out.

The accompaniment phase is as ambitious as the preparation, but again, in theory the air forces are well prepared to undertake it. Supporting the fixed wing aircraft of the Groups of Forces and Military Districts would be the helicopters of the armies, the fighter bombers of the Warsaw Pact allies and possibly additional fixed wing units formed from older aircraft used in training squadrons in peacetime: a total force of several thousand tactical combat aircraft. Moreover, during the last decade combined arms effectiveness, at least in unopposed exercises, has improved considerably. Up to 1977 ground force commanders were frequently criticised for failure to co-ordinate and derive the greatest advantage from the ground, rotary and fixed wing assets available to them. If 'air support' was not in the plan, it was highly probable that it would not be called for even when the 'offensive' clearly needed air support. Criticism, again, of slavish adherence to plans, lack of initiative and, frequently, straightforward lack of combined arms awareness was commonplace. Perhaps this should not have been too surprising. The 1970s saw the introduction into combined arms operations of longer-range close support aircraft, assault and attack helicopters, extended use of electronic combat, all in addition to the modernisation and expansion of the ground forces themselves. By 1978, however, there were signs that the Soviet Union was beginning to get its combined arms act together. The 'Berezina' exercise in Western Russia sought 'to master coordination among the different arms of the service'[24] and the airforce commander was very pleased with the results:

> Personal contacts of air unit commanders with those of ground forces was a pledge of success in their operations. Exchange of experience and knowledge of each other's combat activities helped both sides to attain better mutual understanding and to grasp the peculiarities of a concrete combat situation. All this stood the participants of the exercise in good stead.
>
> For instance, when breaking through the defences of the 'Southerners' army the advance of a motorised infantry battalion of the 'Northerners' army was suddenly checked by fire from emplacements and a tank reserve which they had failed to detect. The offensive could have come to nothing. Through the intermediary of the spotter plane the motorised infantry headquarters asked for a group of fighter-bombers to be sent to the battlefield. Despite poor visibility this group approached the target exactly at the present time and delivered a powerful missile attack. The fire emplacements of the 'Southerners' were destroyed and the advance of their tanks was stopped. The 'Northerners' were thus enabled to press home the attack.[25]

No doubt, as is the custom in the Soviet armed forces, all the ingredients of the success had been frequently rehearsed to word and deed perfection. But there had been pre-'combat' association between ground troops and airmen, a forward air controller was used as a communication relay, close air support was called for allegedly outwith the plan and the 'rescue' was on time in less than perfect weather. But for that operation to succeed, air supremacy was essential and communications had to stay unjammed and working. Such a contribution by fixed wing aircraft is a well-rehearsed procedure, either to add fire power to a rolling offensive or to winkle out stubborn defensive positions such as those denying a river crossing.

It was also significant that General Brazanov, in his observations on Berezina, commented on the continued development of combat helicopter tactics. Much has been made in the Western press of the Soviet Union imitating US helicopter operations in South-East Asia. No doubt those tactics were assiduously studied, although in the late sixties Soviet military comment on Western operations tended to be distorted by ideological commentary much more than is the case in the mid-eighties. But whatever the observations, the Soviet use of the helicopter owes far more to Soviet military history and doctrine than to any foreign example. Of particular importance is the contribution of the helicopter to the activities of the Operational Manoeuvre Groups (OMG):

> ... The 'Air Echelon' of these forces should consist of assault and multi-purpose helicopters (including some equipped with special signals apparatus and adapted to commanding troops from the air). With such helicopters, based and operating directly with the formation of the fighting troops, away from the main forces, it is possible to implement a number of fire and special tasks. It also facilitates a swift reaction to any changes in the combat situation and the gradual adjustment of tasks according to the pace of these changes. Furthermore it reduces the time needed to carry out tasks set in response to requests from the battlefield, and also makes it possible to concentrate aviation assets on the implementation of the most important tasks in a given tactical situation. In these conditions helicopters, owing to their flying and combat characteristics, are capable of providing a systematic surveillance of gaps, open flanks and the rear of troops; of attacking from ambushes in circumstances which place the enemy under the greatest disadvantage; and even of engaging small groups of enemy forces which have penetrated into the attacking formation. Operating in this way, helicopters can increase the combat potential of the raiding and manoeuvring forces, and consequently increase the pace of the offensive of the main ground forces.[26]

This Polish analysis of tactical aviation is typical of more recent studies appearing in Warsaw Pact journals, including the Russian: a more thoughtful, relatively objective study of operational factors comparatively free from ideological distortion. In the study appeared the germ of the idea that more of the close support task should devolve to the helicopters, with fixed wing aircraft providing air cover, detection and destruction of larger enemy groupings (by implication not in contact with Soviet ground forces) and air transport. Such a prospect has a certain amount in common with Western concepts of battlefield interdiction, except that NATO air forces do not have either sufficient helicopters or a coherent doctrine to mount sustained co-ordinated rotary wing close air support operations. Nor would rotary wing operations on that scale be as appropriate to Western defence as to Soviet attack. Helicopters are still relatively vulnerable, slow and range limited. When a general knows exactly where and when the meeting engagement will take place, he can preposition and co-ordinate his helicopters accordingly. Such an advantage will, in any foreseeable conflict in Central Europe, lie with the attacking Soviet commander. If, on the other hand, the defending general is likely to be faced with several large-scale thrusts with minimal warning, and if he cannot confidently anticipate which of them are likely to be exploited by main forces or succeeding echelons, he cannot afford to depend on air support which might not have the range to reach the critical point.

But possession of large-scale air assets is not an unmixed blessing, as the Polish author perhaps implies in his further comment: 'However, air force operations in support of these troops (OMG) are subject to restriction. . . .'[27] Forward deployment of aircraft to support a fast-moving offensive is a time-consuming business; indeed, the static defence of landing sites or fields could be incompatible with the movement of an OMG. Moreover, as the OMG thrust deepened into NATO territory, so the range limitations of the helicopter from its original forward bases would begin to affect both close air support and resupply. Such a situation might present a role for SU-25 Frogfoot and would certainly increase demands on tactical fixed wing transport. Both would require a benign air environment for their operation: another example of the critical importance to both sides of air supremacy. Seldom can Clauswitz's dictum about war being the province of uncertainty have been so appropriate as in any foreseeable conventional conflict in Central Europe. Seldom, therefore, would flexibility of attitude and response carry such a premium. But as in air defence, bomber operations and in many other areas of activity, the potential for success in aerial accompaniment would be threatened by the same old weaknesses. So much so, that when the Soviet Air Forces were preparing to celebrate the annual 'Day of the Air Fleet' on 21 August 1983, *Red Star* introduced a far from celebratory note into its leading article:

> In modern air combat with its rapidly changing situation, in a situation where very powerful fire power is deployed, pilots must have excellent flying skills, a high degree of knowledge of the capabilities of their aircraft, its weapon systems and their employment; also of the strength and weaknesses of the enemy and the effective use of tactics against him.
>
> But in some units there are commanding officers who think that it is enough for their pilots to be able to fly well, to fire a bomb to a high standard on the range under practice conditions. They think that the rest will follow—the skill to employ good tactics and to act boldly and with initiative under operational conditions. Most commanders, of course, do ensure that this knowledge is acquired

by proceeding from the simple to the difficult in stages, not always operating under simple conditions and situations. Pilots should have a wide knowledge of the tactics of all branches of the Armed Forces with whom they have to cooperate. There must be no simplification, no weakness or complacency allowed. Crews must be encouraged to act—without looking over their shoulder for advice, no whispered words or fixed pattern of behaviour.[28]

Perhaps, when NATO aircrew grimly assess the likely numerical odds against them, they could derive a little satisfaction from such explicit criticism. One has only to imagine such comments in *Stars and Stripes*, or *Air Force Magazine*, or *RAF News* or *Air Clues* to realise just how widespread 'weakness', 'complacency,' 'whispered words' and 'fixed patterns of behaviour' must be. It is tempting to believe that as long as the Soviet political system and social conditioning remain in their present form, such weaknesses will remain endemic in the Soviet Air Forces and impair considerably their advantage of numerical superiority. Meanwhile, the reach for technological equality will, hopefully, be similarly impeded by a failure to produce comparable ground crew and ground support facilities. The net result could well be a far greater gap between the concepts of aerial preparation and accompaniment and their practical realisation.

Nevertheless, the determination of the Soviet Union to afford the greatest priority to military requirements; its full understanding of the paramount importance of air supremacy; its identification of weaknesses and willingness to address them publicly; a freedom to challenge existing doctrine and procedures which in some cases exceeds that in the West; all are factors which, if brought to a successful conclusion, could yet allow the Soviet Air Forces to attain their war-making potential. As long as the Western air forces do not let their priceless advantages of technological edge, aircrew skills and ground crew quality in depth fritter away, the balance will be sustained. But if ever the words of the 1983 *Red Star* leading article should become equally relevant to Western air forces, the time might not be far distant when we would become part of its compulsory readership, and deservedly so.

7

Moscow's Lessons from the 1982 Lebanon Air War

BENJAMIN S. LAMBETH

The September and October 1983 issues of *Aviatsiia i kosmonavtika*
(Aviation and Cosmonautics), the monthly periodical of the Soviet Air
Force, featured a two-part article by Colonel V. Dubrov entitled 'Aviation
in the Lebanon Conflict'.[1] Published more than a year after the devastating
Israeli Air Force offensive against Syrian SA-6s and MiGs over the Beka'a
Valley in June 1982, that article was the first sustained treatment of the
Lebanese air war to have appeared in the Soviet literature. The only
commentary on those events that had previously been made available to
Soviet readers was routine propaganda excoriating Israel's 'air piracy' and
grossly distorting its portrayal so as to reflect favourably on Syria's
performance. Dubrov's article, by contrast, offered a more dispassionate
and professional treatment of combat events, with the avowed purpose of
highlighting the various tactical innovations they encompassed and drawing
appropriate operational conclusions for Soviet aircrews. Although it
repeatedly cited 'foreign military observers' and 'the foreign press' (a
common Soviet usage when sensitive topics are being discussed), his article
contained a good deal of material that had *not* appeared in the Western
literature. This suggests that Dubrov's remarks indeed reflected, at least
in part, independent Soviet impressions and interpretations.[2]

Why did the Soviets take so long to produce this 'professional' rendition
of the Lebanese air war (as opposed to the usual propaganda caricature)?
Numerous high-level Soviet teams had long before visited Syria to gather
combat data, beginning with the delegation led by Colonel General Yurasov
that arrived in Damascus only 4 days following the Beka'a Valley shootout.
A plausible answer might be that the Soviets were so perturbed by the
poor showing of their weaponry in Syrian hands that it took them that
long to arrive at an agreed interpretation to communicate to their own
people.

Perhaps a better question might be why the Soviets felt obliged to
comment on Israeli air employment in Lebanon at all. There is no doubt

that they were embarrassed severely by the defeat the Israelis dealt the Syrians as a result of their superior equipment, tactics and pilot proficiency. Given this deep-seated Soviet sensitivity, might it not have been easier just to let the whole sorry episode go unmentioned?

The problem with this approach almost certainly involved an abiding uneasiness at the highest echelons of the Soviet Air Force as to whether rank-and-file Soviet officers would long believe the propaganda line they had been fed in the wake of the Beka'a Valley campaign. It is no secret among Soviet fighter pilots that the Syrians are anything but accomplished air tacticians. The operational prowess of the Israeli Air Force is equally well known. Give the widespread appreciation of this reality that underlies the cover story Soviet audiences are routinely told about the Middle East air balance, the initial wave of propaganda that so blatantly misrepresented Syrian combat performance must have met with disbelief on the part of many thoughtful Soviet military personnel.[3] When one further considers how fast rumours tend to spread in a country like the Soviet Union, where information flow is so tightly regimented, one can imagine the pressures the Soviet Air Force must have felt to put forward at least *some* 'official' accounting of what happened in the skies over Lebanon in June 1982, if only to help offset the corrosive effects of uncontrolled gossip.

This article describes how the Soviets have presented the Lebanese air war to their own pilots. Dubrov's analysis may or may not accurately reflect the more fine-grained impressions privately drawn by high-level Soviet officials from their battle data collection in 1982. It does, however, embody the perspective the Soviets have chosen to convey for broader consumption. As we shall see, it is an image largely devoid of ideological fulmination. Nevertheless, it remains highly selective in the events it reports and is pervaded with omissions and occasional gross misrepresentations. Furthermore, some of the key 'lessons' it cites from its given examples of Israeli force employment appear to be fundamentally misconstrued. Has Colonel Dubrov, knowing better, held out a purposely skewed account aimed at reassuring his readers? Or has he genuinely misinterpreted the significance of the Israeli weapons and tactics employed by looking at them through the distorting lens of Soviet military style? We will speculate on this question below. Before turning to the Dubrov article directly, however, it would seem worthwhile first to present the actual highlights of Israeli air combat over Lebanon as best we can from available evidence, and then review the Soviet propaganda depiction of that combat which preceded the publication of Dubrov's account.

Highlights of the Beka'a Valley Air Campaign

Any attempt to reconstruct Israeli air operations over Lebanon must first recognise that the Israelis have treated this subject as highly classified and have said little in public about what actually happened. Because of this circumspection, available information is both fragmentary and inconsistent, leaving us with no reliable way of distinguishing fact from hearsay and opinion.

The Israeli Defence Force (IDF) has always been extremely security-conscious. Indeed, we cannot rule out the possibility that much of the press comment that has appeared on the Beka'a Valley operation has been a product of intentional Israeli disinformation, both to protect the more sensitive aspects of IAF operational tactics and perhaps also to exaggerate the image of Israel's combat prowess for its psychopolitical effect. Nevertheless, there is enough evidence—starting with the more obvious results of the campaign and the well-known array of equipment the IAF had at its disposal—for us to assemble at least a rough-order portrait of how events probably unfolded.

To summarise the origins of the conflict, an assassination attempt in May 1982 against the Israeli ambassador to London (which left him gravely wounded) prompted limited Israeli retaliatory strikes against Palestine Liberation Organization (PLO) positions in southern Lebanon. This action, in turn, triggered intensive PLO shelling against Israeli civilian settlements in Galilee and further occasioned a substantial reinforcing of existing Syrian SA-6 missile emplacements in the Beka'a Valley, the first of which had been deployed to Lebanon on 29 April the previous year.

Using these developments as a pretext, the IDF on 6 June launched what it labelled 'Operation Peace for Galilee', a massive combined-arms assault intended to destroy the PLO as a military force and neutralise any Syrian combat assets in Lebanon that might interfere with that effort.[4] The air portion of this campaign began 3 days later with a co-ordinated surprise attack against the Syrian SA-6 network in the Beka'a Valley. This was immediately followed by an intense aerial showdown between Israeli and Syrian fighters, in what has been widely acclaimed as the largest single air battle since the Second World War.

The SAM Suppression Phase

For understandable reasons, the IAF was strongly inclined to destroy the Syrian SA-6 sites immediately upon their initial emplacement in April 1981. That departure from the status quo was typical of the ambiguous enemy provocations that have routinely caused the IDF to agonise over whether to pre-empt decisively and accept the ensuing diplomatic consequences or else tolerate the provocation and perhaps incur a long-term military disadvantage as a result. In this case, the IAF was probably torn between a natural desire to take prompt action and concern that by doing so it might compromise its SAM-suppression tactics that could prove critical to Israeli success in a later and more serious confrontation with the Syrians.[5] The issue was resolved in favour of attacking, and the Begin government authorised the IAF to proceed with mission planning. Before the operation could be carried out, however, a heavy cloud cover moved into the target area and obliged the IAF to wait. By the time the weather cleared, US diplomatic efforts to mediate the conflict had begun in earnest. This forestalled any immediate resumption of strike preparations.[6]

The resultant delay gave the IAF over a year to amass tactical intelligence on the Syrian SA-6 positions and refine its attack plans.[7] The latter included, by some accounts, extensive rehearsal sorties against simulated SA-6 sites in the Negev desert.[8] Once the day of the strike arrived, the IAF commanded an excellent threat picture, a cadre of highly experienced and well-prepared aircrews, and a tactical repertoire precisely tailored to the operational situation.

The target complex consisted of nineteen SA-6 batteries deployed at several locations in the Beka'a Valley, an agricultural plain in central Lebanon some 10 miles wide by 25 miles long and flanked on both sides by ridgelines up to 6,500 ft high. Key mission support elements included several E-2C surveillance aircraft orbiting off the coast of Lebanon, a Boeing 707 electronic intelligence (ELINT) platform, and numerous ground and airborne jammers (the latter aboard CH-53 helicopters).[9] The functions of the E-2C were to provide gap-filler support for Israeli ground radars, monitor the airspace over the target area and beyond into Syria, and provide vectoring and battle-management assistance to Israeli fighters in the event that Syrian MiGs rose to challenge the SAM suppression operation.[10] The 707, for its part, was poised to monitor Syrian SA-6 radar activity. Finally, Israeli jammers were to be employed against voice and data-link transmissions between Syrian fighters and GCI sites (and perhaps also against other threat emitters such as enemy aircraft and SAM radars).

Reports about the equipment and tactics employed by the IAF vary widely. Most accounts agree, however, that the mission was accomplished by a combination of F-4s with Shrike and Standard ARM missiles, F-16s with standoff weapons and conventional bombs, and a variety of other systems (notably artillery and ground-launched missiles).[11] The attack reportedly commenced with a wave of remotely piloted vehicles (RPVs) launched as decoys to activate the engagement radars of the SA-6s.[12] As expected, the Syrians rose to the bait, showed poor target discrimination and firing discipline, and initiated a massed launch of SAMs against the incoming drones. Once positive SAM activity was confirmed by the 707, the following sequence of events (or something like it) unfolded in rapid succession:

SAM radars in the southern portion of the Beka'a were attacked by artillery from Israeli ground units that had rapidly moved forward from their positions south of the Awali River, as well as by Israeli ground-launched battlefield missiles.[13]

SAM radars located farther north, outside IDF artillery and missile range, were simultaneously engaged by F-4s using Shrike, Standard ARM, and Maverick.

Once the Syrian SAM radars had been neutralised by a combination of electronic countermeasures (ECM) and physical destruction, F-4s and F-16s employing low-level ingress and terrain-masking tactics entered in simultaneous attacks from multiple directions, delivering stand-off munitions, cluster bomb units (CBUs), and general-purpose bombs against surviving radar vans and the SA-6 missile launchers.[14]

In the course of this highly orchestrated strike, which reportedly took only 10 minutes, Israeli forces destroyed seventeen of the nineteen SA-6 sites in the Beka'a Valley, as well as several SA-2 and SA-3 sites.[15] Throughout the operation, orbiting Scout and Mastiff RPVs provided continuous video coverage of events for the ground-based IAF strike commander. The Boeing 707 continued to monitor enemy radar emissions and transmitted threat data to attacking fighters. Chaff and flares were used extensively by all Israeli aircraft operating within the Syrian air defence envelope. Numerous SA-6s were fired during this evolution. None found their target, and the IAF accomplished the mission without a single aircraft loss. (Several Israeli fighters, however, are reported to have recovered with moderate to severe battle damage.) The two surviving SA-6 sites, as well as some additional batteries that were replenished with new equipment overnight, were destroyed in a similar IAF raid the following day.

The Air Battles

As expected, the Syrian Air Force scrambled a large number of MiGs to engage the attacking Israeli fighters. The IAF was fully prepared. Several F-15 and F-16 combat air patrols (CAPs) were positioned west of the Beka'a Valley to intercept any Syrian fighters that might attempt to disrupt the SAM suppression raid. Intelligence on Syrian MiG activity was excellent. By one account, the Israeli Scout RPV used its electro-optical zoom lens and digital data link to provide real-time video imagery of Syrian fighters positioned for take-off.[16] The E-2C, with its 200-mile surveillance range, was able to pick up the MiGs on radar as soon as they left their runways and relayed intercept vectors to the IAF fighter CAPs. Once the enemy fighter formations were airborne, their communications were massively jammed and they were deprived of any contact with their

GCI controllers. (IAF fighters carry jam-resistant radios and were able to communicate with their own controllers through secure voice and data link, despite countervailing Syrian jamming attempts.)[17] The Israelis also used some F-15s in a tactical AWACS mode to provide gap-filler support for the E-2C and to assist other fighters.[18]

The resultant confrontation was by far the largest in the history of Middle East air warfare. At its height, there were reportedly some ninety Israeli and sixty Syrian jets simultaneously airborne in the combat arena.[19] The IAF enjoyed the combined advantages of tactical initiative, numerical preponderance, superior aircraft and munitions, and confident knowledge of where the Syrian threat would be concentrated. Using their look-down radars and all-aspect missiles (both of which the Syrians lacked),[20] Israeli fighters simply picked off any MiGs that ventured past a pre-established line.[21] Although the IAF maintains that it took no shots at Syrian fighters from beyond visual range, it evidently made extensive use of blind-side tactics by employing the E-2C to vector F-15s and F-16s into beam attacks against Syrian MiGs (where their radar warning systems were reportedly least effective).[22]

Beyond Israel's advantages in equipment and tactics, another notable feature of the engagement was a marked asymmetry in pilot skill. Upon having their communications jammed, the Syrians lost any semblance of air discipline and quickly became split up into isolated pairs and singles. As one Western military attaché who witnessed part of the air battle from the ground later recounted: 'I watched a group of Syrian fighter planes fly figure-eights. They just flew around and around and obviously had no idea what to do next.'[23] This impression was confirmed by the after-action comments of an anonymous senior IAF officer: 'The problem was that [Syrian] pilots didn't do things at the right time or in the right place. They flew in a way very difficult to understand. ... The pilots behaved as if they knew they were going to be shot down and waited to see when it was going to happen and not how to prevent it or how to shoot us down.' Reflecting on this lack of aggressiveness and initiative (and apparent unfamiliarity with air combat) displayed by the Syrians, he added: 'They could have flown the best fighter in the world, but if they flew it the way they were flying, we would have shot them down in exactly the same way. It wasn't the equipment at fault, but their tactics.'[24]

The IAF downed twenty-three Syrian fighters during this engagement while sustaining no losses of its own. The following day Israeli fighters shot down fifteen more MiGs. By the end of July the IAF had destroyed eighty-five Syrian aircraft (half MiG-21s and half MiG-23s) in a cumulative series of air battles without losing a single aircraft to enemy fighter action. According to press accounts of remarks by General Wilbur Creech, at the time Commander of the USAF Tactical Air Command, around forty Syrian fighters were downed by F-15s, some forty-four by F-16s, and one by an F-4. Most of these kills were accomplished by the AIM-9L. By this same account, only 7 per cent of the Syrian MiG losses resulted from gun kills.[25] This suggests that despite some initial impressions, what actually occurred was not a single, swirling, multiparticipant 'dogfight' in the classic sense, but rather a series of independent encounters between smaller numbers of fighters on both sides, with the Israeli pilots maintaining their speed, keeping predictable manoeuvres to a minimum, and capitalising on their all-aspect weapons by taking snap shots of opportunity. Whatever the case, the result was a complete rout that established a new high for IAF kill ratios in air combat.

Overview

Israel's air operations over Lebanon in 1982 constituted the first full-scale test of current-generation American tactical air weaponry. Their distinctive features included combined-arms employment in a real-time electronic warfare environment and thorough integration of high-technology hardware with exceptional training, tactics, and leadership competence. It would be risky to generalise overarching 'lessons' from this experience (and the Israelis themselves have expressly cautioned against trying) because of several circumstances that rendered the Lebanese air war unique.[26] For one thing, the operation was severely limited in scope, intensity, objectives and number of participants. Second, the Syrian SAM threat consisted largely of fixed SA-6s whose positions were well known by the IAF. This posed considerably less of a challenge than the USAF would face against integrated Soviet air defences in Central Europe (or the IAF itself would confront in a major air war over the Golan Heights).[27] Finally, the IAF commanded unprecedented numerical superiority over the enemy and maintained the tactical initiative at all times. Neither circumstance would be likely to favour Israel in a full-fledged war against a coalition of Syria, Jordan and Iraq. They certainly could not be expected to favour the United States and NATO in a conventional war in Europe initiated by the Warsaw Pact.

Nevertheless, the IAF performed very well in this campaign by any measure—so well, in fact, that its leaders were reportedly astonished to have come through it virtually unscathed.[28] By the end of September it had amassed a total score of some twenty-nine SAM sites destroyed in seven raids and eighty-five Syrian MiGs downed—with only two Israeli aircraft losses to enemy ground fire.[29] These numbers are, of course, only approximations from a variety of conflicting accounts, and the IDF has remained silent on most of the operational matters addressed above.[30] Despite continued uncertainty at the margins, however, there is no denying the impressiveness of the IAF's performance in the aggregate. It dealt a serious setback to Syria, deeply embarrassed the Syrian High Command's

Soviet suppliers, and provoked intense Soviet discomfiture over the dismal showing of its front-line weaponry in the eyes of an interested and watchful world.

Early Soviet Reactions to IAF Combat Successes

It is scarcely surprising that the Soviets should have been so distressed by these events. Apart from the widespread humiliation they caused the Soviet leadership, they raised troublesome questions about possible shortcomings in Soviet combat equipment—with implications reaching well beyond Moscow's narrow interests and stature in the Middle East. The SA-6, after all, is a system on which the Soviets themselves depend heavily for theatre air defence in Europe and elsewhere. Likewise, though they lacked the latest-generation Soviet weapons and fire-control systems (the Apex missile and Highlark radar), the Syrian MiG-23s that were so totally outclassed by the IAF were virtual carbon copies of the Soviet Union's best air superiority fighter in current service. They also represented one of the mainstays of the Soviet Union's military aid relationship with many third-world client states. Not long after the Beka'a Valley campaign, Iraq and Peru were among the first of those states reported to have questioned the adequacy of their Soviet weapons as a result of the Syrian debacle.[31] This was only the harbinger of a broader setback sustained by the traditional image of Soviet prowess that had hitherto undergirded Moscow's far-flung international arms trade.

In the immediate wake of the Lebanese war, the US government pressed Israel hard to share the details of its combat experiences so that the USAF, in particular, might benefit from learning how its previously untested equipment had performed.[32] The Soviets, for quite different reasons, had even more urgent interests in deriving appropriate 'lessons' and lost no time dispatching a sizable data collection team to Damascus to gain first-hand answers about why their weaponry took such a drubbing. As a measure of its agitation, Moscow began resupplying Syria with attrition-fillers only a day after the Beka'a Valley dust had settled—well before the Soviets had more than the broadest inkling of what had happened beyond the obvious facts of Syria's extensive combat losses.[33] Following that, the first of four Soviet delegation visits occurred on 13 June under the leadership of Colonel General Yevgenii Yurasov, first deputy commander of the Soviet Air Defence Forces.[24] This visit was only cursorily noted by the Soviet media and was portrayed as a routine 'friendship' meeting to reaffirm Moscow's security commitment to Syria. Although much of the delegation's time was undoubtedly spent negotiating follow-up arms transfers and security arrangements, its main concern was almost surely a searching review of every aspect of Syrian combat performance so that appropriate countermeasures might be introduced into front-line Soviet forces. Concern about possible problems with Soviet weaponry implied by the one-sided outcome was evidently such that the Chief of the Soviet General Staff, Marshal Ogarkov, reportedly visited Damascus the following month to conduct a personal evaluation.[35]

To save face and shore up its political footing in the region, the Soviet Union commenced a major rearmament of Syria in the wake of these consultative meetings. In addition to replacing the MiGs and SAMs that had been destroyed, the Soviets provided Syria with several new weapons types, including the SA-8, SA-9, and most important, SA-5.[36] The latter weapon, never before deployed outside the Soviet Union, has a slant range of 180 n.miles and is capable of engaging Israeli aircraft flying within Israeli airspace and off the Lebanese coast. It thus confronts Israel with a new deterrent challenge. It would have to be destroyed pre-emptively in any future IAF air operation against Syria that envisaged employment of E-2C and 707 aircraft. Yet it is exclusively manned by Soviet personnel, whose presence would almost certainly constitute a powerful restraining factor in Israeli planning.[37] Other developments heralding a deepened Soviet involvement included the dispatch of some 2,000 additional Soviet advisers to the Syrian armed forces, expansion of a Soviet submarine facility at the Syrian port of Tartus, deployment of SS-21 tactical ballistic missiles to Syria, and commencement of heavy ECM activities using helicopter jammers and other countermeasures to complicate future IAF raids.

None of this could disguise the fact that for all their surface appearance of 'solidarity' with the Syrians, the Soviets were severely stung by the visible setback sustained by their hapless Middle Eastern client. On the diplomatic circuit there were widespread private expressions of Soviet disgust over Syria's ineptitude in squandering away what, in more competent hands, should have been perfectly adequate weaponry.[38] Soviet commentators also took the unusual step of publicly refuting Western claims that American weapons employed by Israel were 'superior' to those provided to Syria by the USSR. To help counter internal and foreign tendencies to doubt the technical virtuosity of Soviet weaponry, the Soviet domestic media and TASS immediately proclaimed that 'In a bid to diminish the potentialities of the forces opposing the Israeli-American aggression in Lebanon,' US and Israeli propaganda agencies were 'intensively circulating deliberately false information about Soviet combat equipment.' In this vein, a TASS commentary on 1 July petulantly complained that the 'combat qualities of American arms used by the Israelis are being extolled in every way, while the losses sustained by the interventionists on Lebanese soil are understated'. Although it conceded substantial losses to the Syrian side in the conflict, the TASS statement sought to dismiss this as an inevitable consequence of the IDF's 'sudden and massive blow on Lebanon by all its armed services'.[39]

This argument was repeated 2 days later by the head of the CPSU Central Committee's International Information Department, Leonid Zamyatin. He too acknowledged that Syria's losses were 'higher' than those suffered by Israel, but insisted that this was attributable 'not to the weapons supplied by the USSR but to well-known military advantages traditionally enjoyed by the attacking side'. He added, however, that Israel was deliberately 'minimising' its own losses and that in fact 'up to 40' of its aircraft had been shot down during the preceding month's fighting. As for the conflict itself, Zamyatin said it was initially assumed that the Israelis would not engage Syrian forces during their sweep toward Beirut, but allowed that on 9 June 'a real battle' took place between the two countries. A subsequent TASS statement sought to downplay this by conceding Israel only a 'limited military success' against 'a rather limited anti-aircraft defense force of Syria in Lebanon'. It rationalised Syrian air losses by asserting that the Syrians 'did not have a ramified network of radar stations [which] complicated their action'. It further tried to cast Syrian conduct in a favourable light by noting that 'Israeli planes did not violate the airspace of Syria a single time', attributing this to the IAF's sober recollection of its 'heavy losses' suffered at the hands of Syrian air defences during the 1973 war.[40]

All in all, the thrust of Soviet domestic commentary on the Lebanese conflict was to convey an impression entirely at odds with the facts. For example, following the IAF's destruction of Syria's SAM sites, Radio Moscow spoke of 'serious battles ... in the Beka'a Valley, where Syrian forces have been repulsing attacks by the Israeli aggressors in three directions'.[41] A month later, a *Red Star* article went significantly further in misrepresenting the truth when it claimed that 'Syrian troops, using Soviet-made weapons and material, have inflicted considerable losses on the Israeli forces. ...' 'Several [Israeli] air defence missile batteries have been destroyed', it falsely reported, 'and 67 Israeli aircraft, including modern US-made F-15 and F-16 fighters, were downed'.[42] Echoing this distortion, a TASS dispatch cited Western statements extolling the 'extensive capabilities of the ... F-15 and F-16 ... and the "success" of these aircraft in putting out a number of Syrian air defense missile units' and summarily discounted these as products of an Israeli 'propaganda stratagem'. Instead, it maintained, 'Israeli pilots have learned at first hand the high skills of Syrian pilots and have seen for themselves that ... the Syrian air defence forces have shot down a number of enemy planes, including F-15 and F-16 fighter-bombers.' 'Facts show', it concluded, 'that the Syrian Army possesses modern weapons [and] has shown its capability to repel the aggression.'[43]

The ultimate in Soviet fabrication, however, was a succession of articles by Colonel G. Kashuba (billed as a 'special correspondent' to *Red Star*), whose contrivances in seeking to glorify Syrian combat performance went to such extremes as to be downright entertaining to any reader aware of the facts or inclined toward scepticism over the Soviet propaganda line.[44] In one of his more fanciful flights of imagination, Colonel Kashuba described his visit to a Syrian air base and his recollection of fighter operations that he observed in the wake of the Beka'a Valley engagements:

> An aircraft came in to land. I looked at its streamlined, beautiful contours. I recognized a MiG. . . .

> The aircraft taxied into the standing area. Its turbines were steaming with heat. . . . A thickset figure encased in a G-suit, with lively expressive eyes and curling, oily hair over a high forehead, jumped out of the cockpit. If you were to draw his portrait, you would have a generalized image of a Syrian airman.

> We introduced ourselves. He was Captain Nafi Salmu. He was just 25 years old but already an element lead with about 700 hours of flying time. . . .

> I asked Nafi to describe the battle in which he downed an Israeli F-15. The officer began speaking animatedly, gesturing to represent his plane's manoeuvres. The interpreter couldn't keep up with him and had difficulty translating the aviation terminology. Then Captain Salmu took my notebook and with a few clear strokes drew the picture of his duel with the F-15. The victory had not been easy, the enemy had been subtle.[45]

This nonsense neatly summarises the general propaganda view of the Beka'a Valley operation developed and circulated by the Soviets for domestic consumption. Astute Soviet pilots, especially those with personal experience at dealing with the Syrians, most likely had little difficulty seeing through Kashuba's tale and others like it.[46] All the same, the foregoing examples typify the way in which the Lebanese air war was interpreted for the home front by the Soviet media throughout the year and a half before the appearance of Colonel Dubrov's analysis.

Insights and Oversights in the Dubrov Article

In sharp contrast to the Soviet commentary noted above, Dubrov's remarks are entirely professional in tone and purpose. They are not aimed at foreign audiences or the Soviet population at large, but at officers with special interests in tactical air weapons and operations. Aside from some perfunctory propaganda boilerplate at the beginning and end, the article is devoid of ideological axe-grinding and sticks closely to describing and

analysing technical matters. As such, it should be read as a serious effort
by the Soviet Air Force to communicate a credible account of the Lebanese
air war to its aircrews.

Dubrov addresses equipment and tactics (both air-to-air and air-to-
ground) in equal measure. An interesting question concerns the nature of
his source materials. Undoubtedly the Soviets have done extensive classified
analyses based on their debriefings of the Syrians, but these would not
routinely be shared with Soviet aircrews or alluded to in a general-
circulation article of this sort.[47] Indeed, given the exceptional secrecy and
compartmentation that limit information flow within the Soviet military,
it is a fair question whether Dubrov himself was ever directly exposed to
them. As noted earlier, Dubrov frequently references 'foreign experts' and
the 'foreign press', and his account of the various hardware items used by
the IAF probably does derive from those sources. But he also discusses
matters of an operational nature—formations and spreads, ingress techniques, engagement tactics, weapons-release parameters and the like—
which have not been treated openly in Western publications. In so far as
they ring true, they may derive from Syrian accounts or from direct Soviet
observation. In cases where they appear to run counter to reasonable
inferences about how the IAF most likely employed its forces, they may
be entirely fabricated. In all events, they are hard to corroborate in the
absence of independent Israeli testimony.

The Dubrov article is far more instructive for what it ignores than for
what it includes. For example, the reader is treated to lengthy commentary
on F-15 and F-16 performance characteristics, fighter patrol techniques,
the use of airborne radar surveillance and battle-management platforms,
and how operations among these various assets were co-ordinated. Yet he
is not given the slightest clue that the net result of this activity was a
sustained turkey shoot in which the Syrians lost eighty-five aircraft in the
course of 3 months. For all its detail in describing the set-up, the article
remains virtually silent on the combat itself.

Dubrov also alludes to defence suppression, but offers nothing approxi-
mating a recognisable description of what actually happened to Syria's
SA-6s in the Beka'a Valley. Indeed, he expressly *denies* that SAMs figured
as Israeli targets and leaves his readers to believe that the IAF performed
as well as it did because its operations 'were carried out over a country
that did not have modern anti-aircraft systems' but only 'anti-aircraft
artillery units ... organic to combined Arab forces located on Lebanese
soil'. The effect is like reading a variation on *Hamlet* without any reference
to the prince. Perhaps these distortions are only to be expected, given the
Soviet Union's natural incapacity to concede the unpleasant truth. All the
same, they indicate that for all the earmarks of dispassionate professionalism
conveyed by the article, Dubrov is clearly striving to sweep the more
disturbing aspects of the story under the rug.

Lessons Learned

Among the genuine operational implications (or at least topics for serious thought) the Soviets may have extracted from the Lebanon war, the following points touched upon by Dubrov may be suggestive:

The increased freedom of manoeuvre afforded by using air-superiority fighters in separate patrol orbits rather than in direct support of strike formations. Dubrov correctly notes that detaching counter-air elements from direct escort and allowing them to roam their assigned CAP sectors freely not only enhances their defensive utility but also their offensive leverage against enemy air threats. However, he erroneously describes this as merely a 'minimal' departure from US fighter tactics developed during the Vietnam War. He also goes overboard in depicting as a 'negative feature' of offensive CAPs what he claims to be their dependence on 'positive radar control outside the strike zone'. At several points Dubrov describes the E-2C (or a comparable surveillance platform) as a necessary prerequisite for such employment. In doing so, he overlooks the considerable autonomous search capability possessed by the F-15's onboard radar. Moreover, his assertion that Israeli use of fighter sweeps revealed 'diminished reliability ... in comparison to direct accompaniment of bombers' has a defensive tone, suggesting that the Soviets may remain wedded to direct escort of strike formations in their own operational doctrine.

Nevertheless, Dubrov's special fascination with F-15 employment could indicate serious ferment within the Soviet fighter community. For years the Soviet Air Force has resisted the idea of allowing its pilots much independence and has instead stressed the importance of maintaining close control over its fighters at all times.[48] Recently, however, it has begun to acquire equipment that would allow it, in principle, to go well beyond that restrictive operating doctrine. With the advent of the new MiG-29 and SU-27 fighters that will soon be entering operational service, Frontal Aviation will have aircraft with substantially improved weapons, avionics, and manoeuvring performance.[49] It will not, however, be able to extract anywhere near the full potential afforded by that capability if it continues to operate in accordance with its traditional air combat doctrine. Although it remains far too early to tell (and although powerful stylistic proclivities will have to be overcome before any significant change can occur), the interest in Israel's F-15 operations reflected in Dubrov's commentary may suggest that Soviet Air Force leaders may have this problem increasingly in mind. In all events, it involves an area that will continue to bear careful watching.

The vulnerability of airborne surveillance platforms to enemy fighter and SAM action. However mistaken Dubrov may be in implying that fighter CAPs are 'dependent' on AWACS support, there is no question that AWACS platforms are substantial force multipliers and thus constitute lucrative targets. Dubrov notes that the IAF felt obliged to station its E-2Cs well beyond Syrian SAM range and further took heed to guard them against the Syrian MiG threat with a pair of F-15s. He also suggests that without E-2C support the IAF would have been unable to achieve its air combat results. This may say something about the Soviet rationale for subsequently providing Syria with the SA-5, whose extended range will allow it to engage targets like the E-2C and 707 even in overwater orbits or deep within Israeli airspace. It may also telegraph Soviet thinking about the need to neutralise the USAF E-3A as an early priority in the event of a European war. In so far as this impression is correct, it suggests a derivative 'lesson' for USAF and NATO planners as well.

The value of communications and radar jamming. Although Dubrov mentions this only in passing, there is little doubt that the combat utility of ECM was forcefully reconfirmed to the Soviets by the Lebanon experience. Syrian MiG formations were heavily jammed by the Israelis from the moment they were airborne. As a result, Syrian pilots were unable to receive either intercept directives or evasive commands from their controllers and were thus deprived of any offensive or defensive potential. The Soviet Air Force currently operates under a similar close-control doctrine and would be comparably vulnerable to enemy jamming interference. How (or whether) the Soviets will eventually change their *modus operandi* in response to this threat is a question that cannot be explored here. But the strong implication for any intelligent Soviet planner surely must be an appreciation of the growing need either for electronic counter-countermeasure (ECCM) capabilities that would permit Soviet pilots to talk through enemy jamming measures or else new departures in training and tactics that might reduce this direct dependence on GCI support.

The utility of employing fighters with long-range radars in a mini-AWACS role. Dubrov notes the IAF's use of the F-15 in lending gap-filler support to the E-2C and in transmitting airborne target data to F-16s (which lacked the radar capability of the F-15). He further acknowledges that 'this was the first time such interaction between fighters has ever been practised'. In so far as the SU-27 is expected to have a similar capability, this reference may suggest underlying Soviet efforts to unburden themselves from their current dependence on ground-based management of the air battle by extracting greater force-multiplier potential from their emerging fighter technologies.

The diminished reliability of positive radar control as the depth of air operations into enemy territory increases. Given the close geographic confines of the Lebanese conflict, this was probably less critical a factor in the operations of either side than Dubrov suggests. But his statement that 'radar control over fighters weakens with increasing depth into enemy territory' and thus increases 'the probability of sudden attack—by enemy aircraft with forward-aspect missiles' is correct and has clear implications for Soviet operations planning against NATO. His observation that 'air superiority is fundamentally achieved by shifting the battle to the enemy rather than over one's own territory' (since the latter 'means losing the initiative') likewise has a bearing on Soviet tactical air planning for the European theatre. Both points suggest Soviet recognition of the growing importance of having the capability and option to use fighters beyond the effective range of Soviet ground-based control facilities.

The value of other 'force-multiplier' technologies. Dubrov seems notably impressed by Israeli use of such systems as reconnaissance RPVs, standoff munitions, and even simple things like chaff and flares. The tone of curiosity that accompanies his discussion of these techniques suggests that they may not be routinely practised in the Soviet Air Force. He seems especially attracted to the cost-effectiveness of RPVs as contrasted to manned aircraft and notes that their ability to provide commanders with real-time target data has become 'a most important factor in air power application'. (Although one can only speculate here, this observation could point toward one way the Soviets might seek to solve their problem of locating and engaging NATO's mobile Pershing II and ground-launched cruise missiles in the coming decade.) Dubrov also speaks approvingly of precision stand-off weapons in attacking high-priority targets where enemy defences prohibit armed reconnaissance and multiple passes per target. His remark that 'free-hunt' operations are impossible in areas where enemy defences have not been suppressed has relevance to Europe and is consistent with the common Western assumption that any Soviet air campaign against NATO would begin with an attempt to clear penetration corridors through the Hawk belt and other NATO defences.[50]

Lessons Mislearned or Ignored

These and other insights reflected in Dubrov's article are, on balance, overshadowed by its numerous misrepresentations and errors of fact. The first temptation is to dismiss those cases where Dubrov fails to put the point right as undifferentiated examples of intentional disinformation. Some of them, however, may be merely a natural result of the author's looking at novel events through the subjective filter of Soviet military culture and style. Others, particularly those that appear to deny the real significance of the IAF's accomplishments, may reflect a determination to suppress bad news or an ingrained inability to face up to real challenges. Readers with more authoritative knowledge about what happened over Lebanon will undoubtedly discover multiple holes and faulty interpretations in Dubrov's account. My own discussion that follows below will limit itself to the more obvious problems.

To begin with, Dubrov unduly discredits the IAF's tactical innovations when he equates them with the so-called 'American model' employed over a decade ago in Vietnam. Perhaps he is trying to assure his readers that changes in the Western air threat have not rendered matters tougher for the Soviet Air Force in the years since. But by comparing Israeli air operations over Lebanon with the stereotyped and often predictable mission profiles flown by the US Air Force and Navy against North Vietnam,[51] Dubrov not only misrepresents reality but contradicts his previous remarks about the significance of Lebanon as the first 'proving ground' for current-generation fighter aircraft and weapons. Any discerning reader, Western or Soviet, will readily see through the inconsistencies.

Another distortion, already touched on above, is Dubrov's apparent belief that independent fighter sweeps require the direct support of airborne control platforms. To some extent, this may simply reflect insufficient appreciation of the independent-search capability of the F-15's radar (particularly for situations like that in Lebanon, where the focus of enemy fighter concentration and likely axes of attack were precisely known beforehand). More interestingly, however, it may also reflect unwitting Soviet misperception of events resulting from the insidious interference of Soviet military culture bias. Given the Soviet Air Force's long-standing reliance on GCI close control, it could have a natural tendency to look at other variants of battle management in that idiosyncratic light. In the original Russian, Dubrov describes the IAF's E-2C as a 'VKP' (*vozdushnyi kommandnyi punkt*, or 'airborne command post'). He further claims that Israeli F-15 pilots were obliged to follow 'directives' from the E-2C and that F-15 fighter sweep operations were 'dependent' on those directives. In doing so, he may be misconstruing the E-2C as merely a variant of the ground-based 'KP' (*kommandnyi punkt*) that routinely governs Soviet fighter operations. In other words, he may perceive it as an airborne GCI site fashioned according to Soviet lines, rather than as a largely advisory— as opposed to directive—facility.[52] This would certainly account for the remainder of Dubrov's faulty inferences regarding the problems that he maintains would plague offensive fighter operations in the absence of AWACS-type support.[53]

If this analysis of Dubrov's reasoning is right, it may militate *against* the likelihood that the Soviets are gradually moving away from GCI close control toward more autonomous fighter operations.[54] It may also suggest that if and when the Soviets ever deploy their IL-76 AWACS in a theatre support role, they will be more inclined to use it as an airborne GCI site rather than in the way NATO now employs the E-3A. This will afford greater offensive 'reach' for Soviet fighter operations over NATO territory, but it will also mean continued suppression of individual pilot initiative and continued emphasis on key tactical decisions being made by higher-level commanders.[55]

Finally, and perhaps most important, Dubrov seems to have missed the boat fundamentally in his treatment of the implications posed by the advent of all-aspect air-to-air missiles. Taking issue with Western claims that the forward-hemisphere attack 'has asserted itself as a new element in air combat tactics', Dubrov insists that such missile employment depends on 'various complicating factors' and remains, at best, only the 'wave of the future'. His argument (which considers only the AIM-7F Sparrow and ignores the AIM-9L Sidewinder) rests on these premises:

> That effective positioning for such an attack requires AWACS vectoring and control, which may or may not always be available.
> That the target aircraft can defeat the attack by manoeuvring violently, thus forcing the AIM-7F's seeker head to break lock.
> That the attacking aircraft must 'acquire target data before this information is received by the other side'.

Dubrov adds that forward-hemisphere attacks by IAF fighters 'without transitioning to the manoeuvring phase' were only 'episodes heralding the future [and] were not typical fighter tactics'. His bottom-line 'lesson' from this experience for Soviet pilots sounds more like a counsel for complacency than a call for alarm, in light of its curious suggestion that the more things have changed, the more they have remained the same:

> The practical side of this conclusion derives from an established fact: Aircraft and weapons are ready to carry out manoeuvring combat. What is left is the preparation of the pilot. All the basic propositions of group manoeuvring combat theory and practice formulated during World War II are well known. Each subsequent generation of fighter aircraft has added to and perfected these propositions. But the main idea remains unchanged. Looking for some 'new in principle' way of training, in the view of experts, is a waste of time.

What are we to make of this perplexing conclusion? Perhaps part of the answer can be attributed to doctrinal lag. Since the Soviet Air Force, by all accounts, still lacks a good all-aspect missile of its own, it necessarily also lacks first-hand training experience in the all-aspect arena and remains caught up in planning for aerial combat aimed at manoeuvring toward a classic stern conversion. But this explanation is ultimately unsatisfactory, since we know that the Soviets have for years been seeking to develop missiles with expanded firing envelopes and have spoken openly since the mid-1970s about the tactical advantages that would be afforded by a capability to take forward-aspect shots at the enemy from beyond visual range.[56] Another interpretation may be that the Soviets remain excessively fixated on extended beyond visual range (BVR) systems at the expense of weapons for close-in combat. In this regard, Dubrov's failure to consider the AIM-9L may stem from his sole concentration on expanded firing opportunities made possible by 'medium-range' missiles and from his apparent reduction of all-aspect weapons employment to launches taken against the enemy 'in the face' rather than from *any* off-boresight position within the lethal parameters of the missile (including beam attacks and shots from behind the target's wing line).

Even within its own terms of reference, Dubrov's treatment of the all-aspect issue seems off the mark on several important counts. First, given the extensive proliferation of all-aspect missiles like the AIM-7F and AIM-9L throughout Western tactical fighter forces, it is misleading, to say the least, to maintain that they merely constitute 'the wave of the future' and to imply that there is no need to develop appropriate countermeasures against them. On the matter of AWACS support, Dubrov is certainly right to suggest that this would greatly enhance the effectiveness of a fighter sweep, particularly if the enemy lacked a comparable capability. But he is quite wrong to insist that an all-aspect missile attack 'requires thorough preparation, in which other aircraft must also participate'. Although it will generally be assisted by GCI or AWACS whenever these assets are available, the F-15 is capable of detecting and locking up an enemy on the nose quite unassisted as far out as 50n miles and engaging it head-on—once within range—with both the AIM-7F and AIM-9L (assuming that adequate target identification or prevailing rules of engagement would permit clearance to fire).

Second, it is true—as Dubrov notes—that an AIM-7F attack can be negated by appropriate counter-manoeuvring, but for this to occur the defending pilot must know he is under attack and have visual contact with the incoming missile. He may or may not enjoy this luxury in a heavy electronic warfare environment. It is also true in principle—as Dubrov states—that the attacker must possess appropriate target data and arrive at a firing solution before the enemy becomes alerted if any front-aspect shot is to achieve its maximum possibility of success. Yet the results of the various Beka'a Valley MiG encounters suggest that precisely this occurred on many occasions. It is a fair presumption that many Israeli AIM-7F shots caught their Syrian targets completely off guard—and an in-parameters AIM-9L shot is hard to counter even by the best pilots once the missile leaves its rails. Even assuming that defending fighters could deny the attackers a monopoly on timely target data, this would be of little help in a situation where the attackers had all-aspect weapons and the defenders did not, as was uniformly the case in the Lebanon air fighting.[57]

All in all, Dubrov's dismissal of the all-aspect threat and his claim that missile attacks over Lebanon 'without transitioning to the manoeuvring phase' were exceptions to the rule are strangely at odds with the facts and reflect a basic unfamiliarity with the three cardinal rules of multi-participant air combat (keep your speed up, avoid a turning fight, and stay unpredictable). Virtually all the IAF's MiG kills were accomplished by AIM-7F and AIM-9L shots. And while Israeli pilots are well trained for close manoeuvring combat, the large numbers of aircraft committed on both sides over the Beka'a Valley and the low incidence of reported IAF gun kills make it unlikely that a great deal of hard manoeuvring occurred outside of isolated engagements.

Where all this leaves us is not entirely clear. On the face of the evidence presented by Dubrov, however, at least one interim conclusion seems inescapable: Either the Soviets have failed to comprehend some of the major tactical lessons suggested by Israel's air combat results over Lebanon, or they are intentionally misrepresenting those results to their aviators for a variety of reasons that we can only guess at. Either interpretation offers ground for guarded encouragement among American and NATO European fighter pilots.

Conclusions

Despite its impressive advances in weapons technology, the Soviet Union remains a country heavily dominated by institutional drag, organisational compartmentation, and tenacious adherence to culture-bound practices that often perpetuate existing problems rather than encourage their solution. This is true in the military no less than in other sectors of Soviet society. It is one thing to 'understand' a situation and something quite different to translate that understanding into meaningful change—particularly in the Soviet armed forces, where deep-seated traditions tend to throw up obstacles in every path. This was forcefully underscored by Viktor Belenko, the Soviet pilot who defected by flying his MiG-25 from the Soviet Far East to Japan in 1976. When subsequently asked by his American interrogators to compare his impression of the US armed forces with his more familiar knowledge of day-to-day Soviet military practices, Belenko cited as an example the dissemination and adaptation of new tactical data. In the Soviet Union, he noted, communication of new information, let alone its exploitation, is slow and difficult because of pervasive secrecy and the burdensome effects of military bureaucracy.[58]

This view certainly seems borne out by the way the Soviets responded to their own limited combat experience with the Israelis during their brief

MiG encounter against IAF Phantoms and Mirages over the Suez Canal in June 1970. To summarise that encounter, the Soviets showed no familiarity with basic principles of air combat and lost five aircraft in an intense 4-minute engagement without laying a hand on their Israeli opponents.[59] The following day, the Soviet Air Force Commander, Marshal Kutakhov, was prompty dispatched to Cairo West in search of the 'facts' (and presumably appropriate heads to roll as well).[60] Yet it remains far from clear how deeply the lessons of that experience have penetrated into day-to-day Soviet training in subsequent years. It has been claimed by some that the Soviet Air Force is steadily improving its tactical repertoire in consonance with its ongoing acquisition of advanced fighter aircraft and weapons.[61] How well it might be able to implement that 'improved' repertoire under conditions of actual combat, however, remains an open question, given the rigidities and time-worn conventions that apparently continue to govern Soviet tactical air training.[62] After all, those Syrian pilots who found themselves so outclassed by the IAF over Lebanon in 1982 were flying front-line Soviet hardware and were operating in accordance with accepted Soviet air combat theory and practice.[63] Even with all due allowances for greater Soviet professionalism, technical sophistication, and air discipline, there is no *prima facie* reason for believing that the outcome would have been substantially different had the Israelis been flying against Soviet pilots rather than Syrians.

It is against this backdrop that Colonel Dubrov's article must be considered. By itself, it provides far too little evidence to support any confident conclusion about what 'lessons' the Soviet Air Force has absorbed from the Lebanese air war. (Indeed, the very question of how the Soviet military assimilates 'lessons' from its own and others' combat experiences is a complex one that warrants close examination in its own right.) All we can say for sure is that Dubrov's article accurately reflects what the Soviet leadership has chosen to communicate about that war to its officers. To go much beyond this would require detailed information about trends in Soviet tactical concepts, training practices, and patterns of aircrew supervision and management—information which the Soviet armed forces unfortunately are not generally disposed to share with outsiders.[64]

Taking at face value what Dubrov has indirectly told us in communicating with his own fighter community, the worst-case interpretation is that Soviet military leaders have fully understood the handwriting on the wall from Lebanon and have chosen to keep their aircrews blissfully ignorant while they seek to develop and validate appropriate countermeasures. a less alarmist appraisal would maintain that the Soviet are incapable of facing up to conclusions that would force them to alter fundamentally their reliance on rigid top-down control and have failed to comprehend the essence of the Beka'a Valley experience because of the inhibiting bonds of their entrenched biases and preconceptions.

My own view inclines towards this latter interpretation. Granted, the Soviets are as capable as we are of reading the technical results of the Lebanese war and drawing appropriate technical conclusions. They, like ourselves, are aware that the AIM-9L was a star performer (notwithstanding Dubrov's silence on the matter), and they are undoubtedly well along toward developing a comparable weapon. Likewise, the Soviets learned to their consternation what the USAF itself was gratified to see confirmed, namely, that the F-15 and F-16 are unsurpassed fighters when properly supported.[65] These and similar conclusions have been well appreciated by the Soviet defence bureaucracy and can almost certainly be expected to influence Soviet weapons characteristics in multiple ways—none of them congenial to Western security interests.

Yet to accept such narrow technical findings as the major teachings of the Lebanon air war would be to overlook the larger implications of its outcome. The real 'lessons' of the Beka'a Valley do not concern weapons so much as concepts of force employment. In the end, the Soviets saw the bitter results of a confrontation between two radically divergent military philosophies, in which the Syrians were simply outflown and outfought by vastly superior Israeli opponents. Without question, its very capable American hardware figured prominently in helping Israel emerge from the Beka'a Valley fighting with a perfect score. Nevertheless, the outcome would most likely have been heavily weighted in Israel's favour even had the equipment available to each side been reversed.[66] At bottom, the Syrians were not done in by the AIM-9L's expanded launch envelope, the F-15's radar, or any combination of Israeli technical assets, but by the IDF's constant retention of the operational initiative and its clear advantages in leadership, organisation, tactical adroitness, and adaptability. This is the overarching 'lesson' of lasting significance from the war—and the last one the Soviets seem close to comprehending and assimilating.[67]

None of this should be read as an excuse to underestimate the Soviet Union as an adversary in the large. If only because of their quantitative strength and their apparent indifference to attrition as a necessary price for operational success, the Soviet armed forces have the capacity to create profound problems for NATO—*whatever* tactical weaknesses they may suffer at the unit level. Moreover, the Soviet Air Force's reliance on GCI and its lack of refined air combat skills may not be perceived as a liability by Soviet commanders given the way they intend to fight.[68] Considering the subordinaion of Soviet tactical air power to the imperatives of achieving victory in the land campaign, the Soviets may be quite content to be the losers in an air-to-air slugging contest, so long as Frontal Aviation succeeds in holding off NATO's counter air fighters long enough to allow Warsaw Pact ground forces to accomplish their objectives on schedule. For this reason, Soviet failure to develop an air combat repertoire comparable to that of most Western air arms should not be viewed in isolation as grounds for great optimism by NATO commanders and planners.

Nevertheless, if Soviet pilots genuinely believe and are prepared to act on what they have been told by Colonel Dubrov (about the insignificance of the all-aspect missile threat, about the continued validity of 'tried and tested' tactical principles, and so on), this can only come as good news to USAF and NATO pilots who may someday have to confront their Soviet opposites flying the SU-27 and MiG-29. The axiom that 'you fight like you train' applies to the Soviets no less than it does to ourselves. Only the foolish or the naive would flatly assert that the Soviet Air Force will *never* alter its training and tactics in a manner that might allow it to operate its emerging generation of fighter weapons to the limit of their designed performance. Until that occurs, however, there is great merit in Major General Jasper Welch's admonition that 'there is a certain unbecoming fatalism about routinely allowing the Soviet military a free ride on its existing vulnerabilities just because we "might" be wrong or they "might" fix them'.[69] For the moment, however impressive the emerging Soviet tactical air posture may be on paper, the individual Soviet fighter pilot still appears to have a considerable way to go before he will be allowed the training and latitude to employ his equipment to its fullest combat potential.

8

The Air-Land Battle

GROUP CAPTAIN TIMOTHY GARDEN

Air Power and the Ground Forces

The advent of the military aircraft into the fighting forces of nations during this century has transformed the way in which wars are fought. No longer can the Army commander depend on the nature of the ground to protect him and to constrain his enemy's avenues of advance. No longer can he build obstacles to deflect or direct his enemy's movements. No longer can he assume that the threat comes only from the front or the flanks. The enemy has freedom to operate regardless of terrain, either from directly above or by concentrating his fire power on the all too vulnerable rear areas. At the same time as air power has brought new vulnerabilities, it has also brought a new capability for the land commander to know what his enemy is doing, to relay the information in a very short time, to act on that information with rapid and mobile deployment of forces, or to concentrate aircraft fire power wherever it may be needed.

Air power has transformed the way in which wars are fought. It has brought with it new dangers and new opportunities. The rapid development of techniques in the First World War to support the ground forces, initially through artillery spotting, and then to full reconnaissance and beyond to offensive bombing and defensive air-to-air combat, heralded the types of operations in which air forces were seen in the Second World War. The development and successes of the tactical air forces in that war proved the crucial nature of joint air and land operations. When the Army and Air Force operated in harmony towards a common aim, they could achieve victory in the land battle.[1]

In this essay we shall consider how air power can continue to support the Army commander in achieving his objectives under likely modern tactical situations. What tasks does the Army commander require his air power to carry out? What air threats must he counter? What weapon systems are available today? What tactical doctrine makes best use of the air power resources which are available? In looking at the current

149

situation, those areas which could best benefit from possible technological development will be highlighted. The broader question of allocation of scarce resources to promising new capabilities is beyond the present scope. That question requires a much broader examination of the competing defence needs for the future, which must include relative priorities of strategic forces, maritime operations and independent air operations.

Before looking at the detail of the roles which air power can play, we must define the concept of the Air-Land Battle a little more closely. The term has gained much currency since the advent of the US Army Manual FM100-5,[2] which has become the American national manual for the conduct of Army operations. It is characterised by the use of manoeuvre to fight rather than positional defence.[3] It is not, however, this narrow national single-Service concept, but the much broader question of how air power can be used in support of the ground forces under conditions ranging from the lowest intensity operations, through limited wars to all-out general war which should be examined. No prior assumptions can be made about the organisation of the air power: different nations have different traditions in their organisation. Nor are particular aircraft types necessarily used in the same way by different national forces.

Reconnaissance

The first requirement for the conduct of the Air-Land Battle is for information. The commander must know where his enemy is deployed, what he is doing, in what strength, with what equipment and what options are open to him. He must identify the enemy's weaknesses and exploit them; he must identify his strong points and either weaken them or avoid engaging them. The key to all this is intelligence. Intelligence can operate at many different depths and levels of discrimination.[4] The Infantry commander, whose position is being overrun by an armoured column, knows where the enemy is, and in such detail that he can read the number of every tank. Such detail is unnecessary, and the information is too late to be of use to the hapless soldier on the ground. At the other end of the scale, the orbiting satellite can provide sensor coverage of whole countries. Such a surfeit of information, which may be prone to weather limitations or enemy countermeasures, requires considerable analysis before it can generate practical information. The Army commander needs that intelligence about the enemy which is relevant to his area of operations. Signals information can provide a remarkable amount of such intelligence. Army reconnaissance units can patrol into enemy territory and bring back information, albeit only over relatively short distances and comparatively slowly.

Tactical reconnaissance must depend for the main part on deploying appropriate sensors to a position where they can observe the enemy, and relay their information back in time for it to be of use. This in turn leads to a requirement for a flying platform to support and deploy suitable sensors. The earliest such reconnaissance systems were tethered balloons with a man acting as the sensor. Such a static system suffers from both range and vulnerability disadvantages. To select the appropriate air vehicle for reconnaissance, the sensor requirement must be first examined. In turn, the choice of sensor must depend on an appreciation of the type of information required. If the enemy is a Third World guerrilla fighter hiding in the undergrowth, a sensor which detects body heat might be appropriate. If the target is a large tank army on the move, radar optimised to detect moving vehicles may give the best overall picture of a line of advance. In general, the information obtained will come from the electromagnetic spectrum at wavelengths/frequencies between radio, through radar and infrared to visible light. Different frequencies have particular advantages for different types of targets and sensors, but also have inherent propagation characteristics which will affect the choice. For example, visible light reconnaissance suffers from the need for illumination at night, obscuration by weather or smoke, and the enemy's ability to camouflage. When the sensor is a human eye, there are advantages of rapid analysis of detail, but possible inaccuracies in memory. Nevertheless, visual reconnaissance should not be underestimated as a producer of intelligence. Both specifically tasked aircrew and those engaged on other missions can provide pieces to the information jigsaw. At the same time, however, concerns about aircraft vulnerability are pushing aircraft to lower operating altitudes and higher speeds, which makes such information gathering increasingly difficult.

The traditional method for utilising the visible light region of the electromagnetic spectrum for reconnaissance has been via photographic reconnaissance. The use of specially designed cameras providing both overhead and oblique photographs of target areas coupled with interpretation by specially trained operators has been a powerful combination. But for fast moving operations in a modern general war, this system suffers from some drawbacks. Reconnaissance aircraft must successfully return to a base where photographic information can be processed and analysed. Given increasing difficulty in penetrating modern air defences, some information will be lost during the return from the target area. Additionally, the time in transit from the target plus the time in image processing, analysing and dissemination severely reduces the tactical utility of the data in a rapidly changing battlefield. The cycle time[5] of tasking a photographic reconnaissance mission, executing it, analysing the results, and mounting the necessary tactical offensive operation remains at several hours. For mobile targets this is likely to be unsatisfactory.

What is required is rapid transmission of information back to the analysing centre, which is then able to produce the information in a digestible form to the commander, so that he can decide on the appropriate response. It is in this area that a number of rapidly maturing technologies may come together. The idealised requirement[6] is that the offensive mission should receive targeting information at the same time as the reconnaissance sensor detects the targets. To move in a practical way towards this ideal, we can look at each link in the chain with a view to speeding up operations. First, the reconnaissance vehicle must be able to respond to its tasking in as short a time as possible from wherever it may be located. This requirement might be met by relatively few vehicles with high transit speed and long range, or large numbers of short-range slower vehicles. Manned aircraft are likely to fall into the first category and unmanned drones into the latter. The preference for one or other, or a particular mixture of systems, will depend on relative cost, payload, flexibility and vulnerability as is explained in greater detail elsewhere in this volume. Currently the balance tips towards the manned reconnaissance aircraft, as technology has not yet provided the capability for other than fairly rigidly preprogrammed drone systems at reasonable cost. Remotely piloted vehicles may offer easier prospects of more flexible affordable unmanned reconnaissance systems, but they are inherently more vulnerable to interference with the control links.

Whichever system is used, the key to improving information dissemination time must be the direct transmission of data as it is acquired. This is at its fastest and most discriminating when the information is digitised from the sensors. The advantages of infrared over visible light for penetrating haze and for night operations, coupled with new materials giving much faster response and finer resolution in the infrared region, make this an excellent reconnaissance medium. Processing the information into a data stream for retransmission, either directly, via satellite relay, or on return to friendly territory, can cut hours off the information processing time. The same techniques can be used by airborne reconnaissance assets working from radar imagery, which can also indicate target movement. The analysis of such data streams by computers, especially if the information from many sources can be combined, has considerable attractions. The degree to which this process can be expanded will depend considerably on the hoped for developments in artificial intelligence. Already imagery can be enhanced to produce greater resolution and hence finer detail through computer processing of sensor data.

A final link in the chain is the offensive tasking which results from the analysis. Here it is tempting to forecast that artifical intelligence will bring the prospect of virtually instantaneous display of target requirements in the offensive aircraft cockpit, at the artillery battery commander's command post, or in the armoured division's headquarters. Beyond that, one might speculate about the information activating the targeting system and firing appropriate autonomous weapons.[7] Perhaps such an automated battlefield will one day be an available option. However, in following this chain of logic, which takes us from the observer in the balloon to the unmanned reconnaissance vehicle automatically tasking offensive missiles and further reconnaissance, in a battle which bypassed human intervention for the sake of speed, we must retain a sense of proportion. It makes neither political nor military sense to operate without a man in the decision-making loop. Indeed, eliminating the human brain, with the advantages of intuition and surprise, opens up new vulnerabilities to be exploited by the enemy. It would be a disservice if the opportunities of the new technologies moved us that way.

What the technologies offer is a much faster acquisition of reconnaissance information and much greater discrimination and a capability to remove 'noise' from the acquired information. The ability to process the information and display it should allow the human commander to base his decisions on more accurate intelligence. Having made those decisions, he will be able to task his forces more quickly and more accurately. This must be the way we move forward for reconnaissance operations. We need an appropriate mix of manned and unmanned vehicles with sensors operating from the infrared down to radio frequencies, transmitting information directly to processing centres which provide the information for the commander to task his assets directly. Within this scheme there are still great problems: the vulnerability of the vehicle, the range of the sensors, enemy countermeasures, the prediction of probable enemy options from the available information and the vulnerability of the nodes throughout the system.

Offensive Operations

If the aim of the reconnaissance assets is to provide intelligence, ultimately for defeating the enemy, then offensive operations are the means by which that defeat is to be achieved. We shall consider the need for defensive operations shortly, but it is a truism that defensive measures alone cannot win a battle. They make conditions right for ultimate success, but the defeat of the enemy will only be achieved through the offensive. Can that offensive be separated into ground force offensive and air force offensive operations? In any battle where air power is available to one or both sides, it assumes crucial importance. It can provide the conditions necessary for success or defeat. What it cannot do is provide victory on its own. In discussing tactical operations, we are ultimately looking at questions of gaining or regaining territory. This may be the advance of so many kilometres by armour, or it may be the ousting of insurgents from secured areas. Success is measured by that traditional yardstick of land controlled. The air must therefore be to provide the ground forces with the appropriate power to secure their military objectives. It is when we come to consider this that the peculiar characteristics of air power become of major import.

The ability of air-delivered weapons to extend the offensive range of action beyond the 20 or so kilometres of artillery has been a prime attraction of the use of air power in war. It is, however, more than just this extended radius of effect which makes offensive air action so vital. A typical artillery barrel can fire a projectile weighing some 35 lb out to a distance of less than 20 km at a sustained rate of approximately one round per minute. Compare this with the ability of a single aircraft to drop in excess of 10,000 lb of bombs, out to a distance of hundreds of kilometres. The dramatic increase in fire power is further multiplied by the use of co-ordinated attacks by numbers of aircraft, which can operate from different bases while attacking the same target. Aircraft provide a powerful element in the commander's fire power inventory wherever they are used, and for targets beyond the immediate battle area they may be the only method of attack available. They can be redeployed and retargeted at short notice, and can be used on multi-target missions. They cannot, however, replace ground fire power. They are constrained by weather, vulnerability to enemy defences and problems of target acquisition. Furthermore, they are expensive resources which will always be in short supply.

In employing offensive air power in support of the land battle, a distinction is usually drawn between direct fire power support of the ground forces (Close Air Support) and the deeper penetration of enemy-held territory in order to attack rear area formations (Battlefield Air Interdiction). For this analysis, no such sharp distinction is drawn. The question to be considered is what offensive action can cost-effectively be provided to enable the air-land battle to be won.[8] The winning of the battle can be considered at both the tactical level or at the strategic level. The nature of air power assets, with their ability to be tasked for many different types of missions, may mean that in some circumstances they cannot be allocated to the local battle, as they have a more critical mission to contribute towards achieving the strategic objective. Putting this reservation to one side, let us consider what the Army commander needs in an intense war fought with conventional weapons. He requires fire power to stop the enemy advance of armour and infantry; he requires the elimination of the enemy's fire power directed at his forces; he requires fire power to regain territory lost; and he requires reserves of fire power to compensate for losses, reversals and/or surprise attacks. Air power can provide all of these.

To impede the advance of armour or protected infantry, either the vehicle must be attacked directly or their avenue of advance obstructed. To attack heavily armoured vehicles requires munitions which are aimed with sufficient accuracy to make a direct hit on a part of the armour which can be penetrated by the projectile. Anti-tank weapons can be hand carried

PLATE 8.1 AH-64 Apache, built by Hughes Helicopters Inc. This aircraft is the US Army's most advanced attack helicopter (*McDonnell Douglas Corporation*).

by infantry, fitted to fighting vehicles, fired from helicopters or dispensed from fixed-wing aircraft. Targets can be spotted from the ground or air, and can be marked through illumination with laser light, which subsequently gives range and guidance information to the anti-tank weapon. Current weapons available allow the commander to combat an advancing enemy through the use of fire power provided by his own tanks, specialist anti-tank ground forces, artillery, helicopter anti-tank missiles, bombs, missiles, rockets, and high velocity guns from fixed-wing aircraft. In addition, mines can be used to obstruct the line of advance of the enemy.

Ideally what is required of offensive fire power is instantaneous reaction to task, regardless of the target location, survivability of the weapon system, total accuracy in target acquisition, total certainty of a kill for every weapon used, and the maximum number of kills per mission mounted for the minimum cost. When applied to offensive air assets, these ideals must be carefully weighed against each other, particularly when the overall inventory is constrained by cost. Speed of reaction depends on the nature of the Command, Control, Communication and Intelligence (C^3I) and the tasking organisation which was discussed earlier. It also depends on the location of the weapons systems relative to the target and on the transit speed of the delivery vehicle. The organisational aspect is common to all possible fire power systems, and its efficiency is therefore of critical importance to a successful operation. Transit speed to position for an attack is fastest for ballistic missiles, followed by fixed-wing aircraft and cruise missiles, then helicopters and slowest of all are weapons mounted on ground vehicles. Against this must be set the speed of the reaction if the delivery systems is already within range to attack, when the order may well be reversed. Thus artillery, infantry weapons, and tanks in contact with the enemy can respond in very short time scales, and at significantly less cost than expensive air assets.

The question of survivability of air-delivered systems is one of considerable concern to the commander, and can be considered in two parts: survivability on the ground and survivability in the air. On the ground, most fixed-wing aircraft are tied to prepared operating surfaces. the closer their air bases are to the battle area, the faster their response time, but the more vulnerable they are to enemy attack. The commander must strike a balance between security of his valuable air assets on the ground and extending the transit times on each mission. Helicopters and VSTOL aircraft can disperse from main operating bases and improve their ground survivability as well as reducing response time. In the air, survivability depends on the aircraft's ability to avoid being destroyed by ground-based enemy SAMs and guns and air defence aircraft fitted with missiles and guns. The factors which improve survivability will be high speed, low altitude, agility, defence suppression systems, electronic countermeasures and poor weather and night capability. These factors are most easily obtained in modern high-performance fixed-wing aircraft. Helicopters lack speed and have inherent vulnerabilities in their rotors, but can operate at very low level and in poor weather.

High accuracy in target acquisition is necessary to ensure that offensive air resources are used efficiently. Considerations here have parallels with the limitations of reconnaissance systems already discussed. Indeed, many of the same sensors will be used. High speed and low altitude, both desirable for suvivability, reduce the time available between target acquisition and

PLATE 8.2   Close air support: vertical take off by an USMC AV-8B Harrier II from US Naval Air Station, Patuxent River, Maryland. An AGM-65E Maverick missile can be seen under the port wing.

weapon release, making errors more probable. Laser marking aids target identification, but is limited by weather and the need for a ground or air designator.

Weapon design to give a high kill probability is crucial to the overall effectiveness of offensive air power. There is no point in producing highly expensive delivery systems, able to penetrate enemy defences to weapon release point, if they have no weapons capable of destroying the target. The aircraft is limited in the weight of ordnance it can carry. New weapon designs aim to produce greater kill probabilities for a given weight in order to increase the number of weapons that can be carried. In general, air-delivered weapons range from cannon which depends on high kinetic energy projectiles for penetration, unguided rockets which depend on number and dispersion for area targeting, through gravity bombs with high explosive power, to guided weapons with high accuracy compensating for reduced explosive weight. The appropriate weapon system to be used will depend on the nature and number of targets to be attacked. When multiple targets present themselves in close proximity, greater effectiveness can be achieved using multiple kill systems. In particular, the use of weapons which dispense submunitions can increase the number of kills per weapon release.[9] However, there is a trade-off between the penetrating power, which is a function of the size of the submunitions, and the number which can be carried and dispensed.

Looking at all these facets of offensive air power, how can future systems evolve to improve capabilities? The analysis above indicates a number of competing factors, and in particular greater effectiveness usually requires higher cost for both the delivery vehicle and the weapon, which in turn reduces the number of systems which can be made available. Looking briefly at each of the factors in the offensive air support acquisition, the productive areas for future development appear to be: C³I and data distribution, integral self-protection systems, target acquisition and weapon effectiveness. Further increase in speed of delivery systems, or reduction in transit altitude is unlikely to bring any great benefits. The possible developments in C³I and data distribution were discussed in the section on reconnaissance. The need for self-protection means that an increasing part of the payload must be devoted to air-to-air missiles, defence suppression systems, and ECM pods. Here development should be directed towards reducing the weight and size of these add-ons so that weapon payload is not reduced. New sensor materials, and computer processing of the information can improve target acquisition and discrimination. Developments in artificial intelligence may offer the opportunity for computer allocation of priorities to multiple target displays for the pilot. Major improvements in weapon effectiveness can be achieved by improving the stand-off distance at which the weapon can be released, coupling the target information acquired by the aircraft systems to the weapon systems, and giving individual guidance to submunitions. Reducing the size of each weapon, while increasing its intelligence, allows a greater number of weapons to be carried on each mission. The overall number of weapons may, however, be constrained by their unit costs.

A much discussed question among planners is the form of future delivery systems. There are those[10] who would argue that the vulnerability of the manned aircraft, in the undoubtedly hostile air defence environment of the future, means that its role in offensive air support is declining. Conventional ballistic missiles[11] are suggested as alternatives which offer much greater penetration capabilities. I have argued in detail elsewhere[12] that the cost of such systems, their inherent inflexibility, their political implications and the relative ease with which the enemy may counter them with a change in his concept of operations, make such weapon systems a less useful option than manned aircraft. The increase[13] in use of armed helicopters by the Soviet Union is sometimes taken as a pointer for the future. Indeed, for a strategy which anticipates moving forward rapidly, the helicopter (armed and transport) has considerable attractions. For a defensive and reactive strategy, as exemplified by NATO, a high dependence on relatively vulnerable rotary wing fire power may be less attractive. Certainly the ability to disperse the aircraft with the ground forces improves both reaction time and survivability. This can be coupled to the advantages of speed, range and fire power of a fixed wing aircraft through increased use of VTOL aircraft. The Harrier has proved to be a first rate offensive aircraft for support of the ground forces. There will still remain the need for aircraft able to penetrate defended airspace and destroy targets critical to the ground force commander. These will be expensive fixed wing aircraft tied to airfields. By their nature they will also be needed for other difficult tasks deep in enemy territory. For this reason control of these assets will have to be maintained at an appropriately high level of command. The manned aircraft will remain a necessary, and irreplaceable, part of the fire power available to the ground forces for as far into the future as we can see. Ground-based weapons will improve, so that more fire power will be directly available to the commander. It can be made more mobile by the use of air transport, which will be discussed below. Nevertheless, fast reacting air power will remain the crucial reserve for reversing the situation in the land battle.

Defensive Operations

The battle for air supremacy is considered elsewhere in this volume. This quest to deny the enemy the free use of the air is crucial to the ground battle. In that sense regional air defence and counter-air operations are a part of the Air-Land Battle. With one exception, while they are necessary to make conditions right for success, they can be conducted independently of what is happening on the ground. The exception is for those multi-role aircraft which may be tasked either for the air superiority or the offensive air support role. These assets must be controlled at a high enough level for the proper allocation of priorities to be made.

At the same time as the overall battle for air supremacy is being waged, the ground forces have a need to provide local control of their own airspace. It is this provision of tactical air defence which we shall now consider. The aim is to provide appropriate systems to prevent the enemy using his offensive air power against the ground forces. The targets are therefore the systems discussed in the section above on offensive operations: helicopters, fixed-wing aircraft, drones and ballistic missiles. The elements of a tactical air defence system must include methods for detection and identification of targets and a suitable killing mechanism. Detection and identification may be as simple as a soldier spotting an aircraft making an attack on his position. It may be as sophisticated as an Airborne Early Warning aircraft transferring its data to a ground station, which pushes forward an attack warning to a Corps HQ. The key to successful air defence of the ground forces must be the warning of enemy approach, in sufficient time for the target to be engaged before weapon release. This reaction time is made more difficult by the need for effective identification systems. If ground forces engage and destroy friendly aircraft, they not only reduce the combat strength of their own side needlessly, but they also deplete their ammunition stocks. The soldier with a hand-held air defence missile appears to be a beneficial way of providing local air defence. However, he has very little time between first visually sighting an approaching aircraft, and firing his weapon if he is anticipating being subject to attack. The aircraft will be approaching head-on, and thus be difficult to identify, and may be a returning friendly rather than an attacking enemy. At the other end of the air defence spectrum a comprehensive radar detection system, linked to many source identification systems, may take too long to provide the information for it to be of any use at the local level. A VTOL aircraft, or armed helicopter, may take under 10 minutes from take-off to weapon release.

The air defence systems available to the ground force commander range from small arms, through dedicated anti-aircraft artillery, to surface-to-air and air-to-air missiles. The effectiveness of small arms fire should not be underestimated. Given the low-altitude attack profile of aircraft, they have become significantly more vulnerable to high concentrations of ground fire. While great kill rates may not be achievable, the use of tracer can make weapon attacks more unnerving for the pilot, and reduce their effectiveness. An important element of the use of small arms is in having appropriate anti-aircraft mountings, and carrying out realistic training in the role.[14]

Dedicated gun systems have a number of attractions. They can have integral radar and optical detection and tracking systems, they can have identification systems, and they can achieve high concentrations of lead through rapid fire and multi-barrel mechanisms. The Soviet ZSU 23-4 has developed a reputation for providing excellent mobile air defence for the ground forces. There are two disadvantages: range and cost. The limited range[15] of the projectiles gives a relatively short engagement bracket for a crossing target. This could be acceptable if the units were sufficiently cheap to be positioned with overlapping fields of fire. They are not. This is not to discount the utility of modern air defence gun systems. However, given the cost they are likely to be used more in a point defence role for particularly important targets. Small arms, artillery and even tank armament can be used effectively against slow moving or hovering targets such as helicopters.

Surface-to-air missiles include hand-held systems with ranges out to about 3 miles. Guidance systems can be optical tracking with command guidance, or may be infrared homing. Given that the target needs to be destroyed while approaching, a missile which can engage departing targets only is of limited value. The major difficulty with such systems is in the identification of targets and rules of engagement. In the clear case when an aircraft has been seen to attack friendly forces, identification may be certain, but may also be too late.

Operators of hand-held weapons need to be well trained, especially in aircraft recognition. It might be thought that the more sophisticated surface-to-air missile systems available to ground forces would have an easier task. Certainly, radar detection and longer missile ranges increase target acquisition capability and kill probability. Identification remains a problem despite the availability of Identification Friend or Foe (IFF) systems.[16] They are easily overloaded and unreliable in a hostile electronic warfare environment. The additional detection time may allow the operator an opportunity for more rational assessment of the threat posed by the apparent target. The more sophisticated the system, the more expensive it is, and hence the greater the importance to making every shot count. Aircraft supporting the ground forces can also be fitted with air-to-air missiles. In general these will be designed for self-protection rather than providing local air superiority for the local ground forces.

This somewhat piecemeal picture of air defence available to ground forces stems partly from the fact that the battle for air supremacy is being fought at a higher level, and partly from the difficulties of providing coordinated integrated air defence at the battlefield level. The ideal system for the future would be a hand-held infantry weapon, so cheap and light that it could be universal, with a target identification system that prevents firing if a friendly target is engaged, and a range and speed of operation which ensures target destruction before weapon release. Such an ideal has little chance of realisation. Technical developments will allow earlier detection of targets, and data links may permit information from more remote and powerful sensor systems, such as AEW, to provide attack warnings. Both guns and missiles will continue to have a role to play, with developments being in improved tracking and guidance systems. Against helicopters, artillery has a capability when they are refuelling and re-arming. It may also be that helicopters with air-to-air missiles will be a worthwhile addition to ground air defences in countering the armed helicopter threat. Defence against unmanned air-breathing systems must follow the same lines as defences against aircraft. For many the difficulties of small target size is offset by predictability of flight path. Of greater difficulty is the defence against ballistic missiles. Some of the research currently being undertaken in relation to strategic ballistic missile defences may produce some anti-tactical ballistic capability. It is, however, likely to be expensive option, and has implications for arms control agreements which are beyond the scope of the discussion in this article.

Tactical Air Transport

In considering the contribution that air power has to make to the Air-Land Battle, the use of air transport is often given insufficient credit. Troops, equipment and logistic support can all be moved rapidly to respond to a changing ground situation, to correct an initial maldeployment, or to bring in additional forces to support a critical area. Fixed-wing tactical transport aircraft can carry bulky equipment, or company sized troop formations. Once loaded, the aircraft can travel in a short time between any two airfields within an operational theatre. The requirement for prepared operating surfaces is a significant limitation in considering the use of tactical fixed-wing transport aircraft. It can be overcome at the delivery point by the use of air-drop systems, and they will be considered separately. For routine operations the payload of troops, equipment and stores must be organised and loaded at the air-head, and co-ordinated at the destination airfield, and provided with further transport to their operational locations. All this is time consuming, and requires a tasking organisation which can ensure that transport assets are fully utilised, while at the same time cargo is not delayed. For these reasons, fixed-wing transport operates best when following premeditated plans. It is of great use for carrying out deployment plans, and for regular resupply from theatre rear areas to the forward logistic centres.

For rapid reaction to changing circumstances, helicopter transport offers the ground force commander the opportunity to redeploy troops, move equipment and provide logistic support with little regard to terrain. The benefit of this mobility was demonstrated by the extensive use of helicopters by the United States in the Vietnam War. The potential benefits are great for both offensive and defensive forces in any Central Region conflict. At the same time, there are certain constraints associated with helicopter transport. The range and payload have until recently been much more limited than fixed-wing tactical air transport. Typically, a support helicopter might carry fifteen men, or 2 tons of stores out to a distance of 100 miles. Larger helicopters, such as the CH-47 Chinook, can improve on this performance by a factor of four. Against these performance figures must be put the numbers of men, the weight of equipment, and the rate of usage of ammunition, fuel and other consumable stores in any intense conflict. Most of the in-theatre transport requirements will have to be met by surface transport. The helicopter lift will have to be allocated to those tasks which can crucially affect the outcome of the battle, or for which there is no alternative method. It may be for example that an inaccessible location provides a superior artillery position, so long as ammunition can be supplied by air. Or it might be that forces need to be evacuated from a position in a very short timescale, and that helicopters would be the only way.

Sufficient air transport, and the supporting organisation, to enable the commander to move all of his ground forces at will and be able to support them on a continuous basis is the ideal. Developments in VTOL cargo aircraft may offer some promise of increasing lift capacity, while not being tied to prepared airstrips. Most of the improvement in mobility comes from the independence of the routes from the nature of the ground: rivers, minefields, hills and towns do not slow progress. Once in the general area of operations, transit times are not very sensitive to flying speeds. What is required for the future is increased lift capacity, both in weight and bulk, coupled with the flexibility of operations associated with helicopter operations. These requirements do not alter greatly for major defensive or offensive operations. It is interesting in the light of this analysis to note what has been happening to the Soviet tactical air transport assets over the past decade.[17] The smaller fixed wing tactical transport aircraft have been progressively phased out, as the new larger strategic transports have arrived. This has given a trebling in payload, with a reduction in fixed wing aircraft. To provide tactical flexibility, a large number of cargo helicopters have been built over the past 5 years. The continuing trend is significant with fixed-wing aircraft moving more towards strategic transport, with the development of Condor; and helicopters carrying loads as large as former fixed-wing transports, with the development of Halo. There would seem to be much merit in this structure for military air transport.

Air transport can also be used in a more directly offensive manner than considered so far. The dropping of airborne troops, who then rapidly engage the enemy, is as much an offensive action from the air as the firing of a missile at the enemy. Historical evidence is ambiguous as to the balance of advantage from the use of specialist parachute forces. They can capitalise on surprise, and attack more lightly defended areas. They must either succeed quickly, and join up with the main ground forces, or they will require continuing support from the air, which may become progressively more difficult to provide. Less ambitious in scale, and more easily controlled, is the placing of such battle-ready forces by the use of helicopters. The problems of forming up are much reduced, and the operations may be mounted much more rapidly, without using specialist parachute trained troops. A particular case of either delivery method is the use of air-delivered special forces. Air drop provides a useful and rapid method of inserting small groups of special forces in enemy territory.

Tactical air transport is a crucial factor in any Air-Land Battle, yet in allocations of budget resources it may not fare as well as more fire power centred items. It is also an area which bridges the divide between what is obviously Army or Air Force equipment. No nation will be able to replace all of its ground transport by air transport, which raises the question of the optimum balance between the two. Certainly, the ability to deploy reserve forces in short timescales and then to support them is likely to be a significant factor in the outcome of any future battle.

Limited Nuclear War

The discussion thus far has considered exclusively the use of air power in a non-nuclear environment. While this is a useful artifice, and indeed is applicable to a range of possible future conflicts, the possibility of escalation to a nuclear war in any superpower confrontation must be considered when looking at the Air-Land Battle. Even if nuclear weapons are not used, the possibility of their employment will modify the way the war is fought, the forces which are available and the political control which is exerted over those forces.

A conventional war, which may develop into a nuclear one, poses the commander with particular problems over the use of his air power assets. Many aircraft will be 'dual-capable': able to deliver high explosive or nuclear weapons. If he uses his air power fully from the start of the war, he will progressively lose delivery systems to enemy air defences, systems which could deliver fire power of much greater effect after the nuclear threshold had been crossed. On the other hand, if he saves his dual-capable forces against this eventuality, the conventional battle becomes more difficult to win, and the nuclear threshold is lowered. This is undesirable both from a military and political point of view. In addition the decision to use nuclear weapons, the scale of their use and the delivery method to be used are political rather than military questions.

Against this background, what can air power contribute to nuclear forces, and how is it affected by the enemy's nuclear forces? Nuclear weapons, gravity bombs and stand-off missiles can be delivered by aircraft in the same way as conventional weapons. The destructive power of the weapon would reduce the number of aircraft required to destroy a given target. To determine the number of aircraft required to achieve a particular level of destruction, the analyst must consider aircraft serviceability, attrition on the way to the target, navigation accuracy, target acquisition errors, weapon delivery accuracy and weapon effectiveness. The last two of these factors are markedly less important with nuclear weapons. Thus more targets can be attacked for a given number of aircraft. However, if nuclear weapons are to be used by both sides, the number of aircraft available may decrease very significantly. A single weapon exploded on an airfield will stop operations. There would seem, therefore, to be merit in moving nuclear delivery systems away from fixed base operations. While a move to VTOL nuclear capable aircraft would be one method, missiles (cruise or ballistic) offer a number of advantages. By separating the nuclear and non-nuclear delivery systems, military actions being used as political signals become less prone to misinterpretation. Aircraft can be used fully according to military priorities in all phases of the war. The survivability of mobile missile systems deters the enemy from using his tactical nuclear systems, and hence preserves air resources. It can be argued that the flexibility of targeting, and the lack of public interest in nuclear capable aircraft, make their retention in the role important.[18]

The Future of the Air-Land Battle

Such an analysis of the various contributions which air power can make to any future war, leaves unanswered the question of the priorities in making preparations for deterring or for fighting such conflicts. In indicating that for particular roles future technology trends suggest some routes may be more beneficial than others, the benefits relative to other—perhaps strategically more important—systems have been beyond the scope of this article. However, given that resources must be provided for appropriate forces to conduct future Air-Land Battles, deductions about priorities of allocation within those resources are useful.

A recurring aspect has been the question of Command, Control, Communication and Intelligence. This is scarcely a novel conclusion. The strengths of air power, in its mobility and versatility, place much greater strains on the tasking organisation than do less multi-purpose and slower moving forces. The air assets, which are very costly and hence usually under-provided, must be used to greatest overall effect. From an organisational point of view, this must mean that in war they are controlled at a sufficiently high formation level to ensure that they are tasked where they can have the greatest effect. Once tasked for particular missions, operational control can be delegated to the appropriate lower formation. While factors such as parent Service, national ownership and base location, will all influence the commander in his allocation of air forces to tasks, they must not be allowed to constrain the true advantages that accrue from mobility. To capitalise on this, the commander must have an information and tasking system which can provide data that is accurate, comprehensive and comprehensible, and which is fed in and out in timescales where it can be of use, through systems that are sufficiently redundant to be survivable. This is a tall order, but is the key to the successful use of air power in the future.

Survivability of air assets is another common thread which runs through the use of air power. Measures such as air defence, dispersal and self-defence have been discussed above. The area which poses a common danger to the survivability of all air assets, is airspace management. Friendly aircraft should be able to operate over friendly territory without being destroyed by friendly forces. Reliable identification procedures are essential to the efficient use of air and ground resources. The use of new sensors, coupled to more powerful information processing, and multi-source acquisition of data must offer better identification possibilities for the future. While this may be an expensive area for development, it is of crucial importance. There is little value in developing and fielding weapons able to operate at vast distances from the target, if there is no method of ensuring that the target is enemy rather than friendly.

The next question to be answered is the balance between numbers of weapon delivery systems, numbers of operating crews and the numbers of weapons available. This is based on a complex mix of assumptions about attrition rates, weapon usage rates, type of scenario, replacement timescales for systems, men and weapons, as well as many other imponderables. Some broad deductions are however possible. As technology permits future wars to be conducted without regard to weather or darkness, man continues to need regular rest to operate efficiently. For full utilisation of new weapon systems, the ratio of operating crews to systems will have to increase. Increased utilisation, and recent combat experience,[19] suggest that numbers of weapons provided per delivery system will also need to rise, with the extent depending on expected attrition rates. If the resources available for air power are fixed, these two trends would lead to a declining share of the cake for the delivery systems. As the unit costs of the delivery systems increase, this problem is compounded.

The totally automated battlefield, without human intervention, is neither desirable nor affordable. Any move towards unmanned systems produces penalties in flexibility. Only when these can be offset by reductions in cost, so that quantity can give flexibility, will this be a productive route to follow. Even quite limited technological improvements to weapon systems today are causing unit costs to rise markedly. The man remains relatively cheap, with a computing capacity and an inferential facility unavailable from etched silicon wafers. The prerequisite for successful use of man operated systems is high-quality training. For aircrew this means realistic mission training under similar conditions to those which they would encounter in war.

Conclusion

Any future conflict will have to consider the use of military air power. The roles carried out by aircraft in the past are going to be needed in the future. The tactical environment of the future will make them more difficult and more expensive. The commander will need information more rapidly, and developments in sensor and computer technology offer him that prospect. Offensive air power will continue to provide fire power on scale not otherwise achievable. It will be on call to redress the balance when the ground battle goes badly. It will attack targets beyond the reach of ground forces. Technology will improve survivability, target acquisition and weapon effectiveness. Defensive air power will be necessary to allow the ground forces to continue to operate. Technology will provide new identification methods and more effective surface-to-air and air-to-air systems. Transport by air offers the commander true mobility for operations of all sizes. Widespread availability of large cargo helicopters may change his concepts of land operations.

The vital contribution that all these systems make to the Air-Land Battle is undoubted. In a time of limited resources the relative priorities of one system against another in the context of possible future wars becomes a question of prime importance. As this essay has sought to explain, the factors which should be taken into account when coming to a judgement will not diminish in complexity.

9

Maritime Air Power

GROUP CAPTAIN A. G. HICKS

The lessons of past wars at sea are available to all maritime nations, whatever their military capabilities and the scale and nature of their commitments. Even from the very earliest days in the evolution of air power one message was becoming clear: the war at sea would never be the same again. Thus, for instance, in the last months of the First World War only 257 merchant ships were sunk while they were in convoy; but of these, only two were lost when the convoy escort included aircraft—a harbinger of things to come. But it was in the Second World War that air power, whether shore- or sea-based, was seen to have changed fundamentally the way the maritime war was to be fought in the future.

Examples from the Second World War abound, but lack of space makes any general historical survey in this article impossible. Nevertheless, the words of Lord Tedder, in his Lees-Knowles lectures in respect of the German successes in 1940/41, point to a general lesson:

> Despite her inferior naval strength, Germany was now able to contest seriously our exercise of sea power; given air superiority, air forces were now clearly able to take an effective hand in securing command at sea.

The part played by shore-based air forces in maritime operations during 1939–45, together with the dramatic coming of age of carrier-based naval aviation, clearly demonstrated that the classical canons of maritime strategy no longer applied. Support of surface forces from the air, the neutralisation of the enemy's air capability and above all the maintenance of air superiority were clearly shown to be keys to success in the war at sea.

Discussion of past wars though can only take us so far. Times and circumstances change and the advent of nuclear weapons and, more recently, of developments in surveillance and targeting, missile guidance and warhead effectiveness, bring yet more new dimensions for consideration. The fundamental message though remains. The exercise of power

169

in war inevitably involves a trinity of capabilities: land, sea and air. Maritime war in particular is inherently three-dimensional in nature, and it is dangerously misleading to think in terms of air power or sea power in isolation; they are two totally interactive aspects of the prosecution of the war at sea. This article considers the mix of capabilities which today makes up the complex tapestry of maritime air power, starting with a review of the air power deployed by navies at sea.

Naval Air Power

Sea-based air power remains today an element which most major navies aim to possess. Certainly it is an element which provides a mix of operational capabilities which have proved invaluable in recent history. In the Second World War in the Pacific, and most recently in the Falklands War—to say nothing of many more incidents short of major conflict—the utility of sea-based air power has been demonstrated. This section then seeks to review the continuing development of naval air power.

Inevitably, though, such a task is an invidious one, since so many navies aspire to an air capability and achieve it in many different ways. Nevertheless, it is the attack carrier, capable of operating significant numbers of high-performance fixed-wing aircraft, which represents the application of naval air power in its most flexible and effective form. The power of USN Carrier Battle Groups (CVBGs) greatly adds to the sum of NATO deterrence and war-fighting capability.

In its development of tactical air power, the USN is moving forward both in capability and in thinking. New squadrons and air wings are earmarked for deployment with both nuclear and conventionally powered carriers, and a major conversion programme is in progress. At a conceptual level, too, there is currently considerable high-level interest behind a move to improve the force-mix and mission effectiveness.

Turning to the aircraft themselves, which are after all what give the Battle Groups their teeth, the backbone of the USN carrier-borne air defence capability remains currently the Grumman F-14 Tomcat (a two-engine, two-seat and supersonic fighter) which is deployed in both the Atlantic and Pacific theatres. The main weapon systems associated with the F-14 are the AIM-54 Phoenix, AIM-7 Sparrow and AIM 9L Sidewinder. Increasingly, too, the dual-role McDonnell-Douglas F/A-18 Hornet is being deployed.

A fundamental part of air wing operations will always be airborne early warning, and this is provided by the Grumman E-2C Hawkeye. In its upgraded version this aircraft, working closely with the F-14, provides the deep-field defence for the Battle Groups with their embarked strike/attack assets. The outer air battle is of increasing significance as the air threat to the CVBG is seen to increase. This is a particularly interesting example of the way in which land- and sea-based aviation capabilities interface, because as the range of likely threat systems increases, so the CVBG's organic deep field capability must inevitably be augmented by shore-based AWACS and air defence aircraft.

As part of the overall attack package deployed at sea, USN carriers continue to embark the Grumman EA-6B Prowler. A four-seat aircraft, the EA-6B is a powerful, if expensive, tactical EW system. It provides the full range of jamming, communications and overall EW capability and is an essential adjunct to air wing operations.

In addition to strike/attack and supporting AEW and EW aircraft, most USN carriers embark both fixed-wing and rotary-wing ASW units. However, since it is perhaps in the field of ASW above all that the interdependence of shore-based and sea-based assets is best exemplified, this general topic will be covered separately. Suffice it to say now that eleven squadrons of the S-3A are in service to provide fixed-wing ASW, and the SH-3H (Sea King) remains for the moment the prime ASW helicopter.

This has inevitably been a brief and necessarily selective review of USN combat aircraft. However, it is perhaps pertinent to emphasise one fundamental point of concern, and that is cost. The rapidly increasing costs of sea-based air power are enormous even by American standards. Some examples perhaps will serve to illustrate what is involved. The EA-6B's unit cost has been quoted as $311 million, the F14 Tomcat as $29.7 million, and the F/A-18 Hornet—conceived as a low-cost aircraft to complement the F14—as $22.5 million, with a programme cost of $35.6 billion for 1,336 aircraft. Even when these costs, and those of the carriers themselves, are seen against the US defence programme as a whole it is obvious that capabilities of the calibre of those deployed by the US CVBGs can never come cheaply. Costs must increasingly influence the defence debate in the future and it is against the overall utility of these capabilities alone that they can be judged.

The cost of developing purely naval fixed-wing aircraft is only of direct relevance to the United States, perhaps France, and in the future, the Soviet Union. The smaller maritime nations which have a requirement for a carrier capability (whether it be for potentially world-wide operation in the case of the United Kingdom, France and perhaps Italy, or for much more localised deployment in the case of Argentina, Brazil, India and Spain) generally seek to deploy aircraft which are variants of land-based types. Even so, the cost dynamic is still inescapable, since high-performance aircraft impose their own criteria on ship design, and it is in this context that appearance of the Sea Harrier and the *Invincible* Class carrier has expanded the possibilities for the provision of an element of organic fixed-wing air at sea. The evolution of the Sea Harrier from the RAF Harrier aircraft, developed originally over a period of some 25 years by the UK

Bristol-Siddeley and Hawker Companies (and now continued by Rolls Royce and British Aerospace), is very well known. Development of this aircraft for naval operations took a great step forward with the introduction of the 'ski-jump' concept. Using this simple technique, the Sea Harrier can take off with a 4,500-kg load of fuel and weapons, in a distance of 65–190 metres, which equates to perhaps half the length of the largest USN carriers (the aircraft can, of course, land vertically without requiring the operating platform to steam into wind). It is this Short Take-off Vertical Land (STOVL) capability, making fixed-wing operations from relatively small displacement ships (perhaps 20,000 tons) possible, that has transformed the organic sea-power scene for the smaller nations. Until the emergence of STOVL, the formidable cost of carriers (in conjunction with the inevitable arguments about vulnerability) made their possession extremely problematical for all but the superpowers.

The smaller carrier concept, however, may be extended still further. What matters is not the carrier itself, but the enhancement to air capability in a critical situation which the aircraft impart. For the smaller nations, the future may possibly lie in a cheap and simple air-capable ship. This requirement was highlighted by the Falklands War, and led to the concept of merchant ship conversions, such as the Ship-borne Containerised Air Defence System (SCADS) currently being studied by British Aerospace. The germ of this idea lay in the joint work by the Royal Navy and the USN prior to the Falklands War, in the development of the ARAPAHO system, which was designed to provide a comprehensive modular aviation support facility for rapid installation on merchant ships. Looking to the future, it now seems possible that a converted container ship could accommodate all the equipment necessary to operate Sea Harriers in their STOVL mode, including the flight deck with ski-jump and the necessary command and control facilities. Development of such ships—effectively light carriers—could act as a significant force multiplier and go some way to offsetting the question mark which must surround the availability and cost of conventional carriers deployed in inevitably limited numbers by the smaller maritime powers. This is an idea of considerable tactical significance, which is evoking interest in several NATO nations. There are other approaches too. For instance, Vosper Thorneycroft have proposed a very light (8,000 ton) Harrier Carrier with a flight deck and ski-jump and operated by quiet gas-turbine/electric propulsion; and perhaps the ultimate in the small aviation carrier stakes is the Sky-Hook principle advocated again by British Aerospace. In this concept very small ships would be fitted with a crane device with an arm which could be deployed from the side of the ship. The Sea Harrier would come to the hover under the arm to be gathered by the hook system using advanced sensing and control techniques, the arm being fully stabilised in roll, pitch and yaw.

The fundamental factor, however, is the capability of the aircraft being deployed. At present the Sea Harrier is not a supersonic aircraft, but Falklands experience has shown that when the special handling characteristics of the Sea Harrier are combined with an effective missile system, the aircraft has considerable capability. For the future, British Aerospace and Rolls Royce are looking at plenum chamber burning techniques to give a follow-on to Sea Harrier's supersonic capability. But there is perhaps some way still to go before a true supersonic intercept capability is achievable. In this latter respect, too, it must be remembered that an interception capability implies more than an interceptor aircraft. It implies surveillance and command and control as well, so that it would be mistaken to assume that even very capable aircraft deployed from merchant ship conversions would be the total answer under all conditions.

The USN and the Royal Navy, then, are developing their naval air concepts on lines that are by now generally familiar. France, it seems clear, will develop a new nuclear-powered carrier which at 36,000 tons, while considerably smaller than major USN fleet carriers, will be capable of operating the Super-Etendard and future navalised versions of shore-based fighter/attack aircraft. Meanwhile, the new Italian light carrier, the *Guiseppe Garibaldi*, was recently completed at the Monfalcone shipyard of Italconeri. This gas-turbine driven ship, which is fully described in *Navy International*,[1] is of considerable interest. It is conceived on the same lines as the Royal Navy *Invincible* class, being 'through-deck' from bow to stern, and designed from the outset as a 'sea-control' ship. Although primarily a helicopter carrier (normally embarking twelve Agusta SH-3D, to be replaced by the Agusta/Westland EH 101), the ship will be fitted with a $6\frac{1}{2}°$ ski-jump to enable it to operate as a V/STOL support ship in a NATO Task Group. The Italian Navy clearly has an eye to the future, however, and the design retains the option to provide for full Sea Harrier operation when the ski-jump would probably be increased to 12°. At the western end of the Mediterranean, Spain already operates the AV-8A Harrier (renamed Matador) from the ex-USN *Dedalo*. However, on 22 May 1982 the new Spanish carrier *Principe de Asturias* was launched at the El Ferrol yard of Empresa Nacional Bazan. The basic design was developed to meet Spanish requirements from the original US Navy SCS concept, but the ship incorporates a full 12° ski-jump and can deploy six to eight Matadors.

On the other hand, genuine Soviet organic maritime fixed-wing capability has been a long time coming, and is not with us yet. In a review of the Soviet Union and Aircraft Carriers[2] J. E. Moore makes the point that whilst by 1945 the Soviet Navy had no carriers, the need for organic air support had been well recognised. It was not until 1967 though that *Moskva*, capable of carrying eighteen Hormone helicopters, put to sea. The next step was taken in 1976 when *Kiev* sailed out of the Black Sea: a longer and more capable ship, and one above all which was capable of deploying VTOL aircraft. With a total aircraft complement of perhaps forty-three, however, the *Kiev* class was clearly no match for US carriers and was generally assessed as being designed principally for ASW operations. Development of the Kiev class has been slow: *Minsk* deployed in 1979 and *Novorossiysk* in 1984. This latter ship represents the outcome of several years of fixed-wing experience on the part of the Soviet Navy and incorporates structural modifications, changes to the flight deck layout and weapon and sensor developments which are fully described in an article by John Jordan.[3] The capability of the *Kiev* class, however, has to be seen in relation *to* the aircraft it deploys, the Yak-36 Forger. Since its first deployment in 1976, this aircraft has been roundly criticised in the West for lack of range and manoeuvrability and a less than adequate weapon and sensor fit. These criticisms are generally well founded and are expanded in detail in a valuable article by J. D. Gresham,[4] but the Forger must be assessed as part of the overall Kiev weapons system, and in the light of its probable mission. The main AAW armaments of the *Kiev* class are the SA-N-3 Goblet SAM systems; the Forger is thus a secondary AAW system only. Its main role perhaps lies in the field of 'light' attack against vessels with limited AAW capability. Thus, whilst it undoubtedly has an extremely limited capability, the Forger is a useful 'gap-filler' in the all-round fit of the Kiev class, and it should not be summarily dismissed. Its real importance may well have been in providing the Soviet Navy with that irreplaceable base of operating experience from which to build towards a genuine capability to deploy fixed-wing air power at sea. It has been widely reported that a new Soviet nuclear-powered carrier is under construction at the Nikolaiev South Yard on the Black Sea. The ship could have a displacement of some 75,000 tons and it is estimated that four (and possibly up to eight) of these carriers will be built. Very significantly, too, published assessments[5] suggest that the new Sukhoi SU-27 Flanker all-weather fighter *might* be embarked, and up to sixty to seventy aircraft could be carried. The Flanker is a versatile aircraft, comparable to the F-15. It is thought to be capable of Mach 2.35 in level flight and Mach 1.1 at sea-level. Armed with the AA-10 missile, it has a beyond visual-range capability, and with a *high-level* combat radius in the order of 620 nm it is indeed a potent counter-air aircraft.

A long time coming it may have been, but the apparent Soviet commitment to an organic fixed-wing capability continues, and serves notice that control of the airspace over the sea may be increasingly contested in the future.

Land-based Maritime Air

If the possible future emergence of a true CTOL carrier capability marks a new phase in Soviet naval capability, the growing potential of land-based air power has been incontrovertibly demonstrated by Soviet naval air force developments over the past few years. The *Aviatsuya Voenno-Morskovo Flota* (AV-MF) deploys in the region of 1,300 aircraft and gives the Soviet Navy a range of air support which adds immeasurably to its overall capability. The teeth element of the AV-MF is the Tu-22M Backfire, which now forms the front line of Soviet maritime aviation and has the performance and hitting power to enable it to challenge and attack aircraft carrier strike groups and other high value units. Armed with anti-ship missiles, using variable geometry, supersonic performance and with a maximum unrefuelled combat radius of around 3,000 nm, Backfire has the range to threaten NATO movements in the major ocean areas and along the sea lanes of communication. The Backfire, indeed, operating perhaps in conjunction with Bear aircraft in the over-the-horizon targeting (OTHT) role, amply illustrates the weight and flexibility of the fire power which land-based air power can bring to the war at sea.

These developments are matched in the West. Improvements in precision guided weapons, in the effectiveness of warheads and above all the range and weapon-carrying capability of air delivery platforms are all coming together in the last decades of the century to transform the very nature of the war at sea. If attack aircraft can be tasked in strength against a force at sea, a co-ordinated missile attack can bring to bear such a weight of fire power as to overwhelm all but the most coherent and capable ship-borne air defence systems, and any maritime strategy and procurement policy which does not take this kind of capability into account is failing totally to reckon with the extent to which air power can be the dominant factor in the war at sea.

But it is not only in the ship-attack mission that land-based air power can contribute to war-fighting in maritime operations. At every phase of the maritime battle, land-based air forces can augment and complement fleet organic air power and surface units; in air defence, ASW, ASUW and in the overall combined effort to project power at sea, land-based air power, given that it is within range, can play a part. Range is, of course, a crucial factor, and it is precisely in this area that developments in fuel-efficient engines, in the wider application of air-to-air refuelling techniques and in the capabilities of weapons which can be fired from large aircraft from long range, are having such a profound impact on maritime air thinking. Range is indeed a crucial factor, but the potential reach of land-based air attack is increasing to encompass most of the key operating areas for Western navies worldwide.

Surveillance of the Oceans

But whatever the capability of newly deployed weapons systems, they depend upon surveillance—preferably real-time surveillance—and targeting for their operational effectiveness. Surveillance is a field which is developing fast and many aspects, such as the use of transportable Over the Horizon Radars and long-range passive sensors,[6] are outside the scope of this article. But one aspect to which land-based air power can contribute significantly is in the provision of airborne radar sensors, flying beyond the range of carrier-borne aircraft or systems. Maritime Patrol Aircraft (MPA), such as the P3 or the Nimrod Mk II, although primarily ASW assigned, can all contribute to the surface picture, as can AEW and strategic bomber aircraft (albeit these latter will be primarily assigned to other missions). The problem of keeping a continuous plot of enemy surface activities is, however, considerable and involves not only the provision of airborne and other sensors, but the fusion of all the available data and its dissemination to the appropriate tasking authorities. And it must always be borne in mind that the end result of all this surveillance activity is to target a weapons system against the enemy surface unit, whether by means of a remote (perhaps space-based) sensor or by a tracking aircraft.

Ship Attack

Given that the targeting problem can be solved, targeting is the first stage in the attack process and whether the ultimate attacking system is sea-based or land-based, land-based air power can indeed become a key element in naval strategy. Western air forces and navies deploy a formidable variety of ship attack missile and aircraft combinations. The lethality of the first generation air-launched anti-ship missile was effectively demonstrated during the Falklands Campaign. The Argentinian Air Force used the Exocet AM39 which is typical of a whole range of so-called sea-skimmers. It is the air-launched version of a family of missiles developed from the MM 38, and can be launched at any height down to 50 m, with the missile in the final stages of the flight reducing to sea-skimming height to achieve a hit against the hull of the target. With a range of 50-70 km, Exocet has a 160-kg warhead. The Sea Eagle missile, on the other hand, a second generation weapon now entering service with the Royal Air Force and the Royal Navy, was developed specifically for air launch; it has a range of some 110 km and carries a warhead of 230 kg. This weapon is deployed on the Buccaneer SMk2b aircraft which equips the RAF's dedicated maritime attack force, as well as on the RN's Sea Harrier aircraft. Among other European maritime attack aircraft, Naval Air Wing 1 of the German *Marineflieger* operates the Tornado aircraft from NAS *Schleswig*. NAW 1 is tasked for operations into the Baltic area, a crucial area for NATO because of its proximity to Warsaw Pact bases and military installations, and must therefore be able to react quickly and flexibly and deliver a decisive attack in a critical situation, a classic role for air power. The Tornado, a two-seat two-engine variable geometry aircraft, has the performance characteristics to meet the demands of this role, carrying a

PLATE 9.1   Maritime reconnaissance: a British Aerospace Nimrod MR2 of the RAF (*British Aerospace*).

7.5-ton payload. The main weapon deployed by NAW1 is the MBB (Germany) Kormoran, a high-subsonic missile which has a range of some 30 km and flies at very low altitude using inertial guidance initially and active radar search in the terminal phase. Compared to other systems, the Kormoran is clearly short on range, and a Mk 2 version with enhanced booster and sustainer rocket motors is being developed to overcome this deficiency, with up-rated electronics and ECCM capability being built in at the same time. Finally, one further example of the relatively light missile for carriage by fighter aircraft is the Penguin Mk 3 being developed by Kongsberg Vapenfabrikk for use by some Norwegian Air Force F-16s. The versatile F-16 has an effective sea-search mode available in its AN/APG-66 radar and has successfully test flown the Penguin, which will have a launch range of over 50 km.

But fighter aircraft will not be the only ones to carry sea-skimming missiles. If the missile is developed to have a longer range and bigger punch, it can be launched—perhaps in large numbers—from a variety of platforms, including heavy aircraft capable of very long ranges from base to the operating area. The well-proven Harpoon series of missiles perhaps points the way. Harpoon has been in active development since the early 1970s and is capable of launch in various versions from ships, submarines and aircraft. In its air-launched version it can be carried by MPA such as the RAF Nimrod and the USN P3 which with their very long range capability add another dimension to the long-range interdiction picture. These aircraft, however, have a primary mission of anti-submarine warfare, and whilst their anti-ship capability with Harpoon can be an invaluable augmentation, it is unlikely that a sufficient weight of attack could be brought to bear by aircraft such as this. For the future it is strategic aircraft with the capability of carrying a large load of new generation Air Launched Cruise Missiles (ALCMs) that may be best matched to the sea denial and ship attack missions. In terms of the launch vehicle, the B-52 has already demonstrated its ability to sink ships using a variety of attack weapons, including Harpoon, and it is clear that the B-1 could be similarly adapted.

The key to this concept is the cruise missile itself. In principle, cruise missiles are simple enough. They are designed to be long-range weapons, small enough to avoid detection, with the application of stealth techniques, and equipped with a guidance system sufficiently precise to achieve an accuracy which will permit a significant weapon effect from a small, albeit often specialised, warhead. The guidance system should be autonomous, so that the missile is unaffected by jamming transmissions and undetectable by passive location; inertial navigation is the obvious choice. The inevitable drift of an inertial system must be corrected, and whilst overland systems may use Terrain Contour Matching (TERCOM) or digital scene-matching area correlator (DSMAC) guidance, an over-sea missile will generally use an active-radar terminal seeker.

Possible future developments may therefore be of large aircraft with strategic range and payload, capable of attacking hostile surface units from any direction and overwhelming their defensive systems. Nor may the concept apply simply to bomber aircraft. It would be perfectly feasible to modify a large wide-bodied transport aircraft to deploy very large numbers of ALCMs at great ranges. Range and fire power are the characteristics of large land-based aircraft in the ship-attack role, coupled with the speed of response and flexibility which only air can bring to the war at sea.

Air Defence

The obverse of the ship-attack capability just described is the need to protect friendly surface forces against air attack: the capability of the AV-MF Backfires makes this an urgent mission for all NATO nations which deploy surface forces into likely threat areas. The complete tapestry of maritime anti-air warfare is large and complex, and in its totality beyond the scope of this article. In essence, the tactics developed by Western navies rely on defence in depth. A USN carrier battle group, for instance, would thus deploy E-2C AEW aircraft controlling F-14 interceptors as the fighting system in the outermost zone to pin down and cull the attacking aircraft, with F-18s and F-4s closer in to sweep up the 'leakers'. Area surface-to-air missile (SAM) systems would cover the intermediate zone, and close-in short-range missiles and rapid-firing guns, for instance the Vulcan Phalanx, would be deployed. The Royal Navy would adopt a similar approach based on a mix of organic aircraft and ship-borne SAM and point defence systems. But the discussion in the previous section of a ship-attack concept, based on mass attack using extended range stand-off missiles, and undoubtedly backed by heavy use of electronic warfare techniques, must to some extent call in question the capability of even CVBG forces, with an inevitably limited in-flight refuelling capacity, to deal with the threat in the worst circumstances. What may tip the balance in such a scenario is an extension of the defence-in-depth, as has been suggested earlier, by the employment of highly capable land-based aircraft (supported by tankers) to inflict heavy attrition on the attacking aircraft at long range. The Royal Navy and the Royal Air Force have worked up this co-operative technique over a period of many years, but again it is only recently with the development of extremely capable Airborne Early Warning (AEW) aircraft such as the Boeing E-3A and in future the RAF Nimrod AEW Mk III, together with land-based fighters of the calibre of F-15, Tornado F2 and F-16 and the increasing availability of large tanker aircraft with a very high fuel off-load capability, that the concept is truly coming to fruition. The land-based AEW aircraft available today can provide the long-range gap-free cover against intruders at high and low level, and the data-processing, data-link and communications facilities to take control of the situation and to vector the fighters precisely onto their targets. The AEW aircraft, tankers and their patrolling fighters would be operated well up threat in critical areas such as, for instance, the Greenland–Iceland–UK gap, the Eastern Mediterranean and North-East Asia. The land-based aircraft, and the organic aircraft of the surface forces in such a concept, form two parts of a dynamic whole. The surface ships themselves with their detection systems and area cover form an integral part of the overall anti-air war mission system—and equally by virtue of their own capabilities can add significantly to the protection of the on-station AEW and transitting fighters, and indeed to the general air defence of the region in which they are operating. Perhaps in no other aspect of the maritime battle is the newly emerging complement and inter-dependence of surface ships and carrier-borne and land-based aircraft capabilities so well demonstrated. Moreover, the total picture extends beyond air defence in the classic defensive interpretation, for a fundamental aspect of the anti-air war is attack of the enemy's anti-ship capability on the ground. It is not difficult to envisage a scenario where the forward edge of the anti-air warfare battle would consist of attacks by heavy strategic aircraft using land-attack ALCMs (in concert perhaps with carrier borne assets) against enemy offensive air bases, to suppress the threat at source. Once more the concept involves ships and organic and land-based aircraft operating together, maximising individual capabilities and supporting weak areas and in the overall result producing crucial increases in total effectiveness.

A key element in the anti-air battle is the AEW aircraft. There is little doubt that aircraft such as the E-3, and in the future the Nimrod AEW, have produced a step increase in capability, but they are very expensive; thus their numbers must be limited, and therefore what may be required to complement them are cheaper alternative AEW platforms to augment cover and fill gaps. One way to provide this perhaps would be to develop less complex AEW systems which could be fitted in smaller aircraft and deployed in larger numbers. Proposals to this effect involving the P-3 aircraft and the C-130 Hercules have been publicised. Helicopter AEW (such as the Sea King variant being developed for the Royal Navy using the Thorn-EMI Searchwater radar) is another approach for situations where the limited endurance and operating radius of the helicopter are not a constraint. For the future, perhaps, the airship, proposed in the past for many maritime and maritime associated roles, may become a contender as a vehicle to augment AEW cover. Whilst there is always concern at the capability of airships to operate in difficult environmental conditions, the AEW airship has respectable antecedents. The US Navy operated Goodyear ZPG-3W 'Blimps' until the early 1960s. These airships carried a 40-ft diameter radar antenna in the envelope, had a lift capability of some 10 tons and with a 70-knot maximum speed and long endurance could stay airborne (with occasional refuelling) for very long periods in most weathers. One modern equivalent is the British Airships Industries Skyship 600, which is made of modern materials and has a take-off weight of 6,000 kg. In principle, an airship such as the Skyship 600, or later variants, would be able to provide useful AEW cover relatively cheaply, to augment the more capable and costly large AEW aircraft, and it is perhaps in a mix of systems on which the future anti-air picture will depend.

Anti-Submarine Warfare (ASW)

The final capability area to be considered in this brief review is in many ways the most complex of all. It is certainly an area where sea and air operations by both navies and air forces have been inextricably linked over a very long period and where the recognition of the complementary nature of sea and air capabilities and the necessity to operate a mix of vehicles has gained most acceptance. The threat to NATO is, of course, well documented. The Soviet Navy deploys some 375 submarines which are active worldwide, particularly in the Atlantic and Arctic Oceans and the Mediterranean. With a large and very capable force which ranges from small patrol submarines to the strategic missile force, the Soviet ability to operate their submarines effectively is increasing and the challenge to the Western ASW effort has never been greater.

Land-based air power in the form of the Maritime Patrol Aircraft (MPA) is a fundamental part of the ASW force mix. Although MPA can be operated tactically in many different ways, either in concert with a surface force or independently, they will often be positioned to form the outer layer of protection against the submarine threat, rather as the land-based component can form the outer layer of the anti-air war deployment. The MPA brings to the ASW battle the flexibility and speed of reaction over great distances which characterise the air contribution to maritime warfare in other roles. Advanced MPA combine extensive sensor and information processing facilities, a powerful attack capability and, especially with in-flight refuelling, long range and on-station times. However, it cannot be said too often that the successful conduct of ASW operations requires the complete integration of all available assets, which will generally include surface forces and their organic helicopters, MPA and hunter-killer submarines, and other capabilities.

The range of aircraft types which are operated in the MPA role worldwide is extensive and increasing. Not only does this reflect the differing levels of resources which nations can allocate to the role, but also differences in the submarine threat and the nature of the task, which can range from the provision of a comprehensive ASW capability to protect strategic interests and vital sea lanes of communication in war at one end of the scale, to the surveillance and control of an exclusion zone and the protection of national resources in peace at the other.

In the front rank of the MPA deployed by Western nations are aircraft such as the P-3C Orion of the USN, the RAF Nimrod Mk II and the Breguet 1150 Atlantic. Aircraft of this calibre will carry two main types of sensor for submarine detection and localisation: acoustic and non-acoustic. The acoustic techniques employed are based on the air-droppable sonobuoy, which can be either active or passive. There are many different types of sonobuoy available, and to make maximum use of their capability places great demands on the acoustic information processing capability in the aircraft. Indeed, it is the increase in information handling capacity that modern digital techniques provide which offers the possibility of keeping up with developments in the submarine threat. The non-acoustic sensors include electronic support measures (ESM) equipment for passive detection, radar, Magnetic Anomaly Detection (MAD) and infrared detection. The employment of these equipments against a demanding threat and in a medium as constantly shifting and varying as the sea poses technical and tactical problems of formidable complexity. In essence, when using acoustic search techniques the MPA will set up a barrier of sonobuoys in an area of probability through which submarines are expected to pass. Augmented by radar, ESM and perhaps infrared, in a multi-sensor search, the object will be to reduce the area of uncertainty in the submarine's position perhaps initially to a few miles, then to a few hundred metres, and finally to pin-point its position sufficiently accurately for a torpedo attack. The MAD sensor could be used in the very last stages of this process, since it is essentially short range, but can give a very precise confirmation of target location.

The development of effective systems is a continuing evolutionary process against a steadily advancing threat, and whilst the best of current systems can sensibly be assessed as abreast of the threat, a sustained research and procurement effort will be required to maintain this position. The updated III version of the P3-C, for instance, has a new search radar and the advanced IBM Proteus acoustic processor. The CP-140 Aurora of the Canadian Forces is an Orion variant fitted with avionics based on the Lockheed S-3A system, which is itself due for a major update, including increased acoustic processing and improved ESM. The Nimrod force operated by the RAF has been converted to Mk II standard with the Thorn-EMI Searchwater pulse-compression surveillance radar, which provides greatly enhanced target detection and classification capability, enhanced acoustic processing with dual AQS 901 processors, as well as more tactical computing power and the Loral ESM. The Atlantic is also undergoing an update to G2 standard with enhanced radar incorporating a sideways-looking synthetic aperture mode for target classification, and improved acoustic processing and ESM. The French *Aeronavale* is to be equipped with the Atlantic G2, and the West German Navy, which operates over the very demanding Baltic Sea area, may also re-equip with this aircraft. Looking further afield, the P-3 aircraft has been exported in various versions to many countries over the past 20 years, including Norway, The Netherlands and Australia; Japan produces the aircraft under licence.

It has already been emphasised that ASW requires the integration of a mix of units, and thus the ASW helicopter, mentioned briefly earlier, operating from shore, from a moored platform or from a mother ship at sea, merits further comment. The helicopter continues to play an important part in the ASW team, often acting as a vital extension of the sensor and weapon fit of its parent ship. Medium size helicopters can operate successfully from small ships (down to perhaps 1,500 tons), but to provide a genuine search and attack capability over extended periods requires the numbers of helicopters and crews, which can only be deployed by large units such as the USN carriers, the RN Invincible class, the Italian *Garibaldi* and the Soviet helicopter carriers. Space prevents a full description of the range of helicopters operated by the navies of the world. Suffice it to say that the Sikorsky SH-3 (Sea King) has formed the core of the Western world's ASW helicopter capability for many years. The next generation of aircraft will typically carry more extensive avionics and will be capable of longer on-station times. The Anglo-Italian EH 101 and the SH-60B Seahawk are examples of the way development is going. The latter aircraft is a very expensive project indeed, which incorporates a high degree of automation and linkage to the parent ship: indeed, it may over-extend the concept of the helicopter as an automated component of the ship's ASW system.

Soviet ASW aircraft and helicopters have been operating for many years, and are a fundamental part of Soviet maritime air power. Understandably, in this sensitive and specialised field, it is difficult to be precise as to their capability. The backbone of the ASW force is the Tu-142 Bear aircraft which is deployed in both the Pacific and Atlantic fleets. Also deployed are the obsolescent Be-12 Mail amphibian and a large force of ASW helicopters such as the Ka-25 Hormone and Ka-27 Helix-As. Whether or not Soviet long-range ASW aircraft are as capable as their Western equivalents remains an open question, although it has often been suggested that Soviet capability in the field of sensor technology and information processing lags well behind that of the West. Be that as it may, Soviet fixed-wing ASW aviation has been greatly enhanced over the past 20 years or so, both in qualitative and quantitative terms. This, together with continued emphasis of the ship-based and land-based ASW helicopter, is a process which can only be expected to continue.

The ASW role is therefore extensive for MPA, but there are other related roles which may be undertaken by land-based air power. Ocean surveillance has already been mentioned as a specialist role, but which can to some extent be undertaken by any capable long-range military aircraft. Search and rescue too is a task which falls to maritime aircraft, both fixed-wing and rotary, and either in a specialist role or as a commitment arising from the wide sensor fit, long-range and communications facilities of the MPA. Mine-laying too deserves specific mention, since it is very much part of the ASW battle in both the offensive and defensive phases. Maritime aircraft such as the P-3 have a minelaying capability and transport aircraft are relatively easily modified to this role. The capability of an aircraft to commence laying a minefield quickly once the political decision has been made could be an invaluable asset in a period of heightening tension.

Finally, the surveillance and control of the EEZ (economic exclusion zone) and the protection of natural resources is becoming an increasingly significant task throughout the world. It is a priority which, unlike strategic ASW, is shared by small nations as well as large; indeed the protection of vital maritime resources looms perhaps even larger seen from the perspective of a small littoral state as opposed to that of the traditional maritime nations. Whilst advanced MPA have, of course, the capability to carry out this role, the nature of the task is such that the cost and complexity of a full standard ASW aircraft is arguably excessive. A new generation of simpler and cheaper maritime surveillance aircraft is thus coming to the fore, aircraft which are perfectly capable of the off-shore role in most circumstances, and can sometimes offer the bonus of a worthwhile, albeit limited, ASW capability as well. This is currently a burgeoning market, and any attempt at a survey of the aircraft becoming available would require a chapter to itself, so a few examples must suffice. Fokker, for instance, have produced a maritime version of the F-27 which has been exported to, amongst other nations, Thailand, the Philippines and Spain: primarily a passive search/SAR aircraft, Fokker plan a fit to provide ASW and ASUW capability. The British Aerospace HS 748 has also been proposed as a maritime contender in the guise of the Coastguarder, which could potentially be produced as an armed variant carrying the Sting Ray torpedo and Sea Skua anti-ship missile. Aerospatiale are considering a development of their C-160 Transall to permit the rapid conversion of this light transport aircraft to the maritime role using palletised consoles and equipment. In addition to the examples already quoted, many variants are based on lighter jet aircraft such as the Dassault-Breguet HU-25A Guardian based on the Falcon 20G which will fly with the USCG and the French Aeronavale. Finally, as with AEW, the airship is a potential contender for the off-shore surveillance role; Airship Industries of the United Kingdom are proposing the Sentinel, a development of the Skyship 600, and a metal-clad design is proposed by Wren Skyships.

Conclusion

The Second World War incontrovertibly demonstrated that the outcome of a battle at sea could often be determined in the air, and the increase in the capability of both sea- and land-based aircraft in recent years serves only to emphasise this fundamental fact. Yet air power and sea power are still seen in many quarters as competing methods for the projection of power and the achievement of military objectives, and this is a damaging perception. In truth, air power and sea power are mutually interactive and supportive in the prosecution of the war at sea. From the very earliest days, sea power has always implied more than ships; it has always involved the whole mix of national military and civil assets which make it possible to deny an adversary the use of the sea and to ensure its use for our objectives. With the advent of manned flight, aircraft have been part of that mix. Today, with ever-escalating defence costs, and with technological developments that make many older categories and interfaces between air, land and sea power meaningless, seagoing nations must increasingly seek to bring together all those assets which can contribute to the maritime war. Returning to Lord Tedder's Lees-Knowles lectures, the Second World War made it clear that air, sea and land power are part of the same pattern, but the key to that pattern is air superiority. A naval strategy which ignores this fundamental reality can no longer hope to be effective under modern conditions.

10

Manned and Unmanned Aircraft

AIR MARSHAL SIR MICHAEL ARMITAGE

The use of air power had been a ubiquitous feature in virtually all the operational theatres of the Second World War and it was a decisive factor in many of them, perhaps most notably at sea in the Pacific and over Normandy in 1944. Over Germany and Japan, air power had also fought lengthy campaigns unaided, and by the closing stages of the war the employment of air resources, whether in combat or in support roles such as air transport, was massive. For example, Britain produced 128,775 aircraft during the war, Germany 118,778, Japan approximately 60,422, and the United States no fewer than 272,000 between 1940 and 1945. The total number of aircraft produced by all the combatants was around three-quarters of a million.

The loss rates were also very high. US losses worldwide from all operational causes amounted to 22,600 aircraft; and RAF Bomber Command alone lost 8,953 aircraft, together with 55,573 fatal aircrew casualties.[1]

This scale of effort and losses of this kind had never been foreseen before the war.[2] Indeed, it had been confidently expected by the proponents of strategic air power that aerial bombardment would avoid the long, static and very costly campaigns that had so characterised the First World War. In the event, both in Europe between 1940–44 and in the Far East from 1942 to 1945, only air power offered the means to strike at the enemy homelands; strategically there was no other choice. And if air power was to be employed, then the manned aircraft was its only weapon; there was no other technical choice. The outcome was that, particularly over Germany, a campaign of attrition was fought for 4 years in the air rather than on the ground.[3] In the end, offensive air power triumphed in both theatres of war, but it was only in the very late stages of the European air offensive in particular that losses to the attackers were reduced to levels that were less than very grave.

Meanwhile, the infant state of the technologies that might one day cause the manned bomber to be replaced by rockets or unmanned aircraft were demonstrated by the German V1 and V2 attacks in 1944 on southern

England. The V2 ballistic missile was limited in range and so lacking in accuracy that it could be used only as a weapon against the London area as a whole, while the V1 flying bomb had the same limitations in accuracy but was vulnerable to conventional air defences as well. At the end of the Second World War it thus seemed clear that manned aircraft would be the principal and indeed the only weapon of long-range strategic bombardment for many years ahead. Marshal of the Royal Air Force Viscount Trenchard, for example, looking 20 years ahead, wrote in August 1946 that

> the atom bomb ... would be launched from piloted aircraft, ... pilotless aircraft might be used for shorter or medium distances, and it is possible that the long-range rockets can be made in the next fifteen or twenty years moderately accurate. Then the atom bomb might render the Air Force as we know it today as obsolete as battleships and aircraft carriers are today.[4]

In the shorter term, the introduction of the atomic bomb itself seemed to have over important implications. Whether the strategic bombing offensives against Germany and Japan were ill-conceived or not, and there was a great deal of dispute about the contribution that strategic bombing had made to Allied victory, air bombardment in the future would be a matter not of thousand-bomber missions escorted by hundreds of fighters, but of just one aircraft dropping a single weapon. It was therefore believed that even in the very unlikely event of another major war, the kind of horrendous losses incurred during the strategic air offensive against Germany were very unlikely ever to be seen again.

This view of the secure place of the powerfully-armed manned strategic bomber was, however, to be drastically changed within only a few years, notably by the experience of the Korean War between 1950–53. Before the Korean War it had been widely thought, first, that future conflicts could be prevented by the mere threat of long-range aerial bombardment; second, that if in spite of this threat war did break out, then it would be fought and won by long-range bombardment; and third, the only instrument by which all this could be achieved was still the manned bomber. But Korea showed that the only rational strategic objectives for an air offensive, in this case the industrial and military centres of the Soviet Union and China, which were supplying the war, were too diffuse and too ambiguous as targets to be attacked; and it showed that the air power resources available to the United States were too modest. Worst of all, however, when the newly-emerged Chinese Air Force inflicted such heavy losses on the USAF B-29s that their daylight bombing offensive over North Korea had to be halted, it became clear that optimistic assumptions about the invulnerability of the manned bomber would have to be drastically revised.[5] The war was thus a turning point in air power thinking.

Within a few years other factors emerged to further change the assumptions of the late 1940s and early 1950s. In May 1960 an American U-2 reconnaissance aircraft was shot down over Sverdlovsk, thus confirming that even very high operating altitudes offered no sanctuary from the new guided missile defences. This event came, however, as no great surprise to Western Intelligence. The planners of the Royal Air Force, for example, had been working in the early 1950s to bring the V-bomber force into service in the middle of that decade, but even in those early days they foresaw that the emerging Soviet surface-to-air missiles would pose an increasing threat. It was for this reason that the operational requirement for the Blue Steel was issued in 1954, a weapon designed to allow the manned bomber to stand-off from the worst of the enemy's terminal defences. Beyond that, and again partly because of the foreseen threat of Soviet SAMs, it was planned to diversify the UK deterrent force by deploying Blue Streak ballistic missiles in silos in East Anglia.

There was thus a degree of uncertainty in some quarters about the future, not only of manned strategic bombers, but of manned aircraft as a whole, and it was demonstrated perhaps most clearly, though erroneously, in the British Defence White Paper of 1957, which announced among other things 'that fighter aircraft will in due course be replaced by a ground-to-air missile system'.[6]

With all the benefits of hindsight, it can now be seen that what was missing from this kind of assessment in the 1950s was any indication that the eventual concentration of immensely powerful strategic missiles in the hands of both superpowers might eventually result in a nuclear stand-off that transposed war itself back to theatre operations, and to the battlefields that air power had once promised to make unnecessary. But this is what happened, and although the manned aircraft appeared to be increasingly obsolete in what had been thought of as its primary role, strategic bombardment, its place in conflict at any level less than strategic became the subject of new interest and innovation.

Part of that innovative thinking had to concern itself with the continuing development of Soviet ground-based air defence systems. To the static surface-to-air missile SA-1 that entered the Soviet inventory in 1954 was soon to be added the towed SA-2, and the tractor-mounted SA-3 as well as later weapons such as the highly mobile tracked SA-6 battlefield air defence missile. Meanwhile, the very potent ZSU 23-4 mobile four-barrelled anti-aircraft cannon had been deployed in large numbers since the early 1950s, and by the late 1960s not only was there a comprehensive air defence system covering the more sensitive areas of the Soviet Union, but Warsaw Pact battlefields' air defences had developed into a comprehensive and very formidable threat to any manned aircraft.

Counters to those defences took two main forms. That favoured by the

Royal Air Force and by the other European air forces of NATO was determined by their comparatively small resources. Basically it was to evade the enemy defences by tactical routing and by flying at very low level, supported where possible by stand-off ECM. The solution adopted by the more generously equipped US Air Force was to develop mission packages of tactical aircraft. Some of the aircraft in the package would disrupt and confuse the enemy defences, others would attack and destroy key features of those defences such as radars, while the main attack force went for the target itself. These tactics were tried and proved in Vietnam starting in 1966, when the realisation that manoeuvrability and speed alone were not an answer to North Vietnamese SAMs led to ECM pods being fitted to the tactical aircraft of the 7th Air Force.[7]

In that same air war, radar-reflecting chaff played a major role in the 1972 bombing offensive, and 'Wild Weasel' tactics were introduced as early as 1965. These missions, called Iron Hand, involved four tactical aircraft carrying air-to-ground missiles and two more carrying conventional bombs. These flights of four went in ahead of the main strike force by about 5 minutes, and when a defending SAM radar stated transmitting, a Weasel aircraft would launch a missile at it, followed by an attack with conventional bombs. The successes achieved by these means were not confined only to tactical air operations. Supported by chaff flights, Wild Weasels, fighter cover and ECM, at the end of 1972, B-52 heavy bombers flew a total of 729 night sorties with considerable, and perhaps decisive, success against the heavily defended city of Hanoi for the loss of only sixteen aircraft.[8] The war in Vietnam thus demonstrated among other things that with special tactics and special weapons SAM systems could after all be penetrated and even defeated at the cost of tolerable attrition rates, a lesson that was soon applied by the other air forces of NATO and adopted by, among others, the Israeli Air Force.

The same technologies that had fostered the development of effective SAMs had meanwhile made possible much more advanced versions of the earlier V1 flying bomb. Air-to-ground guided missiles such as the Shaddock, Styx and Kelt appeared in the Soviet inventory, and as early as 1950 the USAF was using the Tarzan air-launched radio-guided bomb against bridges in North Korea.[9] Further progress in the whole field of missiles, stand-off weapons and in remotely piloted vehicles then followed in the 1960s and 1970s as advances were made in the technologies of structures, lightweight power plants, very accurate digitalised mapping techniques and in particular in those of solid-state electronics and computational density.

One advanced system in particular, the US Tomahawk Cruise Missile,[10] aroused great interest, particularly because of its intermediate range nuclear capability. It was developed as an autonomous missile able to map-read its way to the target with on-board radar scanning the features of the ground over which it was flying, comparing that profile with a very accurately surveyed profile of its programmed track, and then automatically making corrections to its flight path so as to fly the preplanned route to the target. This advance in technology contributed to a new interest in the whole topic of unmanned aircraft, particularly since the emergence of the cruise missile came at a time when three quite independent factors were leading to public and professional debate that has continued on and off ever since about the future place of the manned aircraft.

The first factor was that the cost of modern aircraft was again causing concern.[11] The second was that the density, effectiveness and geographical cover of the Warsaw Pact ground-based defences were all continuing to increase. And the third factor was that Israeli air power had suffered unexpectedly heavy losses from enemy ground-based air defences in the early stages of, Yom Kippur War of 1973, when almost a quarter of the Israeli Air Force was destroyed in 3 days. In the debate about the future of manned aircraft, those who expressed doubts about their future operational viability were able to point not only to losses like these, but also to the high capital costs, as well as to increasingly high investment costs in the training and support costs of modern combat aircraft and their crews.

It was true that the support and the training organisations behind the operational front line of any air force of worth had historically proved to be very large. In the case of the Royal Air Force, for example, in 1945 there had been 8,752 aircraft actually in operational units, but another 15,857 in training units. From this peak the huge training machine had wound down to a more normal peacetime establishment so that by 1958, and after the impact of the very drastic Sandys cuts, the figures were 1,249 operational aircraft with another 1,473 in training units. By 1969 the figures were 723 operational aircraft and 860 trainers.[12] After years of painful cuts in resources and successive searches for economics, the general picture in the Royal Air Force has now become one of a very rough balance between operational and training machines.

Crew training and crew wastage in training had always been another area of high cost. For example, a study of pilot intakes between June and December 1940 showed that 17 per cent of the candidates were diverted to become instructors for the later intakes, 11 per cent had been killed, injured or discharged, and only 41 per cent had reached operational units.[13] In 1984 a study[14] indicated that the Royal Air Force required in round terms 2,000 active pilots in service. Two hundred or so retired or were otherwise lost to the Service annually and had to be replaced. Each year between ten and fifteen times that number apply to take their places, and from those two to three thousand candidates, four hundred are selected to start their training. But in spite of the rigorous selection that those figures imply, only about half of those four hundred survived the demanding training and actually reach the front line. For those who do succeed, the total financial cost of their training represents a considerable investment, †2.4 million for a

Harrier pilot and †2.7 million for a Tornado pilot. Thus the expense and the wasted effort involved in maintaining a modern air force are undoubtedly high, even without consideration of the extensive logistic, technical and support costs.

Against that it had to be remembered, first, since high-quality manned aircraft are an essential feature of contemporary military power, that is the kind of bill that virtually all nations with modern military forces would have to meet.[15] Second, although unit for unit aircraft and their crews are expensive, and far more expensive in real terms than they were, say, during the Second World War, their operational impact has been steadily growing so that whereas a fighter-bomber of the 1940s might carry a payload of about 2,000 lb, by 1974 the F-4 Phantom could carry eleven 1,000 lb bombs as well as gun-pods and rockets, and 3 years later the USAF AIOA Thunderbolt was in service with a maximum external payload of 18,000 lb. Not only that, but these higher payloads can be put onto targets with an accuracy that suggests a factor of relative effectiveness several orders of magnitude higher than any simple comparison of war-loads would indicate. As one example, between 1965 and 1972 US air power had launched some 700 sorties against the Than Hoa bridge in North Vietnam using free-fall weapons, without success. It was eventually brought down by a single 3,000 lb laser-guided bomb.[16] And third, one of the benefits that flow from increasing unit effectiveness of that kind is that only a relatively small number of men are actually exposed to the risks of the combat environment. Air power has increasingly become a high leverage weapon with very low investment of human lives.

The proponents of conventional aircraft were also able to point to the well-known conceptual and operational advantages of the manned versions. These fell into three very broad areas. First, there was the factor of mobility, which to a unique degree gives aircraft the ability to focus fire power rapidly at critical times and places, thus making an often decisive contribution to the overriding principle of war—concentration of force at the decisive point. One corollary of this mobility is that it brings with it the potential capability of rapid dispersal in order to avoid the parallel air power initiatives of an opponent. High mobility also brings with it the ability to adopt, if necessary at short notice, an ostentatious alert posture; or to reinforce across very wide geographical areas[17] so as to demonstrate commitment or intent; and once deployed, that mobility also means that a relatively small force can be used to generate a high number of operational sorties in the area of interest.

A second area of advantage remains that of high adaptability. Experience has shown that air platforms can be adapted to carry out an often surprisingly high number of contemporaneous roles, combining, for example, an interception capability with the potential to make deep penetration attacks or reconnaissance sorties; or aircraft built for the transport role can be modified to operate as surveillance, air-to-air refuellers or patrol aircraft, and so on. And even within these varied roles, the adaptability of manned platforms has meant that effort can be shifted, often with little difficulty, from one kind of target array to target arrays with quite different characteristics, for example from columns of vehicles, to parked aircraft or even to ships. In many cases aircraft have also been able to demonstrate a sequential adaptability, that is to say over a service life often much longer than that foreseen by their designers, they have been adapted to meet the changing circumstances of operations as new defences or new tactics were introduced. Aircraft such as the Canberra, for example, originally designed as a high-altitude nuclear bomber, was later to be adapted to low-level conventional interdiction and night reconnaissance roles.

Third, there was the flexibility of the manned aircraft, which perhaps shows itself most clearly at the tactical level. Here, a crew is able to bring real-time observation and reaction to the scene of sometimes distant operations with the result that the operational potential of the aircraft can be used to best advantage. Tactical judgement can be applied to the local choice of target; fire power can be very rapidly switched from one target to another; not least, the mission can be recalled or diverted in flight and tactical judgement can be engaged to deal with all the changed circumstances that this can imply.

Although against all this had to be weighed the vulnerability of the manned aircraft both in the air and on the ground, it was apparent that unmanned platforms were much more vulnerable. In the late 1960s, both were unarmoured and thus inherently vulnerable in the air, but the answer to that was a mixture of tactics and electronics, both of which were more effectively employed to bring operational judgement to bear at the scene. On the ground there was no doubt that the air bases needed to support conventional manned aircraft offered unmistakably large and conspicuous targets. But there were three answers to this: First, the large number of military and civilian airfields available meant that the potential target array offered to the enemy was huge and thus resilient. Second, the obvious vulnerabilities, those of the aircraft themselves, and of their runways and taxiways, proved less susceptible to attack by conventional weapons than had once been thought to be the case.

Not only that, but the aircraft of most major air forces, including virtually all those in the Central Region, were, after the classic attack by the Israeli Air Force on the exposed Arab air forces in 1967, increasingly dispersed in hardened aircraft shelters. These gave a useful degree of protection against anything except a direct hit, but perhaps just as important, the attacker had no way of determining whether the shelters were occupied or not, and a great deal of valuable operational effort therefore stood to be wasted. Unless massive offensive air resources are available, these shelters will rarely qualify as worthwhile targets. Not only that, but airfields themselves are increasingly designed and built to have redundant and therefore reserve operating surfaces. And even if all those operating surfaces could be simultaneously attacked, some could be restored within a few hours by quite simple civil engineering remedies. The search for more effective anti-runway munitions continues, but so does the pursuit of defensive remedies on the one hand and better short-field or VSTOL performance in aircraft on the other. No decisive innovation is in sight on either side, and as in so many aspects of contemporary conventional operations, this rough balance seems likely to continue.

The arguments in favour of unmanned aircraft rather than those simply against manned machines rest basically on the grounds that they need neither crew nor crew support systems, and that they are therefore bound to be much more simple, much smaller and thus a great deal cheaper. This also means that there can be more of them, and sheer weight of numbers should be able to make up for whatever deficiencies resulted from the absence of a crew. There are, however, very real problems both technical and conceptual.

The technical difficulties affect both of the possibilities in unmanned aircraft, that of the Remotely Piloted Vehicle and that of the automatic aircraft such as the cruise missile. An RPV requires not merely a command link of some kind to direct it, but a complex two-way communication system to enable the operator to monitor and adjust the flight programme. The problem for the flight programme is unlikely to be simply a navigational one. The benefits of the unmanned aircraft are likely to be in greatest demand and of most value beyond the range of artillery. But the aircraft will almost certainly have to operate at very low level in order to evade both detection and the worst of the opposing anti-aircraft defences, which means that the communications links will have to operate beyond line-of-sight. This implies that some kind of an intermediate airborne link will be necessary. This in turn means a shift from single-point systems to multi-point systems, and if data has to pass through those several points, then the potential vulnerabilities will be increased since every point has to work in order for the system as a whole to operate successfully. Finally, the unmanned aircraft still has to negotiate the same enemy air defences that had led to its being put into the air instead of a manned aircraft in the first place.

What all this amounts to is that in order for the RPV to operate effectively in a combat environment it will be necessary to give it at least four novel attributes. First, all the technical sensors of the manned aircraft as well as sensors to replace human vision will be needed in the cockpit; second, it will be essential to have reliable communication links that will transmit all those stimuli back to a distant operator; third, an operator will be needed who is capable of reacting as skilfully as aircrew would do; and fourth, complex links back to the RPV must faithfully transmit each of those reactions and activate the controls and equipment of the vehicle. And all this has to be accomplished in a hostile operational environment against an opponent determined to disrupt or destroy critical components of the RPV's systems. Not only that, but the RPV will be moving progressively out of the airspace in which the controller can apply his judgement to the safe progress of the aircraft, and progressively deeper into the airspace in which a skilful opponent can increasingly apply his judgement to its destruction. If the vehicle does survive to reach the target area, then it has to deliver its weapons either by itself penetrating the dense terminal defences, or by using yet another complex link to enable the ground controller to guide a missile from the vehicle down to the target. At this point even a smoke screen might give the remote pilot a few problems, yet the RPV and its links must have the ability to deal with these and with many other natural and contrived difficulties.

At the same time, it had to be admitted that RPVs do offer some clear advantages. One is that their manoeuvrability is not constrained by the frailty of the human body; g limits matter only in terms of aircraft structures, and in theory an RPV can always out-manoeuvre a manned fighter. A second is that the absence of a crew means that a great deal of space and weight in the aircraft can be saved, and combined with a continuing trend of miniaturisation in electronc and other components as well as power sources, the unmanned aircraft can be made very small and very much cheaper. Thus it is possible to reverse the rising spiral of aircraft weight and size and pursue it down to a point at which the RPV becomes so small and so cheap that attrition is of much less importance. It thus becomes possible either to evade the opposing defences by making the RPV so small and so silent that it is virtually invisible, or, by using large numbers of RPVs, the defences can be so saturated that some aircraft are certain to penetrate to their targets.

The difficulty here is that the RPV will then be so small that it is unable, with two exceptions, to carry a useful payload; one is a nuclear warhead, and the other is that of a lightweight reconnaissance pack. The idea of a nuclear payload seems not to have been pursued, perhaps because of the very real possibility of an opponent seducing the vehicle electronically into, for example, reversing its course. As for the reconnaissance mode, since the latitude allowed by the field of view of cameras means that the navigational accuracy of the RPV need not be quite as precise as, say, that of an attack vehicle, the reconnaissance RPV can indeed fill a very useful place in the array of modern airborne systems. It can take on one of the functions in which manned aircraft will be at greatest risk, that of single aircraft activity over a combat area at medium level and in daylight.

In the case of cruise missiles, the absence of a crew either in the aircraft or at a remote control station suggests new vulnerabilities. Most important of all, the missile is committed to fly a steady and thus predictable course

PLATE 10.1   Falconet RPV, as used by the British Army (*Flight Refuelling Ltd.*).

for long periods. Next, if it is to be a relatively small and simple airframe, it cannot be a very high-speed machine; it will certainly be subsonic. Finally, not only will the aircraft be exposed to the new and more effective levels of air defence, including airborne radars that are able to detect even these small and very low-flying targets, but the control package itself offers an entirely new vulnerability for the defender to exploit by electronic means. The cruise missile can be programmed to deal only with foreseen operational circumstances. If the defence can surprise the system, and there will be several options open to him, then the automatic system can be disabled. Whereas a crew is able to monitor, adapt and improvise by using the available systems of an aircraft in flight, with cruise missiles the opportunity will now be there for a defender to intervene and not only disrupt key parts of the system, but also to inhibit the ability of the platform as a whole to react to that kind of operational degradation. In short, if the opponent can exploit a key component of the system, then it can be made to enter a self-destructive cycle.

With nuclear-armed automatic systems this might not be decisive, because if even only a small number of them manage to penetrate the enemy defences they will be enough to inflict very great damage. This was an argument that clearly favoured the nuclear armed cruise missile. But even if cruise missiles could be made sufficiently accurate to deliver conventional warheads onto small targets with extreme precision, the relatively small payload and the inherent vulnerabilities in an automatic system that has been described would make them a very expensive system indeed in terms of their operational capability.

The conceptual difficulty in cruise missiles, other than for the nuclear role, is that three factors have led to a new emphasis on high mobility for ground forces. The first factor is the greatly enhanced techniques for military surveillance that emerged in the decades after the Second World War. Heightened capabilities in electronic intelligence, in optics and in conventional reconnaissance, for example by high-flying aircraft, have all played a part; but the advent of surveillance satellites, and the fusion of near-real time intelligence that has become possible, means that a far more accurate picture of opposing deployments can be made available to military commanders.

That step change in combat intelligence has been matched by progressive improvements in weapons accuracy, leading eventually to Precision Guided Munitions which means that once discharged or launched, a projectile can be directed, or can even find its own way, with great accuracy to the target against which it has been aimed. There are two counters to this ability to find targets in near-real time and then to strike with such certainty: protection and mobility. Protection is valuable up to a point. But it implies a static posture and thus attrition, the very type of warfare for which the Soviet Union, with its emphasis on mass, is best able to fight. Mobility, on the other hand, offers not only the capability to evade the worst of an enemy assault, but also the potential for offensive initiatives, for striking at the key vulnerabilities in his combat array, and thus eventually the possibility of defeating him by disrupting and paralysing his operational capabilites.

The third factor is the availability of nuclear weapons. In all considerations of major conflict, the possibility has to be considered that nuclear weapons might be used, and not only in a strategic role, but perhaps in a theatre or a tactical role. The only defence against such a strike would be extensive hardening, something clearly inappropriate to an army in the field, or dispersal, which again means mobility. And there is one other important implication of the existence of nuclear weapons. If their use is to be avoided, something clearly in the interests of both sides but central in the calculations of an aggressor, then the conventional offensive has to be as fast moving as possible, both to defeat the opposing conventional forces, and to do so before he can make and implement the decision to invoke the use of his nuclear assets. All these demands for greatly enhanced mobility are matched by the universal availability not only of the technical means of providing it in an age of mass production and mechanical transport, but also of the skilled manpower required to operate and maintain it. Thus there is a continuing emphasis on higher mobility in war.

Yet it was only against static arrays targets, and not against mobile targets, that unmanned aircraft were likely to be most successful, and the progressive shift to mobile targets thus raised new problems for the concept of unmanned aircraft at a time when new technologies were offering at least some of the answers to their eventual widespread use.

One valuable insight into the state of the operational balance that might result from some of these concepts that have been discussed, rather than from the theories on which they rested, was given by events during the Israeli invasion of South Lebanon in June 1982, a campaign known to the Israelis as 'Operation Peace for Galilee'. It is not necessary here to describe the whole of that campaign, but a brief outline will put the air power aspects of the conflict into a suitable perspective (for another view of this conflict, see the essay by Benjamin Lambeth in this volume).

In 1976 Syria had, by invitation, intervened in the civil war in Lebanon and a garrison of about 25,000 men was deployed across that country, with the exception of the centre of the country and the southernmost 20 miles or so just north of the Israeli border. By the summer of 1982 there were also about 7,000 trained Palestinian soliders in South Lebanon, but in that same area the UN Interim Force (UNIFIL) was deployed, and an uneasy truce had been in force since mid-1981. On 3 June, however, the Israeli Ambassador in London was shot by Palestinians. The Israelis blamed the Palestinian Liberation Organisation and carried out air-strikes against Palestinian targets deep into Lebanon. The Palestinians retaliated with shell and rocket-fire into Galilee, and on 6 June the Israelis invaded with their three standing army divisions, about five of their eight reserve divisions and several independent brigades supported by the Israeli Air Force.

By 11 June Israeli forces were established on the perimeter of Beirut airfield and they held commanding positions above the Beirut–Damascus road; there they halted their advance. In 10 days the IDF had mobilised, advanced about 100 km on a front up to 60 km wide, destroyed most of the PLO bases, captured most of the heavy equipment held by the Palestinians and inflicted heavy casualties. There had been virtually no interference by the Syrian Air Force because, after a few early engagements, its combat effectiveness was neutralised by the Israelis. The brief Israeli air campaign holds lessons in the use of comprehensive intelligence, in the operational value of AWACS aircraft and helicopters, and above all in the vital task of achieving air superiority. It was in this last aspect that the use of unmanned aircraft came into prominence.

Well before the war the Israelis had invested heavily in an electronic intelligence effort devoted, among other things, to the Syrian target. Frequent ELINT flights and other intelligence activities, particularly in the year before 'Operation Peace for Galilee', had enabled the Israelis not only to plot the precise position of the Syrian SA-6 sites in the Beka'a Valley, but by stimulating the air defence radar transmissions they had also been able to collect invaluable data on the precise characteristics of most of the elements of the whole Syrian air defence network.

On 8 June Israeli aircraft were heavily committed in support on IDF ground formations in the Beka'a Valley, and almost certainly used this activity as a cover for further intelligence collection efforts while standing off by remaining south of the Syrian SAM engagement zones. At least six Syrian MiGs were destroyed in this preliminary phase of the air operations.

But the decisive phase of the air campaign came on 9 June, when the IAF launched their attack against the Syrian SAM system. In the first phase of a very carefully planned and precisely co-ordinated assault, Firebee and Chukkar RPVs were used to simulate overflights by IAF aircraft, which thus brought the Syrian SAM radars into action. These transmissions were picked up by Israeli EC 707 aircraft operating off the coast of Lebanon and thus well clear of the combat area. Using the ELINT that had so painstakingly been acquired and analysed, it was possible to identify and locate the Syrian sites that were transmitting, and these were then attacked by surface-to-surface anti-radiation missiles that were launched from a range of 30 km or more so as to neutralise the closest of the SA-6 batteries. Those batteries at greater ranges were also attacked, this time by air-launched SARM and Shrike missiles. Finally ground-attack aircraft were directed in by the same ECM aircraft to take out the remaining SAM elements before any cohesion could be restored to the thoroughly disrupted Syrian systems.

Meanwhile the radars and the C^3 system of the Syrian Air Force were being jammed by the EC 707 aircraft, and that system was also rendered helpless in trying to co-ordinate any air defence fighter response to these crippling blows. The result of the jamming activity was that when the Syrian fighters came into action they did so piecemeal and without proper ground control, and they found themselves confronted by Israeli F-15s and F-16s controlled by E-2Cs, a combination that cost the Syrians some twenty-two MiG-21s and 23s. Much the same sequence of operations was repeated on 10 June, with the result that on this day the Syrians lost another six SAM-6 sites and about twenty-five MiGs. Even more remarkable than this comprehensive defeat of the Syrian air defence system was the fact that it was achieved with no Israeli Air Force losses; the final score in the air war was 90:0 against the Syrians.

Many factors played a part in this remarkable achievement. Not least were the very high quality of the Israeli crews and aircraft, and the excellence of the co-ordinated intelligence-based training of crews and controllers that seems to have taken place well before the conflict. It is conceivable that something like this overwhelming result might have been achieved even without the RPV aircraft that the IAF employed, but the risks would have been so high as to be unacceptable if manned aircraft had been used for the decoy operation in the first wave, or if they had been employed instead of SSMs for the initial attack on the degraded but still undamaged Syrian SAM sites in the second. Instead, manned aircraft were used where their combat characteristics were essential. This meant in identifying, selecting and attacking those SAM elements still apparently functioning following the SSM assault, and in identifying and destroying the confused Syrian air defence fighters. The 2-day air war was a classic illustration of how, in the balance of manned and unmanned systems, the weaknesses of each can be covered by the strengths of the other.

Something along the lines of that balance between manned and unmanned aircraft has persisted for the past decade or so, weighted in favour of the manned machine. There has, however, been an increasing emphasis on air-launched stand-off weapons, an approach that combines the benefits of each type of system while avoiding the worst vulnerabilities of both. Particularly in the theatre land–air battle, this combination employs all the advantages of the manned platform that were discussed earlier to penetrate hostile airspace and avoid or counter en-route defences up to the point at which the dense, dedicated, and perhaps lethal defences of key targets would be encountered. From that point on, the advantages of the unmanned aircraft or missile can be employed. These stand-off weapons offer a very much smaller target than the present aircraft and they are far more difficult to acquire and destroy—particularly if chaff, ECM or decoys are employed simultaneously. The decoys could be very simple machines that would simulate the radar echo and perhaps the infrared signature of the stand-off weapon, or of the platform itself, yet they would be so small that they could be carried by the attack aircraft without undue loss of payload.

Such stand-off weapons will not be inexpensive, nor will they provide a sufficient answer to all the problems of the land–air battle. They will need to be used judiciously so as to neutralise the key features of opposing air defences and to exploit critical weaknesses in ground-force arrays. But they will substitute for the sheer weight of firepower that will also be needed in order to consolidate the paralysis induced by the employment of high-technology weapons. In very many operational circumstances, numbers will still be a vital factor.

In roles other than theatre penetration attack, the place of a wide variety of manned aircraft seems assured. Maritime patrol and ASW work is one example; long-range interception and the interrogation of unidentified intruder aircraft is another; while the whole field of tactical and strategic transport is an obvious third operational area in which manned aircraft will continue to be indispensable. Indeed, the best summary of the likely future balance between unmanned and manned systems is best reached by summarising briefly those narrower fields in which unmanned machines seem to have an important place.

The first and most obvious one is that of the nuclear-armed cruise missile. In this case, and despite the increasing ability of interceptors to destroy them using look-down shoot-down air-to-air systems, cruise missiles are likely to be in service for some decades. It is impossible to guess what other defences might eventually be deployed against them, but electronic methods of disrupting their automatic progress to the target has already been suggested, and since nuclear cruise missiles are likely to be used against large or important targets, it should not be impossible to deploy these defences in an outer perimeter, or even to mount the electronic-counters in airborne platforms along presumed approach routes.

Another use for unmanned aircraft, this time the remotely piloted vehicle, has been seen in effective use in the Israeli inventory. Whether as decoys or as platforms for reconnaissance sensors, small RPVs offer overwhelming advantages for short-penetration work in the air–land battle. They will remain difficult to detect and intercept, particularly if accompanied by deception techniques, yet their military advantage could be essential in critical tactical situations.

Finally, there is the ballistic missile to be considered. Although not an unmanned aircraft in the sense in which the subject has been discussed in this essay, ballistic missiles could play a key part in future theatre conflict. Short- and medium-range missiles with conventional warheads would be ideal weapons for use against fixed installations such as supply parks, focal points in communications systems and, not least, against large airbases. Fitted with terminal guidance and armed with high-explosive warheads or with a load of advanced sub-munitions, a relatively small number of missiles could neutralise airfields for long periods. Any confusion between nuclear-armed and conventionally-armed ballistic missiles for tactical or for intermediate range work of this kind could be avoided by having dedicated and discretely-based systems. The only active defence against them would be pre-emptive attack on their launch sites, which could, however, be mobile and very difficult to acquire with the necessary speed and accuracy. Passive defence of the targeted airfields could take the form of dispersal to smaller fields, but this would on the one hand stretch and expose to attack the supporting C^3, logistic and technical facilities; on the other hand, it might result in the aircraft being unprotected by hardened aircraft shelters on the ground. Finally, it would be likely to remove them from the comprehensive air defences deployed around their main operating bases.

Although these ballistic missiles would be highly inflexible in role, and although their value limited to specific areas and to particular stages of a conventional conflict in theatres such as the Central Region, they would act as a force-multiplier for conventional air power. They would, above all, release manned aircraft from operations against heavily defended fixed targets and free them to take on targets more appropriate to their characteristics of high mobility, flexibility and adaptability. The future application of air power would, in sum, seem to be a judicious mix of both manned and unmanned systems. The choice will no doubt continue to be influenced by traditional factors in warfare common to air, land and sea; the nature of the objective, its strategic and tactical importance, and all the costs involved in providing any one particular weapon system. Dogmatic over-emphasis of either manned or unmanned aircraft would lead to the conceptual bankruptcy and military disaster which have invariably accompanied exaggerated pretensions or outmoded ideas throughout military history.

Notes

Chapter 2

1. B. Brodie, *Strategy in the Missile Age,* Princeton University Press, 1965, c. 1959, p. 107.
2. General C. A. Spaatz, USAF (Ret.), 'If We Should Have to Fight Again', *Life,* 5 July 1948, p. 35.
3. USSBS, *Overall Report (European War),* Washington, USGPO, 1945, p. 107.
4. Harry Borowski, *A Hollow Threat: Containment and Strategic Air Power before Korea,* Westport, Conn., Greenwood Press, 1982.
5. The ideas expressed in this paragraph benefit from long discussions with R. F. Futrell, Dean of USAF historians, and in particular from an early draft of his 'Influence of the Air Power Concept on Air Force Planning, 1945–1962', Paper prepared for the 11th Military History Symposium, October 1984, Proceedings forthcoming from the USGPO in 1986 under title of *Military Planning in the Twentieth Century.*
6. See H. Borowski, note 4 above, and D. MacIsaac, 'The Air Force and Strategic Air Power, 1945–1951', Working Paper #8, International Security Studies Program, The Wilson Center, Washington, DC, 21 June 1979.
7. For a brief account of the airlift, highlighting its operational and joint/combined aspects, see General T. R. Milton, USAF (Ret.), 'The Berlin Airlift', *Air Force Magazine,* June 1978, pp. 57–65.
8. *Air University Quarterly Review,* Vol. 2, No. 4 (Spring 1949), p. 37. A recent Ph.D. dissertation thoroughly documents the demise of tactical aviation following the Second World War; see Joseph W. Caddell, 'Orphan of Unification: The Development of United States Air Force Tactical Air Power Doctrine, 1945–1950', Duke University, June 1984.
9. Charlotte Knight, 'Air War in Korea', *Air Force Magazine,* August 1950; reprinted in the issue for June 1975, pp. 59–63. Miss Knight touched a sensitive nerve when she decried the loss of '*all* the refinements of tactical air warfare we had developed by the end of World War II, and which were now so desperately needed'. In these respects another recent Ph.D. dissertation is especially helpful; see Philip S. Meilinger, 'Hoyt S. Vandenberg: The Life of a General', The University of Michigan, June 1985, esp. pp. 279–315.
10. In addition to the USAF units assigned to FEAF, the UN air forces in Korea included units from the US Marines, US Navy, South Korean, British, Australian, South African, Greek, and Thai Air Forces. For the best brief analysis of 'Air Power in Korea', see M. J. Armitage and R. A. Mason, *Air Power in the Nuclear Age,* University of Illinois Press, 1983, pp. 20–45.
11. John Schlight, 'The Impact of the Orient on Air Power', in Joe C. Dixon (Ed.), *The American Military and the Far East: Proceedings of the Ninth Military History Symposium,* Washington, DC, USGPO, 1980, pp. 160–71; 166 for quotation.
12. Quoted in Armitage and Mason, op. cit., p. 44.
13. Ibid., pp. 44–45.
14. Quoted in Colonel R. D. Heinl, Jr., *Dictionary of Military and Naval Quotations,* Annapolis, 1966, pp. 35, 8.
15. Quoted in Armitage and Mason, op. cit., p. 45.
16. For brief accounts, see the following articles in *Air Force Magazine:* F. W. Klibbe, 'Fox Able One–The First Transatlantic Jet Deployment', October 1980, pp. 72–80; J. Kosek, 'Fighters Across the Atlantic', September 1975, pp. 101–06; and G. M. Lunsford, 'The First Atomic Fighter Wing', June 1978, pp. 79–81.

17. Historical Documentation, [cf. oral history], Major General John D. Stevenson, September 1966, USAF Historical Research Center [new] file #K230.0512-574.

18. General T. R. Milton, USAF (Ret.), 'Readiness and the Critics', *Air Force Magazine*, October 1984, p. 101. General Milton goes on to note that the nuclear-armed F-100s carried 450-gallon drop tanks and ECM pods. 'Then came Vietnam, for which they were decidedly not ready. The huge 450-gallon tanks were useless in a tactical war, and the ECM pods emerged from classified storage only to prove equally useless against the radar in North Vietnam. They were not ready for what they were being called on to do, any more than the B-52s were ready for their conventional role.'

19. Quoted in Benjamin S. Lambeth, 'Pitfalls in Force Planning: Structuring America's Tactical Air Arm', *International Security*, Vol. 10, No. 2 (Fall 1985), p. 105.

20. US Senator Barry Goldwater published the recently declassified ROEs in three issues of the *Congressional Record-Senate*: 6 March 1985, pp. S2632–41; 14 March pp. S2982–90; and 26 March pp. S3511–20.

21. This and the following paragraph have been drawn, with the author's permission, from John Schlight, 'The Impact of the Orient on Air Power', pp. 168–69.

22. For an intelligent discussion of these issues see Donald J. Mrozek, 'The Limits to Innovation: Aspects of Air Power in Vietnam', *Air University Review*, Vol. 36, No. 2 (January–February 1985), pp. 58–71.

23. Lieutenant Colonel Barry D. Watts, USAF, *The Foundations of U.S. Air Doctrine: The Problem of Friction in War*, Maxwell AFB, AL, Air University Press, 1984, p. 110. Colonel Watts, who completed 100 missions over North Vietnam in June 1968, flew F-4s of the 8th Tactical Fighter Wing from Ubon, Thailand.

24. See Armitage and Mason, op. cit., pp. 114–39; esp. pp. 120–21 and 135–38.

25. This is, of course, the persistent theme of Caspar Weinberger, the American Defense Secretary. His assistant secretary for C^3I, D. Latham, is reported to have told an April 1985 Air Force Association meeting that 'the USSR is now ahead of the US in the key areas of infrared sensors, medium range air-to-air missiles, and the application of digital technology [and that] the MiG-31 is superior to existing US fighters'.

26. Benjamin S. Lambeth, note 18, above, p. 85.

27. Ibid., p. 92.

28. Ibid., p. 96.

29. The last of these comments is quoted by Lambeth in note 23, p. 96, and identified as 'a USAF Harrier exchange pilot with the RAF'. The other statements are by friends the author does not wish to lose.

30. See Colonel Walter Kross, USAF, *Military Reform: The High-Technology Debate in Tactical Air Forces*, Washington, National Defense University Press, 1985; and, for the broader context, F. D. Margiotta and R. Sanders (Eds.), *Technology, Strategy, and National Security*, Washington, National Defense University Press, 1985, esp. pp. 43–76.

31. Two recent books treat this and related questions provocatively. See Lon O. Nordeen, Jr., *Air Warfare in the Missile Age*, Washington, Smithsonian Institution Press, 1985, and Bill Gunston, *Air Superiority*, London, Ian Allan Ltd., 1985.

32. See 'US Sets Hypersonic Spaceplane Goals', *Flight International*, 7 December 1985, pp. 14–15.

33. The argument favouring weapons effectiveness was best put in Armitage and Mason, note 10, above, in 1983.

34. See the case made by James Townsend in 'Unmanned Systems for NATO', *NATO's Sixteen Nations*, 4 August 1945, pp. 72ff.

35. 'Gen Marquez: USAF Flexibility in Trouble', Air Force News Service (AFNS), December 1985.

36. For the kind of radical restructuring of the US services that would be necessary, see Commander John L. Byron, USN, 'Reorganization of the US Armed Forces', *Proceedings*, January 1983, pp. 68–75.

37. For a classic example of the kind of discussion that RAF officers in particular find disquieting, see Lieutenant General Merrill A. McPeak, USAF, 'TACAIR Missions and the Fire Support Coordination Line', in the September–October 1985 issue of *Air University Review*, pp. 65–72. For excellent examples of a more empirical approach,

see the articles by Group Captain Ian Madelin ('The Emperor's Close Air Support') and Wing Commander Jeremy G. Saye ('Close Air Support in Modern Warfare') in the issues of the *Air University Review* for November–December 1979 and January–February 1980—along with the ensuing uproar in the issues for May–June 1980 and September–October 1980.

38. Lambeth, op. cit., pp. 94–95.
39. Watts, op. cit., pp. 53–54 and 105–21.

Chapter 3

1. Literature on the terrible condition of South Vietnam today has become legion. *Time* magazine (15 April 1985) devoted much of an issue to the subject on the 10th Anniversary of the fall of Saigon. See especially Lance Morrow, 'Viet Nam, "A Bloody Rite of Passage"', pp. 22–31, Kurt Anderson, 'Viet Nam, "A Pinched and Hermetic Land"', p. 39, and George Church, 'Viet Nam, "Lessons From a Lost War"', pp. 41–42.

2. Morrow, 'Vietnam, "A Bloody Rite of Passage"', *Time*, 15 April 1985, p. 22.

3. Those who served have been characterised as a 'wounded generation' (author Robert Muller's term), and those who protested were also alienated. The former ask: 'Where are our leaders? Where are the politicians that (*sic*) sent us to war? . . . I can't see these jokers . . . The total abandonment of these people that (*sic*) sent us to war is unbelievable.' Johnson Wheeler, 'Coming to Grips with Vietnam', *Foreign Affairs*, Spring 1985, p. 750.

4. Allen R. Millett and Peter Maslowski, *For the Common Defense: A Military History of the United States of America*, London, The Free Press, 1984, pp. 542–44.

5. Millett and Maslowski, *For the Common Defense*, p. 549. We do not imply here that aviators always applied air power optimally, or even correctly. We recognise, further, the difficult and never resolved command and control problems that existed among the American air forces and even within the US Air Force. We maintain, however, that the surfeit of air power was much more than enough to overcome all errors of application and command and control arrangements *if* the strategy had been correct. The air strategy, as promulgated by civilians in the Department of Defense, was the fatal flaw.

6. M. J. Armitage and R. A. Mason, *Air Power in the Nuclear Age*, Chicago, University of Illinois Press, 1983, pp. 112–13.

7. For an unsurpassed treatment of the nature of the bureaucratic strategic failure of Vietnam Washington, see Leslie H. Gelb with Richard K. Betts, *The Irony of Vietnam: The System Worked*, Washington, The Brookings Institution, 1979. See also Herbert Y. Schandler, *The Unmaking of a President: Lyndon Johnson and Vietnam*, Princeton, Princeton University Press, 1977, for an in-depth view of the way domestic politics and international relations interacted in Johnson's administration. Another excellent work is Harry G. Summers, Jr., *On Strategy: The Vietnam War in Context*, Carlisle Barracks, Pennsylvania, Army War College, 1983. Summers recognised the flaws in the American strategy and also recognised the failure of the President and Secretary of Defense to employ air power properly. Summers quotes South Vietnamese Secretary of Defense Tran Van Don as arguing the United States would have done well to bring under control the infiltration of North Vietnam because until that was done the war could not be won. But the United States scattered its air effort everywhere in Vietnam and failed to focus for a number of reasons on the North Vietnamese who were the locus of the problem. See Summers, *On Strategy: The Vietnam War in Context*, p. 104. Indeed, the entire book is an indictment of American strategy. See especially p. 80, where Summers argues that we failed to focus on any of the North Vietnamese 'centers of gravity'. Summers argues that the war was most certainly, especially after the mid-1960s, not a counter-insurgency and that the United States should have treated the war from the start as a conventional theatre war.

8. There is a whole body of literature now gathering dust in libraries on successful counterinsurgencies. Twenty years ago the Rand Corporation seriously studied this form of warfare and made major contributions to understanding its nature. Readers can

refer to A. H. Peterson *et al.*, *Symposium on the Role of Airpower in Counterinsurgencies in Unconventional Warfare*, Santa Monica, Rand Corporation, 1964; Idem, *Symposium on Airpower: The Algerian War*, 1963; Idem, *Symposium on Airpower: The Malaysian Emergency*, 1964; Idem, *Symposium on Airpower: The Philippines Huk Campaign*, 1963.

9. David Fromkin and James Chase in 'What *Are* the Lessons of Vietnam?' *Foreign Affairs*, Spring 1985, p. 725., acknowledge that the Joint Chiefs of Staff saw the war more clearly than the 'National Security Council and other civilian bodies'.

10. Robert F. Futrell, *Advisory Years*, Washington, US Government Printing Office, 1983, pp. 195–206.

11. William W. Momyer, *Air Power in Three Wars*, ed. A. J. C. Lavalle and J. C. Gaston, Washington, US Government Printing Office, 1978, p. 13.

12. Ibid.

13. Momyer, *Air Power*, pp. 13–14.

14. Momyer, *Air Power*, p. 14.

15. Momyer, *Air Power*, p. 15.

16. Gelb and Betts, *The Irony of Vietnam*, pp. 101, 114–15; Momyer, *Air Power*, pp. 15–16.

17. Gelb and Betts, *The Irony of Vietnam*, p. 137; Momyer, *Air Power*, p. 17.

18. Gelb and Betts, *The Irony of Vietnam*, pp. 136–37.

19. Paul Warnke, one of McNamara's assistants in the Department of Defense, confessed that McNamara's view of gradual pressure with the bombing was bankrupt because the Department of Defense had 'guessed wrong with respect to what North Vietnamese reaction would be. We anticipated that they would respond like reasonable people.' Gelb and Betts, *The Irony of Vietnam*, p. 139. McNamara and company, in other words, believed that the North Vietnamese would calculate, mechanistically, costs and benefits as did he and therefore be willing to lower demands as the price rose—as if Ho Chi Minh managed his revolution the way McNamara managed the Pentagon.

20. US Department of Defense, *United States—Vietnam Relations 1945-1967, IV.C.7.(a)*, *Volume I, The Air War in North Vietnam*, The Pentagon Papers, Washington, US Government Printing Office, 1971, p. 5. (Hereafter *The Pentagon Papers.*)

21. Gelb and Betts, *The Irony of Vietnam*, p. 136; Momyer, *Airpower*, pp. 18–19.

22. Momyer, *Air Power*, p. 19.

23. *The Pentagon Papers*, IV. C. 7.(a), Vol. 1, p. 1.

24. Momyer, *Airpower*, p. 20.

25. Gelb and Betts, *The Irony of Vietnam*, p. 138. General Momyer resented the proscriptions of attacks on North Vietnam airfields, surface-to-air missiles, and anti-aircraft artillery sites. The costs were terrible. Momyer, *Airpower*, pp. 338–39.

26. Gelb and Betts, *The Irony of Vietnam*, p. 53; Armitage and Mason, *Air Power in the Nuclear Age*, p. 85; *The Pentagon Papers*, IV. C. 7.(a), Vol. I, pp. 1–6. Colonel Harry Summers called McNamara's bombing halt 'fatal flaws' in the strategy. See Summers, *On Strategy*, p. 72.

27. Gelb and Betts, *The Irony of Vietnam*, p. 140.

28. *The Pentagon Papers*, IV. C. 7.(a), Vol. I, pp. 33–39. John T. McNaughton was a lawyer and a newspaper columnist. Unquestionably bright (a Rhodes Scholar), he had been a lawyer and professor for more than a decade before joining the Department of Defense as an attorney and as an Assistant Secretary of Defense in International Security Affairs. Although he had served in the Naval Reserves during the Second World War, there is nothing in his background or writing that indicates he had even scant knowledge of air power. McNaughton was apparently chief among McNamara's advisers counselling scepticism about bombing. He argued continually that bombing in South Vietnam would be more effective than bombing in North Vietnam and by mid-1967 he had become so alarmed by the growing public protest against the war that he counselled President Johnson to rethink the entire premise of the war itself. He argued all along that there was no way the air war against North Vietnam could force Hanoi to abandon its war in the south. The Air Force did agree that at the levels McNaughton and McNamara allowed there was no way. *Who Was Who in America (With World Notables)*, Vol. iv, Chicago, A. N. Marquis Cq., n.d., p. 646; Nelson Lichtenstein (Ed.), *Political Profiles: The Johnson Years*, New York, Facts on File, Inc., In.d., p. 395.

29. *The Pentagon Papers*, IV. C. 7.(a), Vol. I, p. 21.
30. *The Pentagon Papers*, IV. C. 7.(a), Vol. I, pp. 17–19.
31. Momyer, *Air Power*, pp. 22–23.
32. McNamara, as is well known, became increasingly disheartened and left office some months before the end of the Johnson Administration. By the end of his days in office he was condemning the bombing, reciting the comparative figures of so many more tons dropped on Vietnam than all of Germany, Japan and North Korea. In fact, more tons were dropped on Vietnam than in all of the Second World War and Korea combined, and he reiterated 'it is not just that it isn't preventing supplies from getting down the trail, it is destroying the countryside in the south. It is making lasting enemies and still the determined Air Force wants more.' Gelb and Betts, *The Irony of Vietnam*, pp. 169–70.
33. Momyer, *Air Power*, pp. 22–23.
34. Gelb and Betts, *The Irony of Vietnam*, p. 147. In 1966 the Central Intelligence Agency called for a drastically heightened air campaign in North Vietnam to drive Hanoi out of the war. Ibid., pp. 249–50.
35. Gelb and Betts, *The Irony of Vietnam*, pp. 147–48.
36. Carl Berger (Ed.), *The United States Air Force in Southeast Asia*, Washington, US Government Printing Office, 1977, pp. 4–10.
37. Momyer, *Air Power*, pp. 10–11, 20–21; Armitage and Mason, *Air Power in the Nuclear Age*, p. 93; Berger, *Air Force in Southeast Asia*, pp. 11–13.
38. Douglas Pike, 'The Other Side', in *Vietnam as History: Ten Years After the Paris Peace Accords*, ed. Peter Braestrup, Washington, University Press of America, 1984, p. 71.
39. Gelb and Betts, *The Irony of Vietnam*, pp. 118–19; Berger, *Air Force in Southeast Asia*, p. 40.
40. Berger, *Air Force in Southeast Asia*, pp. 40–41.
41. Berger, *Air Force in Southeast Asia*, pp. 47–52.
42. Momyer, *Air Power*, pp. 311–13; Berger, *Air Force in Southeast Asia*, p. 56.
43. Momyer, *Air Power*, p. 313.
44. Berger, *Air Force in Southeast Asia*, p. 56.
45. Berger, *Air Force in Southeast Asia*, p. 176; Momyer, *Air Power in Three Wars*, p. 319.
46. Momyer, *Air Power in Three Wars*, p. 318; Berger, *Air Force in Southeast Asia*, p. 56.
47. Ibid.
48. Ibid.
49. Berger, *Air Force in Southeast Asia*, pp. 52, 56; Armitage and Mason, *Air Power in the Nuclear War*, 97–98; Momyer, *Air Power*, pp. 309–10.
50. Momyer, *Air Power*, pp. 307–08.
51. Momyer, *Air Power*, p. 307.
52. Momyer, *Air Power*, p. 310.
53. Berger, *Air Force in Southeast Asia*, pp. 52–56.
54. Berger, *Air Force in Southeast Asia*, pp. 151–57.
55. Momyer, *Air Power*, p. 310.
56. Bernard C. Nalty, *Air Power and the Fight for Khe Sanh*, Washington, Office of Air Force History, 1973, pp. 28–31, 103–05; Berger, *Air Force in Southeast Asia*, pp. 175–76.
57. Armitage and Mason, *Air Power in the Nuclear Age*, pp. 97–98; Momyer, *Air Power*, pp. 307–09.
58. Momyer, *Air Power*, pp. 310–11.
59. Berger, *Air Force in Southeast Asia*, p. 61.
60. Berger, *Air Force in Southeast Asia*, pp. 61–64.
61. Ibid.
62. Ibid.
63. Pike, 'The Other Side', in *Vietnam as History*, p. 76.
64. Doglione *et al.*, *Airpower and the 1972 Spring Invasion*, USAF Southeast Asia Monograph Series, Washington, US Government Printing Office, 1976, Vol. ii, Monograph 3, p. 4.
65. Doglione *et al.*, *Spring Invasion*, p. 31.

66. Doglione *et al.*, *Spring Invasion*, p. 1; Pike, 'The Other Side', in *Vietnam as History*, p. 76.
67. Doglione *et al.*, *Spring Invasion*, p. 14.
68. Doglione *et al.*, *Spring Invasion*, p. 12.
69. Ibid.
70. Doglione *et al.*, *Spring Invasion*, pp. 26–29.
71. Doglione *et al.*, *Spring Invasion*, p. 29.
72. Doglione *et al.*, *Spring Invasion*, pp. 15–16.
73. Doglione *et al.*, *Spring Invasion*, p. 36; Momyer, *Air Power*, p. 32.
74. Doglione *et al.*, *Spring Invasion*, p. 34.
75. Armitage and Mason, *Air Power in the Nuclear Age*, pp. 87, 98–99.
76. Momyer, *Air Power*, p. 32.
77. Ibid., Pike, 'The Other Side', in *Vietnam as History*, p. 76; Doglione *et al.*, *Spring Invasion*, pp. 4, 46; Momyer, *Air Power*, pp. 32, 328.
78. Doglione *et al.*, *Spring Invasion*, pp. 47–51.
79. Doglione *et al.*, *Spring Invasion*, pp. 51, 53.
80. Doglione *et al.*, *Spring Invasion*, pp. 53–54; Momyer, *Air Power*, pp. 327–28.
81. Doglione *et al.*, *Spring Invasion*, pp. 54–56.
82. Doglione *et al.*, *Spring Invasion*, pp. 56–58.
83. Doglione *et al.*, *Spring Invasion*, p. 58; Momyer, *Air Power*, pp. 328–29.
84. Momyer, *Air Power*, p. 330; Doglione *et al.*, *Spring Invasion*, pp. 78–80.
85. Doglione *et al.*, *Spring Invasion*, pp. 80–81.
86. Doglione *et al.*, *Spring Invasion*, pp. 81–85.
87. Doglione *et al.*, *Spring Invasion*, pp. 85–86.
88. Doglione *et al.*, *Spring Invasion*, pp. 86–91; Momyer, *Air Power*, pp. 330–32.
89. Berger, *Air Force in Southeast Asia*, pp. 182–83.
90. Doglione *et al.*, *Spring Invasion*, pp. 92–98.
91. Doglione *et al.*, *Spring Invasion*, pp. 98–104; Momyer, *Air Power*, pp. 332–33.
92. Doglione *et al.*, *Spring Invasion*, pp. 106–07.
93. See section below on strategy, 'Air Strategy Analyses', and also Armitage and Mason, *Air Power in the Nuclear War*, pp. 99–100; Fromkin and Chase, *Foreign Affairs*, p. 738; and Pike, 'The Other Side', in *Vietnam as History*, p. 76.
94. Doglione *et al.*, *Spring Invasion*, pp. 105–06; Berger, *Air Force in Southeast Asia*, p. 65; Armitage and Mason, *Air Power in the Nuclear Age*, pp. 109–10; and Pike, 'The Other Side', in *Vietnam as History*, p. 76.
95. Berger, *Air Force in Southeast Asia*, p. 167.
96. Armitage and Mason, *Air Power in the Nuclear Age*, p. 88; and Momyer, *Air Power*, pp. 33–34.
97. Berger, *Air Force in Southeast Asia*, p. 166.
98. Momyer, *Air Power*, pp. 33–34; Armitage and Mason, *Air Power in the Nuclear Age*, p. 88; and Pike, 'The Other Side', in *Vietnam as History*, p. 76.
99. James R. McCarthy and George B. Allison, *LINEBACKER II; A View from the Rock*, USAF Southeast Asia Monograph Series, Washington, US Government Printing Office, 1979, Vol. iv, Monograph 8, pp. 139–40, 56.
100. McCarthy and Allison, *LINEBACKER II*, pp. 41–44, 68–70, 6–7.
101. McCarthy and Allison, *LINEBACKER II*, 172.
102. Sir Robert Thompson, 'Rear Bases and Sanctuaries', in *The Lessons of Vietnam*, ed. W. Scott Thompson and Donaldson D. Frizzell, New York, Crane, Russak & Company, 1977, p. 105. Those Americans unfortunate enough to be on the ground in Hanoi saw directly the psychological impact of the raids on the North Vietnamese. They have testified to the dramatic change in the guards and the guard's supervisors. McCarthy and Allison, *LINEBACKER II*, pp. 174–75.
103. Pike, 'The Other Side', in *Vietnam as History*, p. 72.
104. Office of the Assistant Secretary of Defense, Comptroller, *Southeast Asia Statistical Summary*, Washington DC, 1973, Table 350A. Armitage and Mason, *Air Power in the Nuclear War*, pp. 112–13, from slightly different numbers.

Chapter 5

1. Air Chief Marshal Sir Peter Terry, 'Air Power in the European Theatre'. The RAF/University of Birmingham Conference on Air Power, September 1982, reprinted in *Defence,* September 1983.
2. Lorenzini Fox, 'How Much is Not Enough?' *The US Naval War College Review,* 1980.
3. General B. Rogers. Quoted in *Military Technology,* May 1983.
4. Lieutenant Colonel D. J. Alberts, *Deterrence in the 1980s: the Role of Conventional Air Power.* Adelphi Paper No. 193, IISS, London, 1984.
5. General Bernard Rogers, '"Follow-On Forces Attack"; Myths and Realities.' *NATO Review,* December 1984.

Chapter 6

1. *Soviet Military Power,* US Government Printing Office, 1985, pp. 49, 64, 82, 101.
2. *Statement on the Defence Estimates 1985,* HMSO, London, p. 1.
3. A. N. Lapchinskiy, 'The Air Forces in Battle and Operations', Moscow, 1932.
4. General Major M. I. Cherednichenko, 'On Features in the Development of the Military Art in the Postwar Period', *Military-Historical Journal,* No. 6, Moscow, 1970.
5. Lieutenant General P. Bazanov, 'Air Supremacy, *Soviet Military Review,* Vol. 9 (1980) pp. 42–44.
6. A. N. Lapchinskiy, op. cit.
7. General Colonel of Artillery P. Levchenko, 'Air Defence and the Combined Arms Commander'. *Military Herald.* April 1976, pp. 40–44.
8. Generalleutenant D. W. Schwabedissen, *The Russian Air Force in the Eyes of German Commanders,* New York, 1968.
9. Lieutenant Colonel G. Drugoveyko, 'Maneuver is a Fighter's Strength', *Kravnaya Zvezda,* 12 October 1984, p. 2.
10. Colonel General N. Moskvitelev, 'Constant Attention Must be Given to Complex Forms of Tactical Employment', *Air Defence Herald,* May 1984, p. 20.
11. Lieutenant General Yu Gudkov, 'Tactics, A Pilot's Second Weapon', *Naval Collection,* August 1984, pp. 29–34.
12. Ibid.
13. Ibid.
14. Ibid.
15. See, for example, Major General B. A. Vasil'yev, *Long Range, Missile Equipped,* Moscow, 1972.
16. Seminar Report in *Aviation Week and Space Technology,* 16 July 1984.
17. 'Soviet Military Concepts', from *Soviet Military Encyclopedia,* translated USAF, 1978.
18. Colonel A. Musial, 'The Character and Importance of Air Operations in Modern Warfare'. *Polish Air Force and Air Defence Review,* December 1981.
19. *Soviet Military Encyclopedia,* op. cit.
20. Lieutenant Colonel N. Stupner, 'Hold Yourself Strictly Responsible', *Aviation and Cosmonautics,* March 1983.
21. Colonel General P. Kirsanov, 'Enhancing the Training of Aviators', *Equipment and Armaments,* August 1976.
22. Quoted in Asher Lee, *Soviet Air and Rocket Forces.* Weidenfeld and Nicolson, pp. 10–11.
23. Engineer Colonel General V. Skubilin, 'Introducing Modern Control Methods', *Aviation and Cosmonautics,* September 1978, p. 26.
24. 'Air Operations at the Berezina Exercise', *Soviet Military Review,* November 1978, p. 18.
25. Ibid., p. 19.
26. Major W. Michalak, 'Aviation in the Raid Manoeuvre Operations of Ground Forces', *Polish Air Force and Air Defence Review,* February 1982.
27. Ibid.
28. 'Tactical Training of the Air Force Pilot', *Red Star,* 17 August 1983.

Chapter 7

1. For a full translation of this article, see Benjamin S. Lambeth, *Moscow's Lessons from the 1982 Lebanon Air War War*, The Rand Corporation, R-3000-AF, September 1984, pp. 35–46.

2. Colonel Dubrov also wrote the earlier *Aviatsiia i kosmonavtika* series entitled 'How Has Air Combat Changed?'. That series, published in 1978, dealt successively with the search, closing, attack, manoeuvre, and disengagement phases of an air battle. It remains one of the more thorough Soviet discussions of air-to-air theory and practice and established Dubrov as a prominent Soviet spokesman on air combat tactics development. In consonance with well-known Soviet operational practice, it placed heavy stress on the importance of GCI (ground controlled intercept) directives in shaping the contours of the engagement. Full translations may be found in *The Soviet Awareness Red Eagle Reader* (Washington, Directorate of Soviet Affairs, US Air Force Intelligence Service, 1980), pp. 39–79. For a condensation, see *USAF Fighter Weapons Review*, Spring 1981, pp. 23–27.

3. There is good reason to suspect that Soviet pilots routinely dismiss much of what they hear from the propaganda mill. In this regard, Lieutenant Viktor Belenko (the former Soviet Foxbat pilot) recounted having been told once by his superiors at the Armavir flight school that USAF 'Wild Weasel' pilots were willing to fly on SAM suppression missions over North Vietnam only because they were either well-paid mercenaries or under the influence of narcotics. He said he believed neither story and instead felt nothing but admiration for those aircrews. John Barron, *MiG Pilot,* New York, Readers Digest Press, 1980, p. 157.

4. For a thorough, if sympathetic, description of the Israeli rationale for this operation, see Avner Yaniv and Robert J. Lieber, 'Personal Whim or Strategic Imperative? The Israeli Invasion of Lebanon', *International Security*, Fall 1983, pp. 117–42. A more critical account is offered in Amos Perlmutter, 'Begin's Rhetoric and Sharon's Tactics', *Foreign Affairs*, Fall 1982, pp. 67–83.

5. See John Yunna, 'Those SAM Missiles in Lebanon–Why Israel Would Be Willing To Risk a War To Get Them Out', *Christian Science Monitor*, 15 May 1981.

6. The IAF had been poised on 30 April to attack the three Syrian SA-6 batteries that were then in Lebanon, but was forced to postpone the mission three times in 4 hours because of weather complications. Prime Minister Begin later noted that the strike would have occurred the following day had the United States not appealed for a delay. See David K. Shipler, 'Begin Says Syrians Have Increased Missiles in Lebanon and on Border', *New York Times*, 12 May 1981.

7. Short of destroying the missiles, the IAF continued to monitor their activity through overflights by Mastiff and Firebee drones, occasionally drawing Syrian fire. It also conducted low-level supersonic fighter passes over the emplacements in an effort to keep pressure on the Syrians. Both activities provided valuable target data for IAF mission planners. See 'Israeli Drones Keep an Electronic Eye on the Arabs', *New York Times*, 23 May 1981, and 'Syria Vows to Maintain SAM Sites', *New York Times*, 31 May 1981.

8. Mismatch in the Sky, *Newsweek*, 21 June 1982.

9. Drew Middleton, 'Soviet Arms Come in Second in Lebanon', *New York Times*, 19 September 1982.

10. 'Washington Roundup: Mideast Air Battle', *Aviation Week and Space Technology*, 28 June 1982.

11. This reconstruction draws from numerous second-hand journalistic accounts. Among the more interesting reports on IAF tactics employed in the SAM strike are Clarence A. Robinson, Jr., 'Surveillance Integration Pivotal in Israeli Successes', *Aviation Week and Space Technology*, 5 July 1982, pp. 16–17, and Russell Warren Howe, 'DoD Opts for Untested U.S. Drone', *Washington Times*, 28 September 1982. See also Richard Homan, 'Israel Inflicts Heavy Air, Missile Losses on Syria', *Washington Post*, 10 June 1982; Michael Getler, 'Superior Weapons, Pilots, Tactics Seen as Key to Israeli Victories', *Washington Post*, 11 June 1982; David B. Ottaway, 'Israel Said to Master New Technology to Trick and Destroy Soviet-Made Missiles', *Washington Post*, 14 June 1982; Charles Mohr, 'New Wars Show the Powers of Military Basics', *New York*

Times, 18 June 1982; and Craig Oliphant, 'The Performance of Soviet Weapons in Lebanon', *Radio Liberty Research,* RL 68/83, 7 February 1983.

12. The story continues to be muddled on this point. Some versions have the IAF using its slow-flying Scout and Mastiff reconnaissance drones in this capacity. Others indicate that the Israelis used Samson and Delilah drones, the former air-launched from F-4s and the latter ground-launched (see Middleton, op. cit.). Syrian SA-6 operators would have been more likely to react to this second set of systems, since they presumably would more closely approximate the speed and radar signature of fighters than the Scout and Mastiff. It is possible, however, that all four types of drones played a part in the attack—the first two to induce the Syrians to activate their tracking radars (thus providing IAF antiradiation missiles with emitting targets to guide on) and the other two to add to the confusion factor and perhaps goad the Syrians into firing.

13. Little is known about this weapon. Some accounts describe it as a ground-launched antiradiation missile. Others depict it as a long-range artillery shell with terminally homing submunitions. In all events, it appears to have played a prominent role in the operation (though by no means the near-exclusive one attributed to it by Colonel Dubrov). See Robinson, op. cit., p. 16. See also the interview with IDF Chief of Staff Lieutenant General Rafael Eitan, 'We Learned Both Tactical and Technical Lessons in Lebanon', *Military Electronics/Countermeasures,* February 1983, p. 100. General Eitan confirmed that 'heavy aerial bombardment' was employed in the attack, but added that 'our forces were advancing at such speed that within a short period of time the battery sites were not only under ground-force artillery range but within the range of our family of computer-guided surface-to-surface missiles'.

14. Paul S. Cutter, 'ELTA Plays a Decisive Role in the EOB Scenario', *Military Electronics/Countermeasures,* January 1983, pp. 135–37.

15. By one account, the IAF additionally destroyed several SAM sites within Syria near the Lebanese border, presumably through standoff attacks. (The Israelis have publicly maintained that their pilots never penetrated Syrian airspace proper.) See Anthony H. Cordesman, 'The Sixth Arab-Israeli Conflict: Military Lessons for American Defense Planning', *Armed Forces Journal International,* August 1982, p. 30.

16. Robinson, op. cit., p. 16.

17. John V. Cignatta, 'A US Pilot Looks at the Order of Battle, Beka'a Valley Operations', *Military Electronics/Countermeasures,* February 1983, pp. 107–108.

18. Getler, op. cit.

19. Homan, op. cit.

20. George C. Wilson, 'Israel Proves U.S. Arms Effective, General Says', *Washington Post,* 17 June 1982.

21. In General Eitan's words, the Syrian MiG pilots 'were very irrational in their attack on our Air Force, literally bashing their heads against a wall. Anyone who crossed an imaginary line in the direction of our forces was destroyed . . . The imaginary line was actually the range of the emplaced missile batteries in Syria proper.' Interview in *Military Electronics/Countermeasures,* February 1983, p. 101.

22. Cignatta, op. cit.

23. Quoted in Vincent J. Schodolski, 'Soviet Arms Replacing Syrian War Losses', *Chicago Tribune,* 23 March 1983.

24. 'Beka'a Valley Combat', *Flight International,* 16 October 1982, p. 1109.

25. 'Foxhound Gives Soviets First Look, First Fire Against F-15', *Aerospace Daily,* 5 August 1982, pp. 193–94. See also 'U.S. Arms Used in Lebanon War Outstrip Soviets', *Wall Street Journal,* 5 August 1982.

26. The IAF commander at the time, Major General David Ivry, declined to participate in press interviews after the Beka'a Valley offensive because of his concern, as reported by a respected Israeli defence journalist, that his remarks might inadvertently be used to feed unwarranted Israeli 'self-aggrandisement . . . spilling over into euphoria'. Ze'ev Schiff, 'The Danger of Mistaken Conclusions', *Ha'aretz* (Tel Aviv), 27 August 1983. Note also the following comment by an anonymous IAF officer: 'We should be very careful in drawing lessons from this very limited, restricted war. . . . We flew within a space of 15–30 miles, we didn't cross the Syrian border. We didn't attack their military bases or other strategic targets.' 'Beka'a Valley Combat', op. cit.

27. Remarks by Major General Perry M. Smith, USAF, cited in 'Menachem Begin's America', *Foreign Report*, 23 September, 1982.
28. Robinson, op. cit.
29. For a well-researched summary of Israeli combat accomplishments during this period, see Cynthia A. Roberts, 'Soviet Arms Transfer Policy and the Decision to Upgrade Syrian Air Defenses', *Survival*, July-August 1983, pp. 154–64.
30. The former Chief of Staff, Lieutenant General Eitan, has confirmed at least some of the key points on Israeli weapons and tactics employed. These include employment of RPVs for real-time target surveillance and the use of a 20-km range missile, described as a cluster bomb with '1200 separate explosive units, which proved devastating to the enemy, especially against radar emplacements and field artillery'. 'We Learned Both Tactical and Technical Lessons in Lebanon', op. cit., p. 96.
31. Ernest Conine, 'Red Faces in the Kremlin: Soviet Arms Failures in Lebanon Could Lead to Danger', *Los Angeles Times*, 4 October, 1982.
32. After much Israeli resistance, this finally occurred in the spring of 1983. See Bernard Gwertzman, 'Israelis to Share Lessons of War with Pentagon', *New York Times*, 22 March, 1983.
33. Roberts, op. cit., p. 156. See also James F. Clarity, 'Moscow Replacing Syrians' Materie', *New York Times*, 24 October 1982.
34. William Branigin, 'Soviet General Said to Assess Syrian Losses', *Washington Post*, 15 June 1982; John F. Burns, 'Moscow Stresses Worry over Military Actions Close to Its Border', *New York Times*, 15 June 1982.
35. Drew Middleton, 'Mideast War: Things Soviets Learned in '82', *New York Times*, 2 January 1983.
36. Thomas L. Friedman, 'Syrian Army Said to Be Stronger Than Ever, Thanks to Soviets', *New York Times*, 21 March 1983, and 'Syria and Russia: For Russians Only,' *The Economist*, 7 May 1983. For detailed discussion, see Roberts, op. cit. An Israeli F-4 was downed by one of the SA-8s introduced into the Beka'a Valley in August 1982, during a raid sent out to eliminate the new Syrian missile units '(Soviets Order SA-8s into Action in Beka'a after Israeli Successes', *Aviation Week and Space Technology*, 9 August 1982). Another F-4 was promptly dispatched to destroy the wreckage of the downed aircraft to prevent its ECM equipment from falling into Soviet hands. Unconfirmed reports later indicated that between 11 and 200 Soviet technicians who had been combing the wreckage were killed in the Israeli attack (see Frank Greve, 'U.S. Air Strikes Against Syria Could Hit Soviet Advisors', *Philadelphia Inquirer*, 7 December 1983, and '200 Soviets Died in Israeli Raid, Magazine Says', *Philadelphia Enquirer*, 14 December 1983). Needless to say, none of this was mentioned by the Soviet domestic media or acknowledged by Soviet foreign propaganda.
37. 'Israelis Reporting a Soviet Buildup', *New York Times*, 29 April 1983. According to this account, both SA-5 sites are off limits to Syrians and have direct communications links to Moscow. For further discussion, see also R. W. Apple, Jr., 'Soviet Puts New Missiles in Place at Russian Bases in Western Syria', *New York Times*, 16 May 1983.
38. 'Russia and the Arabs: Where Were You?' *The Economist*, 3 July 1982, p. 29. See also Galia Golan, 'The Soviet Union and the Israeli Action in Lebanon', *International Affairs* (London), Winter 1982–83, p. 8.
39. Serge Schumann, 'Moscow Defends Quality of Arms It Sells to Arabs', *New York Times*, 2 July 1982. See also A. Vlasov, 'Strategic Allies' Aggression', *Izvestiia*, 20 June 1982, for an earlier Soviet reaction to the poor showing of Soviet weaponry during the Beka'a Valley bouts.
40. Quoted in Dusko Doder, 'Moscow Denies that Israelis Proved Superiority of U.S. Weapons', *Washington Post*, 4 July 1982.
41. Radio Moscow domestic service, 11 June 1982.
42. *Krasnaia zvezda*, 18 July 1982.
43. TASS communique (in English), 20 July 1982. As a measure of the depth of Soviet sensitivity on this score, the same argument was replayed a year and a half later in the Soviet military's English-language magazine intended for foreign consumption. After debunking Israel's 'fantasies' concerning the performance of its American equipment against Soviet products flown by the Syrian Air Force, the article proceeded to accent

the technical virtues of the MiG series, even going so far as to claim that the United States 'scrupulously copied the MiG-21's best features in designing the F-15 fighter'. Lest the message that mattered be forgotten, however, it also concluded that 'to fully use these capabilities, those who exploit and maintain this equipment must possess comprehensive and deep knowledge. The aircraft may be a formidable and reliable weapon *only* in the hands of well-trained pilots' (emphasis added). Colonel N. Yelshin, 'Simple and Reliable MiGs', *Soviet Military Review*, No. 1, January 1984, pp. 26–28.

44. 'Airborne Fighters on the Alert: Dispatch from Unit X of the Syrian Air Force', *Krasnaia zvezda*, 28 August 1982; 'In the Beka'a Valley', *Krasnaia zvezda*, 31 August 1982; and 'First-Time Hit', *Krasnaia zvezda*, 30 September 1982. The last of these articles recapitulates a Syrian newspaper report entitled 'Our Weapons Are Good and Our Fighters Are Capable of Using Them with the Utmost Efficiency'. In it, Colonel Kashuba notes that Syria's 'Soviet antiaircraft missiles ... proved their effectiveness whenever used ... [and] showed once again that Israeli pilots are by no means as "invincible" as Zionist propaganda makes out'.

45. Kashuba, 28 August 1982, op. cit.

46. Indeed, it would not be surprising if the Soviet armed forces were rife with private jokes about Syria's pathetic conduct during the Beka'a Valley campaign. Following Israel's victory in the October 1973 war, it was common to hear sarcastic remarks attributed to the Soviets about a new Egyptian tank requirement for back-up lights and how the Egyptian Defence Minister had lamented during a postmortem in the Kremlin that he had studiously followed all the lessons of Soviet military doctrine from World War II ... and was still waiting for the 'long Russian winter' to set in over Suez. After the Lebanon war, similar stories began to circulate about how the Syrian Air Force maintained a Departure Control but no Approach Control and how a Syrian general, upon being told by his Soviet patrons that he already had the best Soviet surface-to-air missiles, replied that what he really needed was some good surface-to-*aircraft* missiles!

47. Responding to a question on a related matter back in the mid-1970s, a former Soviet pilot told me that he had heard through the grapevine about a study having been done on air combat events during the Vietnam War, but that any such study would have been far too highly classified to be shared with the likes of him and his contemporaries.

48. According to a writer with extensive recent exposure to the USAFE community, 'Soviet doctrine requires that most missions be flown under positive ground control, with the added provision that if contact with the ground controller is lost, the mission is to be aborted.' He also notes that 'the USAF spends much more time and money educating fighter pilots than the Russians do' and that the 'highly realistic training regimen introduced to American pilots after Vietnam War has no equal in the East'. Michael Skinner, *USAFE: A Primer of Modern Air Combat in Europe*, Novato, Calif.; Presidio Press, 1983, p. 122.

49. Both aircraft are reportedly optimized for air-to-air combat and feature exceptional acceleration and agility, medium-range missiles with active terminal guidance, and pulse Doppler fire-control systems with extended-range, track-while-scan radars. See Clarence A. Robinson, Jr., 'Soviets Deoplying New Fighters', *Aviation Week and Space Technology*, 28 November 1983, pp. 18–20.

50. See Phillip A. Peterson and John G. Hines, 'The Conventional Offensive in Soviet Theater Strategy', *Orbis*, Fall 1983, p. 708.

51. A notable exception was Operation Bolo, an offensive MiG sweep into the Hanoi-Haiphong area led by Colonel Robin Olds in January 1967. This successful ruse involved a large number of F-4s using the formations, frequencies, and call signs of a typical F-105 strike package to lure the enemy into battle. It was of a piece with the creative imagination that has routinely accounted for the IAF's tactical superiority in air warfare. For details, see *Air War–Vietnam*, New York, Bobbs-Merrill, 1978, pp. 241–47, and Mike Spick, *Fighter Pilot Tactics: The Techniques of Daylight Air Combat*, New York, Stein and Day, 1983, pp. 151–52.

52. It is common to hear assertions in the West that the Soviet fighter force is 'heavily dependent on GCI'. This formulation is correct as far as it goes, but it confuses more than it describes. Soviet Air Force literature on operational training makes it quite clear that the function of the command post '(KP)' includes not only GCI vectoring but

overall mission management as well. In other words, the *rukovoditel' poletov* (or 'supervisor of flying)' who sits in the command post does much of the thinking and decision-making that would routinely take place in the cockpit in USAF and Navy tactical air practice.

53. This is not to suggest that IAF fighter formations, especially those heavily wrapped up in air combat engagements, were not subject to direction as necessary from higher authorities who may have had a better grasp of the tactical situation. It is, however, to take issue with Dubrov's intimation that offensive fighter sweeps would have been ineffective without supporting assets like the E-2C. More likely, IAF flight commanders would simply have altered their tactics to compensate for their increased autonomy (and hence exposure) in such a case.

54. For a contrary view, see Captain Rana J. Pennington, USAF, 'Closing the Tactics Gap', *Air Force Magazine*, March 1984, pp. 83–88.

55. In the words of former USAF Chief of Staff General Lew Allen, 'the Soviets are fairly predictable, doctrinaire, very determined in their approach to things, very strong in a hierarchical sense of how to do things, with less initiative given to people ... One of the advantages we seek to exploit is that they're a fairly predictable force.' Interview in *Armed Forces Journal International*, February 1979, p. 28.

56. For example, a Soviet article in 1976 noted how 'the first launchings of missiles from maximum range can destroy the enemy even before he detects the interception'. Colonel A. Krasnov, 'Forestalling by Maneuver and Fire', *Krasnaia zvezda*, 27 June 1976.

57. Beyond that, if the attacker has a front-aspect capability and the defender knows this and lacks a comparable weapon, the attacker can make the defender predictable. In the Lebanese case, according to one report, 'some Syrian pilots refrained from engaging in dogfights and simply ejected the moment they knew that the Israelis had spotted them' (Roberts, op. cit., p. 163). This hardly squares with the unperturbed view of the all-aspect threat presented by Dubrov.

58. Barron, op. cit., p. 189.

59. According to a rare first-hand account of this engagement, the Soviet pilots appeared to panic and break up in complete disorder once the first two MiGs were shot down. In the words of one of the Israeli pilots who participated in that encounter, the Soviets flew into combat 'like a bull after a red flag. As though they were knocking their heads against a wall. They were like ripe fruit waiting to be picked.' Quoted in Ze'ev Schiff, *A History of the Israeli Army, 1870–1974*, San Franscisco, Straight Arrow Books, 1974, p. 200. It goes without saying that the Soviets have never acknowledged this episode. A former Soviet pilot who defected some years later told me that he had never heard of the incident.

60. Alvin Z. Rubinstein, *Red Star on the Nile*, Princeton University Press, 1977 p. 125.

61. According to a Defense Department report, 'the Soviets have recently made significant changes in their air combat tactics and training programs. Pilot independence and initiative are now stressed....' *Soviet Military Power*, Washington, U.S. Government Printing Office, 1983 p. 43. Although we have abundant reason to be concerned about technical trends in Soviet fighter weapons development, the combined record of Soviet writings on pilot training, the Syrian debacle over Lebanon, and Soviet operational conduct leading up to the downing of Korean Airlines Flight 007 suggest that this assertion is considerably overdrawn.

62. A former USAF Aggressor Squadron commander, well acquainted with enemy weapons and tactics, has put forward what, for me, is the last word on Soviet air combat prowess until available evidence clearly points the other way: 'Exactly how good is the enemy? Is he a ten-foot giant? Not exactly. In fact, without exaggerating, one could place him in the mediocre to poor category when it comes to air combat capability. Certainly his equipment has not improved at nearly the rate ours has.... Most important, however, Soviet training is so inferior to ours that this could well be the deciding factor in the outcome of the next conflict.' Lieutenant Colonel Mike Press, 'Aggressor Reflections'. *USAF Fighter Weapons Review*, Summer 1981, p. 4.

63. By all indications, the Soviets routinely export their operational style along with their arms transfers to client states. One Western observer noted after the Lebanon War how the Syrians, despite their possession of modern Soviet Weapons, were apparently

hampered by the 'highly centralized and unimaginative Soviet tactics that accompany that equipment'. Friedman, op. cit. A similar view was expressed by the former technical editor of the IAF's magazine, *Bita' on Chel Ha'avir:* 'Soviet doctrine calls for wave assaults by fighters to substitute for the denial of airspace to the enemy by missiles.... The Syrians sent their air force up by the book, maintaining some 100 fighters in the air in an attempt to frustrate Israeli air strikes.... Their tactics and operational procedures were very close to those of Soviet Frontal Aviation' Yosef Bodansky, 'In the Wake of Lebanon: The Soviet Union in the Middle East', Washington, Jewish Institute for National Security Affairs, September 1982. pp. 1–2.

64. Occasional glimpses into Soviet operational practice can be found through a careful study of the sort of things Soviet pilots and commanders routinely complain about. For example, in commenting on the rigidities of Soviet tactical training, one Soviet pilot some years ago pointed out that while 'it is all very well that GCI operators should assist us fighter pilots, ... one should not rely on their support for everything'. Captain A. Potemkin, 'Respond to the Situation,' *Aviatsiia i kosmonavtika*, No. 12, December 1975, p. 15. Senior Soviet officers also periodically give vent to such frustration. The Soviet air commander for the North Caucasus Military District, in criticising an exercise failure that stemmed from blind pursuit of rote procedures and an incapacity for improvising, faulted his pilots for having 'simply not thought out the situation. How can someone go into real combat', he lamented, 'without the necessary skills?' Lieutenant General A. Pavlov, 'The Inexhaustible Reserve', *Krasnaia zvezda*, 4 August 1976. The best evidence, however, suggests that despite such expressions of disaffection, the problems that they address only change slowly when they change at all.

65. It has been publicly reported that the IAF maintained a 100 per cent mission-ready rate for its F-15s and F-16s throughout the Beka'a Valley fighting ('U.S. Arms Used in Lebanon Outstrip Soviets', op cit.). This performance record drove a stake through the heart of the argument, most vocally propounded by James Fallows, *National Defense*, New York, Random House, 1981, that there is an inverse correlation between the sophistication and operability of modern fighter aircraft. But the qualification about adequate support remains critical in explaining the IAF's success on this count.

66. Senior IDF commanders would probably agree with this judgement. As one indication, when asked what Israel learned from Syria's use of the MiG-25 in Lebanon, Lieutenant General Eitan replied: 'Answering that question is difficult, because the Syrians don't know how to fly or operate the MiG-25. If we could have been sitting in a MiG-25, nobody could have touched us 'We Learned Both Tactical and Technical Lessons in Lebanon', op. cit., p. 102). Although Israeli planners deeply value the advantages provided by their American equipment and are determined to maintain as sophisticated a force as they can afford, emphasis on the primacy of the human variable remains a core premise of their military doctrine. Their attitude on this score is perhaps best captured in the following remark made some years ago by former IAF commander Ezer Weizman: 'The human factor will decide the fate of war, of all wars. Not the Mirage, nor any other plane, and not the screwdriver, or the wrench or radar or missiles or all the newest technology and electronic innovations. Men—and not just men of action, but men of thought. Men for whom the expression "By ruses shall ye make war" is a philosophy of life, not just the object of lip service.' *On Eagle's Wings*, New York, Macmillan Publishing Company, 1976, p. 178.

67. Reinforcement for this conclusion can be found in Moscow's approach toward strengthening Syria's combat arms in response to their battlefield experiences gained in Lebanon. This effort has featured numerous hardware improvements (especially in the realm of electronic warfare) but has entailed virtually no changes in Syrian training or force employment doctrine. See Anthony H. Cordesman, 'Syrian-Israeli C3I: The West's Third Front?' *Armed Forces Journal International*, March 1984, pp. 87–90.

68. There is a tendency in the West to regard this regimented Soviet approach to air combat as a significant operational deficiency. For some circumstances, that may be a valid assessment. Yet the Soviets may not see matters that way. Two senior RAF officers, M. J. Armitage and R. A. Mason, have cautioned that the Soviet Air Force appears to regard centralized command and control not as a potential weakness which would induce rigidity or reduce local initiative, but as a means of deriving the greatest possible

flexibility to concentrate forces over great distances whenever it should be required.' *Air Power in the Nuclear Age*, Chicago, University of Illinois Press, 1983, p. 176.

69. Major General Jasper A. Welch, Jr., USAF (Ret.), 'The Role of Vulnerability Analysis in Military Planning for Deterrence and Defense of Invasion Threats to NATO' (unpublished paper, June 1976).

Chapter 8

1. In a lecture to the RUSI on 23 May 1984, General Sir Nigel Bagnall, Commander of NATO's Northern Army Group (NORTHAG), showed that the lessons are valid today. 'I wish to stress that there is no such thing as a NORTHAG concept of operations in isolation. There can only be a joint Land/Air battle. ... To my mind, the only way one can develop a truly integrated Land/Air battle is to have a concept of operations, or design for battle, for the army group which the air forces have agreed and use as a basis for their own planning and allocation of scarce resources.' Quoted in *RUSI Journal*, September 1984, p. 59.

2. FM 100-5, Operations. Washington DC, Department of the Army, 20 August 1982.

3. For a good description of the main points from FM 100-5 see Robert A. Gessert. 'The Air-Land Battle and NATO's New Doctrinal Debate'. *RUSI Journal*, June 1984, pp. 53–60.

4. A comprehensive review of all aspects of the gathering of intelligence can be obtained from William V. Kennedy, *The Intelligence War*, Salamander, London, 1983.

5. In calculating the cycle time, the pre-flight preparation, tasking and aircraft preparation time must be taken into account. The mission time must include start-up, taxi and recovery times as well as the flight time en route with evasion of enemy defences. To all of this must be added the image processing and analysis with crew debrief time. This inevitably leads to a significant delay from original tasking to the time that the offensive operation can be mounted.

6. Air Chief Marshal Sir Peter Terry as DSACEUR speaking at the 1982 conference on The Future of Air Power at Birmingham University said: 'By far the most important of the tactical trends is a growing awareness of the need for better, faster and more integrated tactical intelligence of both the land and air situations, to enable better and more responsive command control to be exercised over all our forces.' Air Power in the European Theatre'. *Defence*, January 1983, p. 9.

7. Such a possibility is explored in Frank Barnaby, *Future War*, Michael Joseph, London, 1984, pp. 72–82.

8. For the 2ATAF/NORTHAG concept of operations, Air Marshal Sir Patrick Hine has said: 'Although CAS can still be very effective, it is usually more profitable to use air power in the BAI role against concentrated target groups, leaving the land forces with their organic weapons to deal with the enemy in contact'. *RUSI Journal*, September 1984, p. 66.

9. Speaking at the 1982 Future of Air Power conference, Mr Peter Earthy of Hunting Engineering Ltd said: 'Ideally, a future weapon system should be capable of multiple target kills per weapon, preferable launched to give some stand-off range, but certainly without the need to vector directly over the target. A good measure of effectiveness would be to attack and deal with some 10 targets per weapon launched.' Unpublished script of lecture delivered on 29 September 1982.

10. See, for example, Professor Neville Brown. 'Air Power in Central Europe', *World Today*, October 1983, pp. 378–84.

11. Detailed proposals appear in a paper by Donald R. Cotter in *Strengthening Conventional Deterrence in Europe*, Macmillan, London, 1983, pp. 209–53.

12. T. Garden. 'Strengthening Conventional Deterrence: Bright Idea or Dangerous Illusion?', *RUSI Journal*, September 1984, pp. 32–37.

13. In the decade from 1973–83, the Soviet Union has increased its number of helicopter gunships from 100 to 1475, and its cargo helicopters—which can be armed—from 1,100 to 2,550. John M Collins, *US/Soviet Military Balance*, Library of Congress, 27 August 1984.

14. John Clements would go further: 'Indeed, it can be argued that the main contribution of any air defence system is the emotional stress that the knowledge of its existence causes to aircrew.' 'Air Defence Mythology', in *RUSI Journal*, September 1982, p. 31.

15. Ranges of typical air defence guns are given at 2,500 metres for the Soviet ZSU 23/4, and 1,500 metres for the US Vulcan M-163. (John M. Collins, *US/Soviet Military Balance*, Library of Congress, 27 August 1984.

16. For a comprehensive analysis of the identification problem, and some pointers to possible solutions, see P. F. J. Burton, 'The Identification Problem', in *RUSI Journal*, December 1983.

17. Developments in Soviet military transport are deduced from data in Collins, *US/Soviet Military Balance*, and *Soviet Military Power 1985*, US Department of Defense.

18. The detailed considerations for and against dual-capable aircraft systems are well covered in J. Michael Legge, *Theater Nuclear Weapons and the NATO Strategy of Flexible Response*, RAND, April 1983, pp. 56–76. He concludes that but for the political climate, new land-based mobile nuclear missiles should be acquired to free more dual-capable aircraft for conventional operations. But adds that because of their flexibility, particularly against mobile targets, some aircraft would be needed for a nuclear role (p. 74).

19. See, for example, 'The Falklands Campaign: The Lessons', Cmnd. 8758, HMSO, London, 1982, para. 243.

Chapter 9

1. Antonio O. Ciampi, 'Helicopter Carrier for Italian Navy', *Navy International*, 1983.

2. Captain J. E. Moore, 'The Soviet Union and Aircraft Carriers', RN, *Navy International*, January 1980.

3. John Jordan, '*Novorossiysk—the New Soviet Carrier*', *Defence*, March 1984.

4. John D. Gresham, 'Their Sea Based Fighter', *Proceedings of the USNI*, February 1985.

5. 'Revealed: Flanker on Soviet CVN', *Jane's Defence Weekly*, 28 June 1985.

6. Dr Norman Friedman, 'Real Time Ocean Surveillance', *Military Technology*, September 1984.

Chapter 10

1. From all causes, including accidents, but only those that occurred on operations; the figure includes air and ground accidents in the United Kingdom. Middlebrook and Everitt, Viking Press, *The Bomber Command War Diaries*, p. 707. See also figures quoted by John Terraine in *The Right of the Line*, Hodder & Stoughton, 1985, p. 682.

2. Air Chief Marshal Sir Edgar Ludlow-Hewett, C-in-C Bomber Command, could say in a report on the state of his command in 1939: 'I am convinced that the idea that we shall be able to fight the war with mass-produced pilots and crews as we did in the last war is fallacious.' Quoted in Terraine, *The Right of the Line*, p. 86.

3. It is a striking fact that the number of aircrew losses in Bomber Command exceeded the officer fatalities of the whole British Empire in the First World War (38,834). Terraine, op. cit.

4. Trenchard, 'Air Power and National Security', August 1946.

5. See Armitage and Mason, *Air Power in the Nuclear Age*, University of Illinois Press, 1983, for an account of this and other relevant campaigns.

6. Defence White Paper, Cmnd. 124, HMSO, April 1957.

7. W. W. Momyer, *Air Power in Three Wars*, p. 127.

8. In 1967 the rate had been one aircraft destroyed for each fifity-five missiles fired. Momyer, op. cit.

9. Armitage and Mason, op. cit.

10. It is an indication of the striking technological advance represented by this system that it is widely referred to as the Cruise Missile, when there had of course been very many other less sophisticated types.

11. For example, there was at this time a lively public debate about the cost of the MRCA, later the Tornado aircraft.
12. Figures from Stats Form 603, courtesy of the Air Historical Branch, Ministry of Defence.
13. Figures supplied by the Air Historical Branch.
14. By Air Commodore Thomson, submitted as his Thesis at the Royal College of Defence Studies, 1984.
15. Apart from the nations of NATO and the Warsaw Pact, there are some twelve air forces with around a hundred reasonably modern combat aircraft, nine with between one and two hundred and eight with more than five hundred.
16. Armitage and Mason, op. cit., p. 104.
17. In other words, a lateral flexibility across many potential theatres of operations, as opposed to flexibility in depth of penetration to enemy targets.

About the Authors

Air Vice Marshal R. A. Mason, CBE, MA, RAF, is Air Secretary and Director General of Personnel for the Royal Air Force which he joined after reading history at St Andrews University. He was awarded an MA with Distinction in War Studies at King's College, London in 1967 and since then, in association with his RAF duties, he has written and lectured internationally on defence matters with particular reference to air power and the Soviet Air Forces. Previous publications include *Air Power in the Next Generation* (ed.), *Readings in Air Power*, *Air Power in the Nuclear Age* (with M. J. Armitage), *The Royal Air Force Today and Tomorrow* and *British Air Power in the 1980s*. His *Air Power and Technology* will be published by Brasseys, and *The Soviet Air Forces* by Janes later in 1986.

David MacIsaac (Lieutenant Colonel, USAF, Ret.) was born in Boston, Massachusetts, and holds Degrees in History from Trinity College (Hartford, Conn.), Yale University, and Duke University. He has taught military history and strategy at the US Air Force Academy, the US Naval War College, and US Air War College. During 1978–79 he was a Fellow of the Woodrow Wilson International Center for Scholars at the Smithsonian Institution in Washington. He is the author of *Strategic Bombing in World War II: The Story of the US Strategic Bombing Survey*, New York and London, Garland, 1976, and most recently "Voices from The Central Blue: The Air Power Theorists", in Peter Paret (Ed.), *Makers of Modern Strategy from Machiavelli to the Nuclear Age*, Princeton University Press, 1986. Shortly after writing this article, he was appointed Associate Director for Research at the USAF Air University's Air Power Research Institute in Montgomery, Alabama.

Colonel Alan Gropman, USAF, is the Deputy Director of US Air Force Plans for Planning Integration. He joined the USAF after graduating from Boston University AB (cum laude). He subsequently received his MA and PhD from Tufts University. He has held senior appointments on the Faculty of the National War College in Washington and the US Air Force Academy and has for many years been associated with long-term planning in the Pentagon. He has been awarded the Distinguished Flying Cross and eight other decorations. He is the author of two books: *The Air Force Integrates 1945–1964* and *Airpower and the Airlift Evacuation of Kham Duc*.

Colonel Gropman is a regular contributor to professional journals and lectures widely on defence matters in the United States.

Air Commodore P. D. L. Gover, AFC, BSc, RAF, Commandant of the Aircraft and Armament Experimental Establishment, was commissioned into the RAF in 1960 after taking an Honours Degree in Physics at Reading University. On completion of pilot training his first tour was as an instructor on Jet Provost aircraft. Subsequent flying tours were associated exclusively with fighter aircraft including Hunters in the Fighter Reconnaissance role, command of a Phantom Reconnaissance and Attack squadron and Station Commander of an Air Defence base. Staff appointments have included tours in HQ 2ATAF, Military Assistant to the Chief of the Defence Staff, and Deputy Director Air Plans responsible for the size and shape of the RAF. Before his present appointment Air Commodore Gover attended the Royal College of Defence Studies.

Air Chief Marshal Sir Michael Knight was, until recently, the senior logistics officer in the RAF. However, his background has been almost exclusively in the front line, where he has experience of operational roles throughout the world. His command appointments have included RAF Laarbruch in Germany, and No. 1 Group. He served as Military Assistant to successive Chairmen of NATO's Military Committee, and also as Deputy Chief of Staff for Operations and Intelligence at HQ UKAIR. He is now the United Kingdom Military Representative to NATO. The Air Marshal is a Fellow of the Royal Aeronautical Society and a member of the Council of the Royal United Services Institute for Defence Studies.

Benjamin S. Lambeth is a Senior Staff member of the Rand Corporation, Santa Monica, California. He has a Doctorate in Government from Harvard University, specialises in Soviet military affairs and tactical air warfare issues, and has flown over twenty different types of fighter aircraft with the US Air Force, Air National Guard, Air Force Reserve, US Navy, and Canadian Forces.

Group Captain Timothy Garden is a serving officer who currently commands Royal Air Force Odiham operating Chinook and Puma helicopters. A graduate of both Oxford and Cambridge universities, his Service career has included a tour on strike Canberras, flying instructional duties, command of a Vulcan Squadron, the Ministry of Defence, and he was recently Director of Defence Studies for the RAF. He writes on air power, defence and nuclear issues, lectures internationally, and is a Council Member of the Royal United Services Institute.

Group Captain Alan Hicks joined the RAF in 1957 and initially flew Shackleton aircraft in the anti-submarine and internal security roles. In early 1965 he was posted to Northern Ireland, and later served during the Indonesian Confrontation. After a period of teaching at the College of Air Warfare—specialising in radar systems and electronic warfare—he flew Nimrod aircraft in the Mediterranean and from the United Kingdom. In 1978 he completed a Fellowship at Cambridge University and joined the Directing Staff at the RAF Staff College. Since 1980 he has served with the Central Tactics Trials Organisation, HQ Northern Maritime Region and the Joint Maritime Operational Training Staff. He is now Assistant Director of Studies (Air) in the Central Defence Concepts Staff.

Air Chief Marshal Sir Michael Armitage joined the Royal Air Force as a Halton Apprentice in 1947 and was commissioned as a pilot in 1953. His career has included a wide variety of flying, command, staff and academic appointments in the United Kingdom and overseas. Most recently he spent four years in Defence Intelligence, one of them as the Chief of that branch in the Ministry of Defence, London. He is at present the Air Member for Supply and Organisation in the Air Force Department of the MOD.

Index